THE BIG
New York sandwich
BOOK

99 DELICIOUS CREATIONS FROM THE CITY'S GREATEST RESTAURANTS AND CHEFS

Sara Reistad-Long & Jean Tang

RUNNING PRESS
PHILADELPHIA · LONDON

**To all the creative New York chefs who take
sandwiches to the next level**

Printed in China

9 8 7 6 5 4 3 2 1

Digit on the right indicates the number of this printing
Library of Congress Control Number: 2010941021
ISBN 978-0-7624-4048-1

Cover and interior design by Jason Kayser
Food styling by Katrina Tekavec
Typography: Chronicle, Cyclone, Futura, and Volta

The publisher would like to thank the following retailers for
their invaluable assistance in the production of this book:
Crate & Barrel, King of Prussia and Sur La Table, King of
Prussia

Running Press Book Publishers
2300 Chestnut Street
Philadelphia, PA 19103-4371

Visit us on the web!
www.runningpresscooks.com

All photos are courtesy of the respective restaurants unless
otherwise noted.

Photos on pages 39, 49, 53, 61, 70, 77, 80, 104, 107,
119, 123, 132, 149, 153, 161, 181, 193, 200, 208,
213, 223, 235, and 245 by Steve Legato

Photo on page 4 (tomatoes): ©iStockphoto.com/Stephan
Zabel

Photo on page 4 (taxi): ©iStockphoto.com/Xavi Arnau

Photo on page 11: ©iStockphoto.com/Linda Stewart

Photo on page 19: ©iStockphoto.com/tbradford

Photo on page 27: ©iStockphoto.com/Jill Fromer

Photo on page 33: ©iStockphoto.com/Juanmonino

Photo on page 75: ©iStockphoto.com/Matej Michelizza

Photo on page 97: ©iStockphoto.com/FreezeFrameStudio

Photo on page 143: ©iStockphoto.com/Caziopeia

Photo on page 145: ©iStockphoto.com/Roberto Tartaglione

Photo on page 166 by Ted Axelrod

Photo on page 205: ©iStockphoto.com/Aleksandar Rosic

Photo on page 221: ©iStockphoto.com/Todd Taulman

Photo on page 227: ©iStockphoto.com/Alexander
Sherstobitov

CONTENTS

INTRODUCTION

A very warm welcome to *The Big New York Sandwich Book*! Between these pages, we've assembled a compendium of gorgeous, sandwich recipes from some of New York's most talented and beloved chefs and restaurants. Among the project's nearly one hundred participants are four-star celebrities, industry up-and-comers, skilled ethnic innovators, and longstanding neighborhood legends. It's taken us almost two years since our start date, and together with this incredible group of contributors, we've brought together what we hope will be, well, a definitive sandwich tome. Each recipe has been developed and adapted to not only reflect the chef's taste and cooking style but also to be made with minimal effort, maximum deliciousness, and, perhaps most importantly, without breaking the bank.

For those who want to know more about where the sandwiches come from and why their tastes work the way they do, we're excited to be able to offer that, too: a virtual map—in sandwiches—of a diverse, warmly hospitable, yet still gritty corner of the world. Each chapter, through its recipes, restaurant contextualization, and quotes from featured chefs is a walk down a different sandwich avenue. From classic deli sandwiches to exotic concoctions, the sum of all the parts offers a story about how flavor, open-mindedness, and improvisation can lead to something fresh, new, and entirely delicious.

WHY SANDWICHES?

First off, who doesn't love a sandwich? Believe it or not, these days we're now far more likely to fix a sandwich than cook a meal, according to a survey of 2009 recession eating habits conducted by the market research firm NPD Group. No wonder: Sandwiches present an extremely quick and affordable way to stick to flavorful and fresh food. They're perfect for making ahead, storing, and packing—important considerations if you're eating for one, on-the-go, or eating at different times than your other family members.

We fell in love with this book idea for another reason, too, though. What better introduction to today's varied and incredible flavors, ingredients, and techniques than a food so easy, you can fit it between two slices of bread? With the right recipes, sandwiches can be a foolproof ticket to mind-bogglingly delicious food anybody can easily make. To put a sandwich together, you don't have to be a five-star chef or rogue culinary genius. You can, however, take some of their tips, and give a few of their recipes a try. Sandwiches represent food and ingredients at their simplest. And when conceived right, the absence of all those other culinary bells and whistles can reveal combinations and concepts that are nothing short of pure and effortless great taste.

WHY NEW YORK?

Melting pot, salad bowl—if New York has been described as any one thing, it's as a mix and blend of the many. So much so that, to this day, 36 percent of the city's population is foreign-born, and nearly 50 percent speak a second language at home. It's a reflection of the myriad palates that chefs must consider and influences they can draw from—exactly what you need for a cookbook meant to be high on ideas and adventure, one that's replete with original approaches and surprising discoveries.

New York is also, specifically, a town where the bar is set high. It's always had a reputation for superior sandwiches—be they classic, overstuffed deli fare (think juicy pastrami on crisp rye, or melting hot cheese over smoky turkey); authentic, high-quality street bites (tender chicken, dripping with tahini and stuffed into soft, warm pitas, or peppery sausages and secret sauce); or countless other combinations of quality ingredients using a vast array of techniques and flavors.

Over the past few years, this ante's been upped. First there was the panini craze—delicate, griddle-melted (and melt-in-your-mouth) concoctions brimming with pear, Taleggio, and prosciutto, or maybe mortadella, ham, and tangy red pepper relish. Next came sliders, with all the hipster chefs worth their salt crafting bite-sized sandwiches in the tradition of the croque monsieur, BLT, or tiny pizzetta. Latin sandwiches soon gained a new following, with Cuban sandwiches, Spanish bocatas, and Mexican tortas elbowing in with tacos, arepas, and empanadas for those craving something spicy, hearty, and toothsome. And then, onto pork buns: Suddenly, New Yorkers couldn't get enough pork belly and cucumber slivers tucked into steamed bread and smeared with a dab of Hoisin sauce.

Most recently, city diners have been jonesing for all things báhn mì: Vietnamese pâté, sweetly pickled vegetables, fresh herbs, and spice piled into a warm, crusty baguette. It wasn't long before báhn mì-loving chefs began experimenting with the form, tucking their baguettes with everything from bacon and shrimp, to Polish kielbasa, to the key ingredients of pho, a rich beef soup scented with anise, cinnamon, and basil.

Sandwiches also have been an important element in the movement toward local, organic, and "whole" farmstead produce. No New York meat lover can seem to get enough artisanal bacon (the thicker the better) or hand-cut, house-cured ham (the thinner the better). Meanwhile, vegetable lovers are all about their wild mushrooms, heirloom tomatoes, beets, and ramps—colorful ingredients that taste of the sun and the soil, of life and vitality.

And from there, the flavor and ingredient medleys grow even more eclectic and interesting. With each invention, the new sandwich offers a story about open-mindedness, fusion, and improvisation—some of our most beloved themes in New York City.

HOW TO USE THIS BOOK

Part of the sandwich's appeal is that the directions are easy to follow. They're even easier to riff and improvise on. As much as this book is about offering thoroughly impressive, exciting recipes, it's also about providing an approachable way to sample food from a range of cultures and cooking styles. Try something once—or even just skim the recipe—and subsequently use it as a jumping-off point for your own tastes and the ingredients you have on hand. Cut corners, experiment, and, most of all, have fun.

To make the experience as interesting and user-friendly as possible, each sandwich is framed with context, comments, and tips. Often, you'll find recipes for sauces and condiments alongside. Rest assured, the sandwich gods will not judge you for using store-bought or, indeed, for substituting just about anything you happen to feel like on a given day. At the top of each page, you'll find a combination of four easy-to-use icons:

1 DIFFICULTY: ranges from one (assemble on the fly) to three (you'll really be cooking).

P PACKABLE: refers to whether it's long-lasting or un-messy enough to wrap up for lunch.

H HEALTHFUL: tells you if it is (or can be made) especially good for your waistline or overall wellness. If there are adjustments necessary to help get you there, or if certain ingredients pack an extra punch, you'll get that information here.

M MAKE-AHEAD: warns you if you need to start a day ahead. If something can be made with an easy adjustment or substitution, you'll find that out, too.

Chapter 1

THE BASICS

---

* * *

MAKING YOUR PANTRY (AND FRIDGE) SANDWICH-FRIENDLY

For sandwich lovers, keeping the basics at the ready isn't difficult. We've compiled a list of items, many of which will keep in your pantry or refrigerator for months.

Breads won't keep—unless you freeze them. And you can freeze almost any bread. There are clear trends here; stock accordingly. Rich egg-type breads such as challah and brioche are favored by our chefs. They often keep longer; if they go stale, use them to create wonderful French toast, or, if you bake, crumble them in crusts, such as in Paul Liebrandt's Welsh Rarebit (page 113). Ditto with pita. Keep rye (Jewish and country-style) and wheat breads, white breads and rolls, and focaccia closer to the date you'll use them, or double-wrap and label them for the freezer.

In terms of spices, seasonings, and dried herbs, the most important thing to have is good salt. Table salt is fine, but kosher salt and sea salt contain flavorful minerals, and often have a grainier texture that imparts a pleasing crunch. Very high-end salt includes flaked sea salt, such as Maldon (an English brand). Keep a plentiful supply. Some recipes call for smoked salt; look for the naturally smoked kind. (Store it in a closed container, or the salt will lose its smokiness.) Also keep a good supply of black peppercorns around, and a sharp grinder. (White pepper will impart a milder flavor and is good for seafood.) Other picks include bay leaves, cayenne pepper (or good Spanish paprika), cumin, curry powder, garlic powder, and dried Greek oregano.

---

* * *

Keep extra virgin olive oil handy, and store it away from sunlight. But read carefully: Sometimes a recipe intentionally calls for simple olive oil, not the vividly green, first cold pressing. It's up to you what you'd like to use. We've got a few recipes that involve frying, and for those we recommend canola, grapeseed, peanut, or otherwise neutral oils with high smoking points.

This book contains a lot of recipes for homemade aïolis, relishes, and pickles. To make these items, you'll need a couple of mustards (a whole grain and a Dijon should do the trick), a mayonnaise, some vinegars (white and balsamic as basics; rice, sherry, and white or red wine vinegar as bonuses), and a selection of pickles (dill, cornichons, capers, pepperoncini), and olives (such as pitted Moroccan olives). Pimientos are key—and can save crucial time when it comes to fire-roasting your bell peppers. (Keep in mind, however, that they are more tart and wet than home-roasted peppers.) Buy a few jars; they go quickly. Also useful: Tabasco and Worcestershire sauces and ketchup.

The book also contains recipes for lentil and hummus sandwiches. Both keep easily, of course. When it comes to hummus, there's nothing like starting from dried garbanzo beans. This involves a few easy extra steps (an overnight soak and a one-hour simmer), but they truly make a world of difference.

Scan our recipes for fresh herbs and citrus fruits to keep on hand. Parsley is ubiquitous, as are lemons (and lemon zest). Less ubiquitous, but common, herbs include tarragon (good with chicken or salmon), thyme (chicken), dill (fish and yogurt), rosemary (beef, fresh focaccia), and basil.

In jars or cans, look for almond butter (unless you'll be making your own), peanut butter (ditto), and canned tomatoes and tomato paste.

Now we come to the specialty items. These vary widely according to the recipe and genre. But since this book is intended to inspire you with concepts, flavors, ingredients, and techniques as well as give you step-by-step recipes, we recommend you keep the following items around: toasted sesame oil (widely available), Sriracha (spicy Asian sauce, distinguished by the rooster on the label), pomegranate molasses (marvelous Middle Eastern binding agent with a magnetic tartness), and Mexican chiles (we love the texture and mildness of guajillo). Other helpful items: coconut milk (for Thai dishes), kewpie-style (a sweeter, Japanese-style) mayonnaise, liquid smoke (for instant barbecue action), panko breadcrumbs (for foolproof— and beautiful—deep frying), and pink peppercorns (gorgeously rosy and pungent).

For sweet sandwiches, all-purpose flour comes in handy, as does sugar: granulated, confectioners', and brown. Note: Almost all of our sweet sandwich recipes involve chocolate, and nearly all of those combine milk (about 40 percent cacao) with bittersweet (70 percent) bars or chips.

Chapter 2

HEALTHWICHING

***

THE NEXT TIME YOU BITE INTO ANYTHING FROM A ROAST TURKEY TO A TUNA club, congratulate yourself for having made an extremely healthful choice. Sandwiches rely on balanced ingredient ratios, easy assembly, and whole foods—meaning they're a practically effortless way to eat very well.

Only so much can fit between two slices of bread, and a good mix of ingredients is essential for maximum flavor. As luck would have it, that same harmony of variety and moderation is just as important to good health. Meats, cheeses, sauces, and oils can be fattening in large quantities, for example. But scale your portions to sandwich-size and you're downplaying those hazards, while getting critical building blocks for energy, stamina, and nerve function. Vegetables, fruits, and spices—for their part—add texture and punch, while helping the body function optimally and fight off disease. Each offers unique benefits, so stuffing your sandwich with several different kinds is as good for your body as your palate. And grains, when they're whole and served in sensible portions, keep metabolism going throughout the day.

Because sandwiches are, ultimately, assembled, it's also easy to adjust them to individual needs. Be it for weight-loss or a food intolerance, going light on or eliminating say, a piece of cheese, means nothing more than skipping that step. You don't have to readjust an entire recipe.

Indeed, the very simplicity of these dishes can promote health. Choose a quality prosciutto over processed ham and you'll be rewarded with big flavor and fewer harmful additives. Look for great, ripe produce and you're making good taste as simple and good-for-you as can be; there's no need to over-sauce, salt, or sweeten. At their best, sandwiches can be a natural, deliciously nonrestrictive path to staying well. Here, what you should know to make the most of them.

***

SLOW FOOD: An Overview

**by Jerusha Klempurer, Networks and Partnerships
Program Manager at Slow Food USA**

Slow Food is a movement, a philosophy, and a worldwide organization, forming a network of chapters all over the globe, with nearly 250 in the United States alone. It began in Italy in the late 1980s as a response to the explosion of fast food chains around the country, most egregiously the one on the Spanish Steps in Rome. Slow food is the opposite of fast food—so that means if it's made with real, fresh ingredients, if it's connected somehow to the place where it's made, if it's delicious and nourishing, and you're not eating it alone in your car, it might just be slow food. Sandwiches, with their throw-it-together appeal, are one of the easiest ways to get in on the movement.

SIX WAYS TO INCORPORATE SANDWICHES INTO THE SLOW FOOD PHILOSOPHY:

1. Look for fresh-baked. Be it something from your bread machine, or bought from a local baker, you'll be supporting an artisan and your community, as well as cutting out a whole bunch of additives and preservatives.

2. Choose in-season produce. Is it finally asparagus season? Put those bad boys on a sandwich. Add tomatoes? Best. Sandwich. Ever. Food that's in season is ripe, which translates to delicious, luscious taste and maximum nutritional value. You're also helping make sure farms and soil are thriving in the most natural way possible.

3. Take advantage of what's around you. Find a producer near you who makes terrific cheese or outstanding salami. Or maybe pickles or chutney from your local farmer. Helping these people thrive is ensuring that good, real food continues to have a place in our diet. Plus, you're eating food that hasn't used a ton of fossil fuels to be transported to you.

4. Add an ingredient you love. Food should bring pleasure. A sandwich is basically a vehicle for whatever it is you go cuckoo for.

5. Consider making at least two sandwiches. This isn't so you can overeat, it's so you can eat with friends/family—slow food is about eating together.

6. Have a seat, pop a squat. Even though a sandwich is the perfectly portable meal, it's nice to be a little mindful and enjoy what you're eating by taking the time to sit down.

WELLNESS: Sandwiches as nutrient powerhouses

by Keri Glassman, nutritionist and antioxidant expert

Foods rich in antioxidants are some of the lowest in calories and best for you, promoting energy, strength, and mental focus by combating free radical damage caused by UV exposure, environmental pollution, stress, and even some foods we eat. A diet rich in antioxidants will help maintain healthy brain function, protect against cancers, prevent heart disease, slow down the aging process, improve overall health, and promote weight loss.

SEVEN EASY TIPS FOR USING ANTIOXIDANTS TO SEND YOUR SANDWICH'S NUTRITION THROUGH THE ROOF:

1. Look for color. A quick way to choose high-antioxidant foods is to go by color. The darker or more vivid, the more nutritious your choice. In particular, a deep yellow, orange, or red pigment signals the presence of carotenoids, especially potent antioxidants. You've probably heard of many of them: Beta carotene, for example, is found in several foods that are orange in color, including sweet potatoes, carrots, squash, pumpkin, and mangos. Some green leafy vegetables (such as collard greens, spinach, and kale) are also strong sources. Lycopene, for its part, comes from tomatoes, among other foods. Lutein—best known for its association with healthy eyes—is abundant in green, leafy vegetables such as collard greens, spinach, and kale.

2. Add a slice of avocado. The vitamin E in avocados acts as an antioxidant to stop free radicals from damaging organs in the body, especially the heart. On the phytochemical front, avocados contain glutathione, an antioxidant with anti-carcinogenic potential. Plus, avocados are full of monounsaturated fat, which may reduce your risk of developing atherosclerosis and may increase your HDL (good cholesterol) levels.

3. Slip in yellow or red peppers. Yellow and red peppers have twice the amount of vitamin C as green peppers—and they're packed with vitamin C and fiber (3.3 grams). Yellow peppers, too, have more folate and iron.

4. Top with sprouts. Numerous varieties of sprouts are great with any meal. They're a powerful source of protein and vitamin C. Try adding them to any dish, and your immune system will get a boost.

5. Include chile peppers. These bright red peppers, which fuel the fire in cayenne pepper, contain an antioxidant called capsaicin. While the substance gets a lot of attention for its medical applications and is even used as a topical pain reliever, it also seems to have some effect on human appetite. Some studies have found that people who eat meals with plenty of this delicious (and hot!) spice feel less hungry as a result.

6. Sprinkle in cilantro. Technically a dark, leafy vegetable, it has beta carotene and plenty of vitamins, including A and K. It also contains a natural antibiotic, which may help in warding off illness.

7. Whenever possible, add tomatoes. Try sun-dried for a change. It's no accident that ketchup is the number-one consumed "vegetable"—what's not to love? Besides having plenty of vitamin C, tomatoes are—as mentioned earlier—especially rich in lycopene. Researchers have found that the higher the serum level of that antioxidant found in people's blood, the lower the level of heart disease and other chronic illnesses.

TOP 5 CALORIE SAVING TIPS

1. Ditch the mayo: save 180 calories

2. Substitute low or no-fat Greek yogurt for mayo: save 165 calories (and about 20 grams of fat)

3. Cut out bacon: save 150 calories (but, really, who would want to do that?)

4. Ask for one slice of cheese instead of two: save 100 calories

5. Go open face: save 100 calories

WEIGHT LOSS: Cutting Calories with Sandwiches

by Stephanie Middleberg, nutritionist

Want to build a healthy sandwich? Start with the bread. Multigrain doesn't mean anything unless the grains are whole. Aim for 100 percent whole wheat. On the ingredient list, "whole wheat" should be first. If you see "enriched," stay away. The natural nutrients have been stripped out.

Moving on to the "bulk": If you lay out your ingredients on a plate, half should be vegetables, a quarter protein, and a quarter toppings. The leanest meats include turkey, chicken, ham, roast pork loin (anything "loin" is lean), and roast beef. Choose fresh meat when you can and on packages look for labels indicating hormone free, nitrate free, and free of antibiotics. If you're a sucker for egg salad, you can pare down the fat by going for a ratio of one whole egg to three egg whites. Similarly, you can cut out fat and keep flavor for anything requiring mayonnaise by blending one part low-fat mayonnaise to three parts Greek yogurt (which is also high in protein). Vegetarian healthy proteins include tofu, beans and hummus, eggs, quinoa, tempeh, and seitan.

For toppings, naturally low fat cheeses include Parmesan, mozzarella, goat, and feta. In general, aim for one ounce per sandwich. If you're still craving creamy, try a quarter of an avocado. It's delicious and packed with nutrients.

Finally, condiments. Aged balsamic vinegar offers bold flavor; a little goes a long way. Likewise, tahini, tapenades, and fruit compotes. For spreads, when in doubt, keep it to two tablespoons max. If you're looking for a default oil, you can't go wrong with extra virgin olive. When cooking, however, the heat destroys some of the extra benefits, so regular olive oil is fine—and for a bit more kick, sesame oil is an excellent choice. Always, always cook with real butter over margarine, which contains unhealthy soybean oil and a host of additives.

Love sandwiches but need to eat less bread? Toss the bread and place all the other ingredients in the same proportions over lettuce. Aim for green leafy veggies (spinach, kale, swiss chard, romaine, arugula). Always include at least two colors and at least one healthy fat.

FLAVOR: How to Step It Up a Notch

by Monica Bhide, food writer and spice expert

As a child growing up in the Middle East, I was totally obsessed with a strange contraption my mother used for making sandwiches: a stovetop toaster. It looked like a tiny waffle iron on a stick. Each afternoon when I returned from school, she would be ready and waiting to make me a hot snack. She would open up the toaster-on-a-stick and on one side place a slice of bread. She would top that with whatever was left over from the previous night's dinner—pieces of tandoori chicken, cumin-scented potatoes, turmeric-hued paneer, even scrambled eggs. Then she would slather a mint-cilantro chutney or fiery chili ketchup on the other slice of bread and place it on top of the leftover delight. She would close the toaster and place it over a flame on the stovetop—and in less than two minutes, I would be treated to a warm, toasty sandwich that was the best comfort food on the planet.

What I learned from my mother, besides a great way to use leftovers, was that warm sandwiches are a terrific bed for spicy ingredients. Accordingly, I spice up my sandwiches with everything from Sriracha sauce to tamarind chutney. If I am in the mood for something creamy, then of course mayo comes to mind, but never plain—I have spiced it up with toasted saffron or smashed-up chipotle peppers or harissa (a Middle Eastern spread made with garlic and red chiles) or sambhal. These mayo combos slathered on bread can enliven any plain chicken or vegetable stuffing.

Chutneys and revved-up mayo are not the only ingredients that add sassy spice to a sandwich. I dry-roast slivers of garlic and coconut and then sauté them in a smidgen of oil along with crushed red chile pepper. This combination sprinkled over boring sandwich fillings always adds some oomph. Sliced jalapeños, minced serranos, and oven-roasted peppers also find their way into my sandwiches. Recently, I was introduced to a Yemeni version of salsa called z'hug. With its wonderful flavors of lemon, garlic, chili, coriander, and more, it makes a perfect base for piling up anything on bread.

But zing-adding ingredients don't always have to be savory. One of my personal favorite sandwiches is an open-faced turkey sandwich with melted cheese, topped with sweet-tart cranberry chutney.

(In case you are curious, I never could find that toaster contraption here in the United States. Luckily, a panini press works just as well.)

Chapter 3

THE DELI SANDWICH

* * *

WORLDWIDE, THE NEW YORK DELI HAS AN ENORMOUS REPUTATION. DELIS such as Carnegie and Katz's are famous for piling groan-worthy amounts of pastrami, roast beef, Swiss cheese, and pepperoncinis on fresh rye, challah, and hero rolls. Not only do their fans not complain of lockjaw, they also tip the servers extra to give them more.

As always, the celebrity chef version of these classic sandwiches adds a nifty twist (or five). Generally, the sandwiches in this chapter involve more delicate (i.e., normal portions) amounts of meat (excepting Carmine's generously proportioned cheesesteak). That meat will often (although not always) require brining, braising, or marinating, such as Michael Ferraro's slow-braised Reuben, or Elisa Sarno's Mediterranean Grilled Chicken Sandwich. It's an extra step, but one that's worthwhile. Rather than slathered mustard or mayonnaise, or dashed oil and vinegar, the sandwiches in this chapter often incorporate interesting homemade condiments.

* * *

For example, there are the pickled relishes, such as Anne Burrell's garlicky Spicy Pepper Relish, made with generous (and necessary) quantities of salt and sugar. There are the herbed mayonnaises, such as Jennifer Sant'anna's fresh Rosemary Aïoli or Nikki Cascone's brightly citric Lemon Herb version. There are classic touches, meticulously reproduced, such as the Olive Salad in St. John Frizell's Muffuletta, which hails straight from New Orleans and involves a three-day pickling step. (Don't be intimidated—it's easy.) Of course, you can always substitute a store-bought version of something like Russian Dressing (either Delicatessen's or Aureole's), but we can assure you, if you take the trouble to make this stuff fresh, it'll be a revelation. Even our mayonnaise-phobic friends are excited.

There are melts, such as the Oak Room's distinctly unclassic Tuna Melt, which is paired with trendy accompaniments such as cilantro, avocado, and capers. There are deli sandwiches assembled then pressed, for maximum melt. There are European meats fast-gaining popularity, such as shaved mortadella flecked with pistachio, and gleaming soppressata.

Then, there's bacon. In a city that loves its bacon thick-cut, chewy or crispy, smoked doubly or with applewood, with and without nitrates, at lunch and dinner, in pasta, and even coated with chocolate, you can be sure that fatty cured pork isn't going to be left out of our sandwiches. Nikki Cascone sneaks some in hers—and although that probably cancels out the health benefits of her Simple Salmon Sandwich, it's worth the flavor. Vincent Nargi and Phil Conlon, of Café Cluny, put bacon in their Breakfast Club—all the more effective for their original hangover remedy. Kenny Callaghan, of Blue Smoke, gives his bacon a southern spin in his BLG.

ARTIE'S MOSHE DAYAN HERO SANDWICH

JEFFREY BANK, CEO OF ALICART ✳ ARTIE'S DELI ✳ WWW.ARTIES.COM

1 **P**

ARTIE Cutler may be one of the greatest New York restaurateurs you've never heard of. In Cutler's *New York Times* obituary, Drew Nieporent—owner of top-tier Corton and Tribeca Grill, as well as legendary sushi house Nobu—called him "a quiet genius in our business." Cutler's vision was to bring user-friendly themed food to the masses. By the end of his career, he'd opened Italian restaurants, a Chinese restaurant, and a Mexican restaurant (his partner for this last one was his Mexican housekeeper). Artie's Deli was Cutler's most personal project. The son of a diner owner and the grandson of a herring stand purveyor, he wanted to bring something of the 1930s-style New York deli to the Upper West Side.

More than a decade later, it looks like Cutler succeeded. With thick salami hanging from the ceiling, not to mention display cases beckoning with knishes, cheesecake, rugelach, and a pastrami that the eminent food critic Florence Fabricant called "luscious," Artie's all but overflows with diners looking for that perfect fix. Here, the chefs at Artie's have worked up a make-at-home version of one of their most coveted sandwich orders, named (for reasons we may never know) after a controversial Israeli military leader. "At the restaurant we serve this on a three-foot-long challah," said Jeffrey Bank, CEO of Alicat, the company that now owns Artie's. "It's a spectacle and a half. And the taste lives up. The flavors are just timeless."

✳ ✳ ✳

Smear the condiments on either side of the bread and add the meat in layers: pastrami, corned beef, roast beef, and ending with turkey. Finish with lettuce and tomato as desired.

SERVES 4

Mustard
Mayonnaise
Russian dressing
4 (1-foot) loaves challah bread
4 ounces pastrami
4 ounces corned beef
4 ounces roast beef
4 ounces fresh turkey breast
Lettuce
12 (or more) tomatoes, sliced

NOTE: The hero is, it turns out, a true New York sandwich name. Legend has it that in the 1930s, a *New York Herald Tribune* reporter took one look at the sandwich and noted that only a hero could finish off something that big.

SPICY HAM, MORTADELLA & PROVOLONE SANDWICH
WITH SPICY PEPPER RELISH

ANNE BURRELL * FOOD NETWORK'S SECRETS OF A RESTAURANT CHEF

2 **P**

SERVES 4

4 hero-size ciabatta sandwich
   rolls, split lengthwise
   (not all the way through)
½ cup red wine vinegar
½ cup extra virgin olive oil
½ pound provolone cheese,
   thinly sliced
Spicy Pepper Relish
   (recipe follows)
½ pound ham, thinly sliced
½ pound mortadella, thinly
   sliced

CHEF Anne Burrell discovered this sandwich while traveling around Italy as a student on a limited budget. To really soak in the local flavors, she'd buy cured-meat sandwiches. "Mortadella in Italy is so huge—two feet in diameter—that men had to carry them in slings. Ham is hard to avoid in Italy. I loved the combination of the two," she recalled.

Back in New York, she served her favorite new sandwich at Centro Vinoteca, where she was the opening executive chef. "I perfected it with provolone cheese and squished it, and it became something a little more special," she said. Burrell's recipe for a ham and mortadella sandwich with provolone and pickled hot pepper relish includes silky mounds of mortadella and ham and an astoundingly vivid and spicy pepper relish that's a cinch to make ahead and chill.

* * *

Preheat a panini press, if using. Scoop out the inside of the rolls and discard.

Combine the vinegar with the oil. Brush the mixture inside each roll evenly and thoroughly. Each filling component (oil and vinegar mixture, cheese, relish, meats) should completely cover the insides of the rolls. ("Don't miss any corners!" said Chef Burrell.) Place 2 slices of cheese in each roll.

Spread each roll with an even layer of pepper relish. Crinkle 2 slices of the ham, and lay them in a fluffy, even layer on top of the pepper relish. Make sure the meat is crinkled, not flat. Add a slice of provolone and a slice of mortadella. Repeat with the remaining ham, provolone, and mortadella. Close each sandwich. Press to secure.

Grill each sandwich in the heated panini press. (If you don't have a panini press, place sandwiches on a hot grill or skillet. Top with a sandwich press, cast-iron skillet, or other heavy weight. Grill 1 to 2 minutes on each side.)

SPICY PEPPER RELISH

MAKES 1 TO 2 CUPS

½ **pound Fresno peppers (or**
   ¼ **pound jalapeños)**
2 red bell peppers
3 garlic cloves, thinly sliced
½ **red wine vinegar**
1 tablespoon salt
1 tablespoon sugar

Grill the peppers on a grill, or directly over a gas flame, using tongs to turn them until the skin is charred. Place in a bowl. Cover with plastic wrap for 10 minutes. Uncover the bowl and allow the peppers to cool; then remove the blackened portions of skin and seeds.

Coarsely chop the peppers and combine them with the garlic, vinegar, salt, and sugar. Let sit for an hour before using.

Bacon Lettuce Tomato or "BLG"

KENNY CALLAGHAN * BLUE SMOKE

1 **P**

SERVES 1

3 slices bacon
Ice water
Kosher salt
2 green tomatoes, sliced
2 cups all-purpose flour
6 eggs, slightly beaten
2 cups panko breadcrumbs
½ cup grated pecorino cheese
4 tablespoons chopped fresh
   parsley
2 to 3 cups neutral oil, such as
   canola or peanut
2 slices white bread, toasted
3 tablespoons Barbecue
   Mayonnaise (recipe follows)
1 red lettuce leaf

TUCKED away on a side street in Gramercy Park, Blue Smoke combines two American preoccupations: beloved regional dishes and jazz. By substituting the regular tomatoes usually used in a BLT with fried green ones, this recipe merges two classics: a BLT and a fried green tomato. "At the restaurant, we make the sandwich with our own house-cured bacon, and we serve it on Tom Cat white bread," said Chef Kenny Callaghan.

* * *

Preheat the oven to 375°F. Place the bacon on a baking sheet. Bake in the oven for 18 minutes, or fry in a pan until crisp.

Fill a large shallow bowl with ice water. In a separate pot, bring 3 cups of water to a boil. Add a dash of salt. Blanch the tomato slices in the boiling water for 2 minutes. Using a pair of tongs, remove the tomato slices, and add them to the ice water bath.

Place the flour in one bowl, the eggs in a second bowl, and the panko breadcrumbs, cheese, and parsley in a third bowl. Coat the tomato slices in the flour. Dust off the excess, and coat the tomato slices with the eggs. Allow the excess to drip off, and coat the slices in the panko mixture.

Heat about 2 inches of the oil in a skillet to 375°F. Fry the tomato slices for 1 to 1½ minutes, until golden brown. Drain on a platter lined with paper towels.

Spread 1 side of each bread slice with the Barbecue Mayonnaise.

Build the sandwich with the Fried Green Tomatoes, the bacon, and the lettuce. Close the sandwich. Slice in half and serve.

BARBECUE MAYONNAISE

MAKES 1½ CUPS

1 cup mayonnaise
¼ cup barbecue sauce
¼ cup ketchup
Kosher salt
Black pepper

Combine the mayonnaise, barbecue sauce, ketchup, and salt and pepper to taste. Chill until needed.

SIMPLE SALMON SANDWICH

NIKKI CASCONE

2 **H** **P**

SERVES 4

8 slices thick-cut, naturally
smoked bacon
4 (6-ounce) salmon
fillets (preferably
wild-caught Alaskan)
Salt and pepper
Lemon Herb Aïoli (recipe
follows)
8 slices brioche, or multigrain
or rye bread
8 slices beefsteak tomato
Small head red leaf lettuce

NOTE: To avoid sogginess, pack the
bread and aïoli separately.

DESPITE the steady traffic at 24 Prince, Nikki Cascone's former Soho restaurant, the vibe was always Zen. It's no accident: the Top Chef winner is dedicated to simple, healthful cooking, and 24 Prince's airy interior, peaceful garden, and clean menu thrummed with healthy vibes.

Although 24 Prince is closed and Cascone is cooking at a new spot (unopened as of the date this book went to press), we still love the "organic" story behind this sandwich. In Soho, Cascone and her team liked to cook with salmon. They'd use the fillets and set aside the tails. One day, it occurred to Cascone that the tail pieces would make perfect sandwich fodder—for herself.

"The tail of a salmon is sandwich sized. I'd cook it and put it on top of toasted brioche that we had baked. Then I added tarragon mayonnaise, which we were using for another dish at the time," she said.

Her sandwich was so delicious that she decided to add it to the menu, with smoked bacon. "They always sell out at brunch," she added.

The sandwich is a cinch to make. The Lemon Herb Aïoli is key, and it's stained cheery yellow with (healthy) turmeric, in contrast to the bright green herbs. Make the aïoli ahead of time; you'll have to wait for it to cool.

* * *

Preheat oven to 350°F, put the bacon on a baking sheet, and cook in the oven for 18 minutes, or fry in a pan until crisp.

Add a couple teaspoons of bacon grease to a sauté pan over medium heat and pan-sear the salmon to desired doneness. While cooking, season with salt and pepper to taste. (You may have to do this in batches, depending on the size of your pan.)

Spread the aïoli on each slice of brioche. Divide even portions of salmon (if fillets are too thick, break into 2-inch chunks), bacon, tomato, and lettuce among half the bread slices. Top the sandwiches with the other brioche slices, slice in half, and serve.

LEMON HERB AÏOLI

½ cup white wine
¼ cup finely chopped shallots
1 to 2 garlic cloves
4 rosemary sprigs, finely
   chopped
8 thyme sprigs, finely
   chopped
½ tablespoon turmeric
1 cup mayonnaise
1 tablespoon finely chopped
   tarragon
1 tablespoon finely chopped
   chives
Pinch of cayenne
Juice of ½ lemon

Place the wine, shallots, garlic, rosemary, thyme, and turmeric into a sauté pan. Sauté over medium heat until reduced by half. Set aside to cool.

When completely cool, incorporate the mayonnaise, tarragon, chives, cayenne, and lemon juice. You can store this in the refrigerator in an air-tight container for up to two weeks.

NOTE: Requires 30 minutes of cooling time.

Reuben Sandwich

MICHAEL FERRARO * DELICATESSEN * WWW.DELICATESSENNYC.COM

3 **P**

SERVES UP TO 7

1 (3- to 4-pound) beef brisket
Salt and pepper
2 yellow onions, cut into
  2-inch dice
2 carrots, cut into 2-inch dice
2 celery stalks, cut into
  2-inch dice
3 garlic cloves, halved
2 sprigs fresh thyme
2 tablespoons pickling spice
  (a blend of allspice,
  cardamom, cinnamon,
  cloves, coriander, cumin,
  ginger, mustard seeds,
  and peppercorns)
2 bay leaves
1 dill sprig
1 teaspoon caraway seeds
6 cups chicken stock
10 (if large) to 14 (if small)
  slices Jewish rye bread
1 Brisket (recipe follows)
1¼ cups Russian Dressing
  (recipe follows)
½ to ¾ cup sauerkraut
15 to 21 thick slices
  high-quality Swiss cheese
5 to 7 sour pickles, for serving

DESPITE the name, this isn't a real delicatessen. The Soho restaurant may have begun that way, but the fashionable blocks that surround it have worked their Darwinian magic, so that Delicatessen has morphed into a sort of hip bar and diner, with a penchant for "truffling" side dishes like French fries and artichoke dip, and attracting models who hardly eat at all. But as the restaurant evolved, one recipe remained: the Reuben.

"My mom opened a delicatessen. This sandwich—though not my mom's recipe—is just a favorite. We braise our own brisket, make our own sauce, and the best cheese we can find," said Chef Michael Ferraro, who recommended that you do the same.

* * *

Preheat the oven to 250°F. Season the brisket with salt and pepper to taste. Place it in a large, lidded braising dish. Add the remaining ingredients. Cover and braise the brisket until fork-tender, about 4 hours.

Leave the oven on. Transfer the brisket from the cooking broth onto a cutting board. Let it sit for 10 minutes and then slice the meat thinly against the grain.

Strain the broth into a large saucepan, discarding the solids. Add the sliced brisket to the strained broth. Cover, and braise over low heat for 1 hour.

Lightly toast the bread. Remove the meat from the broth. Top each toasted bread slice with about 1½ tablespoons of the Russian dressing.

Preheat the broiler. Top half of the bread slices each with even portions of the brisket, about 2 tablespoons of the sauerkraut, and 3 slices of the cheese. Line the brisket-loaded slices onto a baking dish. Broil until the cheese is melted, about 1 minute. Close the sandwiches with the remaining dressed rye slices. Garnish each sandwich with a pickle, and serve.

RUSSIAN DRESSING

1¼ cups mayonnaise
½ cup ketchup
⅛ cup diced shallots
⅛ cup chopped capers
⅛ cup chopped cornichons
½ teaspoon minced dill
½ teaspoon minced tarragon
½ teaspoon minced chervil
½ teaspoon minced chives
½ tablespoon extra virgin
   olive oil
1 tablespoon red wine
   vinegar
2 tablespoons lemon juice,
   about ½ lemon
Kosher salt and freshly
   ground black pepper

In a large mixing bowl, whisk mayonnaise, ketchup, shallots, capers, cornichons, dill, tarragon, chervil, chives, oil, vinegar, and lemon juice. Season with salt and pepper to taste.

MUFFALETTA

ST. JOHN FRIZELL ✳ FORT DEFIANCE ✳ WWW.FORTDEFIANCEBROOKLYN.COM

1 **P** **M** 3 DAYS

SERVES 6

SANDWICH

Muffaletta bread loaf, about 11-inches round

9 ounces Emmental cheese, sliced

9 ounces mild provolone cheese, sliced

8 ounces hot coppa, sliced

8 ounces mortadella, sliced

8 ounces sweet soppressata, sliced

OLIVE SALAD

¼ cup sugar

¼ cup water

¼ cup vinegar

½ carrot, roughly chopped

3 cauliflower stalks, roughly chopped

1 celery stalk, roughly chopped

1 shallot, halved

⅓ cup kalamata olives, pitted

⅓ cup green olives, pitted

1 tablespoon chopped pimientos

1 garlic clove

4 parsley sprigs

1 teaspoon capers

1 tablespoon extra virgin olive oil

1½ teaspoons canola oil

IF this sandwich were an Olympiad, it would resemble fourteen-time gold medal-winner Michael Phelps. It's been recognized by *New York Magazine*, the *Village Voice*, and other top local publications as one of the best sandwiches in NY. Not bad, considering its inception at a Red Hook cocktail pub, by a food writer-turned-mixologist-turned bar owner, and former New Orleans dweller called St. John Frizell.

"There are two things that define the muffaletta sandwich: the olive salad, and the round, nine-inch diameter bread. But outside of New Orleans, you'll find lots of 'muffalettas' that contain neither of these elements. I asked a friend to buy a couple of the sandwiches at Central Grocery in the French Quarter—the sandwich's home, according to some—and overnight them to me. I gave half to the chef [to] reverse-engineer the olive salad, and half each to two local bakers to duplicate the bread. I ate the last half. We poked the sandwich; we prodded it; we picked it apart. After a few rounds of trial and error, we came up with a sandwich I can serve proudly," said owner Frizell. The pickles and olives complement the piles of sandwich meat and cheese.

✳ ✳ ✳

For the sandwich: Slice the muffaletta bread in half lengthwise. Spread the olive salad on the bottom half. Add the Emmental, provolone, hot coppa, mortadella, and soppressata. Close the sandwich. Slice into 6 wedges, and serve. Store any leftover olive salad in the refrigerator.

For the olive salad: Place the sugar, water, and vinegar in a saucepan to make a brine. Heat to a boil over high heat; then reduce the heat to medium and boil until the sugar is dissolved.

Place the carrot, cauliflower, celery, and shallot into a large, heat-proof container. Pour the brine over the vegetables to cover. Refrigerate for at least three days.

Remove the vegetables from the brine. In a large mixing bowl, combine the pickled vegetables, olives, pimientos, garlic, parsley, and capers. Working in small batches, add the vegetable mixture to a food processor, and pulse until chopped, but not puréed. Toss with the olive and canola oils.

SMOKED TURKEY AND BRIE SANDWICH WITH ROSEMARY AÏOLI

JENNIFER SANT'ANNA HILL ✳ 508 ✳ WWW.508NYC.COM

1 **P** **H** HALVE OR QUARTER THE BRIE, AND SUBSTITUTE LOW-FAT OR NONFAT PLAIN YOGURT FOR MAYONNAISE IN THE AÏOLI.

SERVES 4

Butter or oil for frying
2 onions, thinly sliced
15 sage leaves
1 pound roasted turkey
4 ciabatta buns
2 teaspoons fresh or 1
     teaspoon dried rosemary
¼ cup mayonnaise or yogurt
½ pound Brie, sliced
2 tomatoes, sliced
Salt and pepper

IT took two couples—owners Lynne Fisher and Fred Hill, and chef-owners Anderson Sant'anna De Lima and Jennifer Sant'anna Hill—to get 508 off the ground, but the effort worked. The space is warm and easy-on-the eye, and the well-considered Mediterranean menu hits just the kind of spot many longtime Soho residents (among them, Lynne and Fred) need. A good example: the house turkey sandwich.

Read how it came about and you'll see 508's hands-on, detail-oriented approach at work: "When we first opened 508, my father begged us to add a turkey sandwich to the lunch menu. He said he wanted something moist, with taste—and good ingredients. Something that tastes specially made, not thrown together," said Sant'anna Hill. "I'm glad we relented because I can assure you, this is a killer sandwich. All the components really work off of each other, from the sweetness of the caramelized onions to the wetness of the tomato to the crackle of sage."

✳ ✳ ✳

Heat some butter or oil in a sauté pan over low heat. Add the onions and cook until they're brown, stirring occasionally.

Put enough extra virgin olive oil in separate pan so the sage leaves will float. Heat the oil over high heat and fry the sage leaves for about 25 seconds or until crispy.

Heat the turkey in the oven until it's warm. As you wait, slice the ciabatta rolls. Combine the rosemary and mayonnaise to make an aïoli. Spread the aïoli on each bottom half.

Place a few slices of the warm turkey on the bottom half of each sandwich, and top that with some of the Brie. The heat from the turkey should cause the Brie to soften and melt a little. Finish with the onion, tomatoes, sage, and salt and pepper to taste. Close the sandwiches and serve.

NOTE: Tryptophan, the ingredient in turkey long-blamed for making us sleepy, might have a redemptive purpose: New studies are linking it to increased production of mood-boosting serotonin.

TUNA MELT

ERIC HARA * THE OAK ROOM * WWW.OAKROOMNY.COM

1 **P**

SERVES 4

8 slices cheese, preferably
   Swiss

8 slices country bread

4 (5-ounce) cans tuna in oil,
   drained

8 sprigs cilantro, chopped

⅓ cup minced red onion

4 teaspoons capers, chopped

10 tablespoons mayonnaise

½ avocado, sliced

1 tomato, sliced

4 leaves lettuce

NOTE: Until 1937, the Oak Room was exclusively a gentlemen's club. In fact, through the 1950s, ladies were not allowed in unaccompanied.

WITH its dark wood-paneled walls, cocktail-hour lighting and—in the bar area—sweeping views of Central Park, the idea of drinks or a meal at the Plaza Hotel may be very nearly as alluring now as it was back when the restaurant opened in 1907. Drop by today, and you'll find plenty of guests—locals and tourists alike—soaking up the New Yorkness of the scene. (The Plaza is, after all, the hotel where Eloise ran wild, where the Beatles first stayed in the United States and where Truman Capote hosted the White Ball.)

For this, the food is entirely fitting: full of big, classic American dishes—from tomato soups and Cobb salads to top-quality steaks and fish sauced about ten ways. Here, chef Eric Hara (a noted pro with seafood) shares the recipe for the restaurant's tuna melt, a lunchtime favorite. "The tuna melt is such a classic sandwich, and The Oak Room is the epitome of classic New York, so when I was playing around with this recipe I wanted it to reflect traditional flavors that would elicit a sense of nostalgia," he said. "On the other hand, I also wanted to add a bit of something new to keep it current, so that's where the avocado and cilantro come into play. It tastes how you remember it, but with a little extra pop."

* * *

For each sandwich, preheat the broiler. Place the cheese on both slices of bread and broil for 2 to 3 minutes, until the cheese is melted.

Mix the tuna, cilantro, onion, capers, and mayonnaise well until uniform. Top one side of every sandwich with a heaping scoop of the tuna mixture. Add the avocado, tomato, and lettuce, place the other slice of bread on top, and serve.

"Marco's Favorite" Prosciutto Panini

MARCO MOREIRA ✳ TOCQUEVILLE ✳ WWW.TOCQUEVILLERESTAURANT.COM

1 **P**

TUCKED away near Manhattan's bustling Union Square Farmers' Market is Tocqueville, its entry an unassuming door. Only the lavishly scrolled name hints at the striking restaurant within.

Since opening in 2000 (and now in its second location, just a few buildings down from the original), Tocqueville has lured in some of the city's most glamorous personalities. The draw? Chef Marco Moreira—a Brazilian-born, Japanese and French–trained New York chef who, like his restaurant, has garnered a reputation for infusing fantastical flavors and high-quality ingredients in simple dishes, like "Marco's Favorite," his eponymous Prosciutto Panini.

"When we first opened, I found myself constantly making this particular sandwich for myself and my friends. The saltiness of the prosciutto, the gooeyness of the cheese, the crispiness of the bread, and the aroma from the truffle oil with the other ingredients, makes a great feast for all the senses. It has a casual opulence and simplicity that everyone enjoys," said Moreira. "As the word spread to friends of friends, and their friends, they were told to ask for 'Marco's Favorite.' The name stuck. We now serve it as an hors d'oeuvres cut in small squares paired with a glass of red or white wine and it is heaven!"

✳ ✳ ✳

Preheat a panini press, if using. Drizzle each bread slice (or side) with the truffle oil. Place the cheese and prosciutto on 4 slices of the bread (or half the flatbread), and close the sandwich.

Grill the sandwiches in the hot panini press. (If you don't have a panini press, place the sandwiches on a hot grill or skillet with a sandwich press, cast-iron skillet, or other heavy weight on top. Grill 2 minutes on each side.) Serve while hot.

SERVES 4

8 slices white bread, or 4 pieces flatbread, or pizza bianca

2 teaspoons truffle oil

8 ounces Asiago cheese, thinly sliced

8 ounces (about 12 slices) prosciutto, thinly sliced

BREAKFAST CLUB SANDWICH

VINCENT NARGI AND PHIL CONLON ✳ CAFÉ CLUNY ✳ WWW.CAFECLUNY.COM

1 **P**

Vincent Nargi

SERVES 4

12 slices double-smoked, thick-cut bacon

4 tablespoons unsalted butter, divided

8 eggs

Salt and pepper

8 slices whole wheat, or multigrain bread

Spicy Mayo (page 175)

1 to 2 large beefsteak tomatoes, thinly sliced

2 large Haas avocados, sliced lengthwise

WITH its cottage-like feel, quaint West Village location, and racks of magazines that beckon one to linger, Café Cluny epitomizes the cozy, accessible, neighborly café—that is, until mealtime, when the food shines far brighter than an average coffee shop.

So it's no surprise then that Cluny's sandwich is an outstanding example of comfort food. It was borne out of the search for a hangover remedy by former sous chef Phil Conlon. After a long night out, Conlon found himself facing a busy Sunday brunch shift with a splitting headache. So he made this sandwich. The smoky bacon, crisp tomato, just-runny egg, and stealthy heat cleared his head—and once cleared, he realized it was also delicious. That day, Conlon ran the sandwich as a brunch special. Soon, customers began requesting it. The "breakfast club" is Café Cluny's best-selling item.

✳ ✳ ✳

Preheat the oven to 350°F. Lay the bacon on a sheet pan and bake until crispy, about 18 minutes.

Place a nonstick skillet over medium heat, and add 1 tablespoon of the butter. Crack 2 of the eggs into the skillet, and season with salt and pepper to taste. Cook for 3 minutes. Gently flip each egg, and cook on the other side for 1 minute.

Toast the bread until golden brown. Spread the Spicy Mayo (to taste) on 4 slices. Top with 2 eggs, then 3 slices of bacon. Add 2 slices of the tomato, and season to taste. Add 2 slices of the avocado, and season again. Repeat, cooking 2 eggs at a time in 1 tablespoon of butter, until all the sandwiches are made.

Top each sandwich with the remaining bread, and cut diagonally. Use toothpicks to secure and serve.

Carmine's Cheesesteak Sandwich

GLENN ROLNICK, DIRECTOR OF OPERATIONS * CARMINE'S * WWW.CARMINESNYC.COM

1 **P**

SERVES 4

¼ cup olive oil

1 green bell pepper, sliced

1 red bell pepper, sliced

1 medium white onion, sliced

24 ounces rib eye steak,
   shaved thinly

1 teaspoon salt

¼ teaspoon ground black
   pepper

2 teaspoons dried oregano

4 Italian hero rolls
   (about 9 inches each)

4 tablespoons Garlic Butter*
   (recipe follows)

12 slices aged provolone
   cheese

IF even for a second you think that the raucous, family-style, over-portioned (not to mention mouthwatering) New York Italian restaurant was a dying concept, try going to Carmine's in Times Square. "Generous" doesn't even start to describe the size of your veal chop or the pile of noodles you'll be tackling if you order, say, the rigatoni.

For more than twenty years, Carmine's has been playing to the palates of office workers, theater-goers, and tourists alike. At the restaurant—or, for that matter, its uptown outpost—dishes are all about pastas and other large-plate items. But for this book, the chefs have translated those big, hearty tastes to a sandwich—a savory cheesesteak built to impress. "People don't necessarily think of Italian food when they think of Philly cheesesteaks," said Glenn Rolnick, Carmine's director of operations. "But our take on this classic sandwich is truly as delicious as the original . . . the smell alone will drive you insane."

* * *

Preheat a broiler on high or oven to 400°F.

Place the olive oil in a 12-inch sauté pan over medium heat. Add the peppers and onions to the pan. Sauté until lightly browned, about 5 minutes. Add the shaved meat, salt, pepper, and oregano. Sauté until the meat is fully cooked, about 5 to 7 minutes. Remove from the heat.

Slice the hero rolls in half lengthwise. Remove the insides of the bread halves. For each sandwich, spread about 1½ tablespoons of the garlic butter over both insides of bread. Toast the bread in the oven or under a broiler until it's crispy.

For every sandwich, put ¼ of the filling in the bottom half and top with three slices of the provolone cheese. Cover with the sandwich top, cut all in half, and serve.

GARLIC BUTTER

½ pound (2 sticks) unsalted
  butter, softened
1 tablespoon olive oil
½ teaspoon dried oregano
½ teaspoon garlic powder
Pinch of onion powder
¾ ounce Romano cheese,
  grated
1 teaspoon fresh parsley,
  chopped
½ teaspoon fresh garlic,
  chopped
¼ teaspoon salt
Pinch of ground white pepper

Combine the butter, olive oil, oregano, garlic powder, onion powder, cheese, garlic, salt, and pepper together in a bowl. Mix well and store in the refrigerator.

*NOTE: If you're in a hurry, mix 1 to 2 minced garlic cloves per 1 stick butter.

GRILLED TUNA BLT SANDWICH

LAURENT TOURONDEL ✳ BLT FISH ✳ WWW.BLTRESTAURANTS.COM

1 **P** **H**

I T'S difficult to imagine a more convincing hybrid than Tourondel himself. The French-born chef has applied his hometown techniques to the broad New York palate in a way that's more broadly successful—and more appealing to the mainstream—than his contemporaries. Tourondel spent his early years in New York creating expertly seasoned haute French food at an Upper East Side restaurant called Cello. After receiving rave reviews, he was able to leverage that flavor savvy and finesse to add his unique stamp to all facets of classic American cuisine. Today, along with BLT Fish, there's a Steak, a Prime, a Market, and a Burger outpost. Each restaurant seamlessly blends his New York present with his culinary roots.

The BLT in this recipe makes use of a double entendre: It alludes to New York's hugely successful series of high-end Bistro Laurent Tourondel restaurants as well as one of America's most beloved classics. "This Grilled Tuna BLT really embodies my taste and culinary philosophy. It's a little bit American classic (BLT, avocado, basil) and a little bit Niçoise (tapenade, hard-cooked egg, tuna)," said Tourondel. For true decadence, he adds, serve the sandwiches with a shallow dish of extra virgin olive oil and invite your guests to dip with impunity. The result is a refreshing, pleasing sandwich that captures the Mediterranean in a crusty ciabatta.

Preheat a panini press, if using. Toast the roll halves. Fry the bacon on both sides, until crispy, about 2 minutes on each side. Drain on a paper towel–lined plate. Season the tuna with the oil, garlic, and salt and pepper to taste. Sear the tuna on a hot grill or pan, until sides are cooked but the centers are raw, about 2 minutes on each side. Set aside.

Spread each roll bottom with 1 tablespoon of the tapenade. Top with a few slices of the tomato, onion, basil, avocado, eggs, cheese, arugula, 2 slices of bacon, and 1 slice of tuna. Spread each roll top with 1 tablespoon of the mayonnaise. Close the sandwiches.

Grill each sandwich in the heated panini press. (If you don't have a panini press, place the sandwiches on a hot grill or skillet with a sandwich press, cast-iron skillet, or other heavy weight on top. Grill for 1 to 2 minutes on each side.) Cut each sandwich in half and serve.

SERVES 4

- 4 soft ciabatta rolls, halved lengthwise
- 8 slices bacon
- 4 (3-ounce) slices tuna (sushi grade, if possible)
- 2 tablespoons extra virgin olive oil, plus extra oil for dipping
- 1 garlic clove, sliced thin
- Salt and pepper
- 4 tablespoons olive tapenade
- 2 large beefsteak tomatoes, thinly sliced
- 1 small red onion, thinly sliced
- 12 basil leaves
- 1 avocado, sliced lengthwise
- 4 hard-boiled eggs, sliced
- 4 slivers Parmigiano-Reggiano cheese, sliced with a vegetable peeler
- 1 bunch arugula, stems removed
- 4 tablespoons mayonnaise, divided

Chapter 4

THE RUSTIC SANDWICH

＊ ＊ ＊

IT'S DIFFICULT TO IMAGINE WHAT THE NEW YORK RESTAURANT SCENE WOULD be like *sans* greenmarkets. To those of us who care about supporting conscionable farms, rediscovering heirloom varietals, and preserving heritage cooking, "slow," "local," and "sustainable" foods are critical. We're glad—and lucky—to have not only fresh farm sources at our fingertips but also talented chefs who care deeply about these concepts and put their concerns into practice. As we scouted the sandwich landscape, we found great examples of not only delicious but sustainable sandwiches everywhere.

Many of these sandwiches use Mediterranean ingredients and components: Orhan Yegen's lamb ragu, the tender kebabs of Michael Psilakis' Chicken Souvlaki, Marco Canora's sun-kissed Egg Sandwich, and a plethora of pillowy focaccia and sturdy ciabatta rolls. Cheese abounds: from the stinky Reblochon in Terrance Brennan's "Tartiflette" sandwich to the (slightly) less stinky Gorgonzola in Manual Trevino's Grilled Hangar Steak and Mint Pesto Sandwich. The sandwiches in this chapter are typically hearty, and use meats such as veal and duck—rich and tasty. These meats feature in Cal Elliott's Meatloaf Sandwich, Eric Bromberg's Duck Confit, Kurt Gutenbrunner's Wiener Schnitzel, and John Fraser's Patty Melt Madame. That Patty Melt features an over-easy egg with a rich, sunny-yellow yolk, similar to the egg in Craig Hopson's Aussie Steak, Egg, and Bacon Sandwich (yes, more bacon!).

We hope you enjoy these sandwiches, and eat conscionably.

＊ ＊ ＊

WARM LAMB CLUB WITH LEMONY AÏOLI

RYAN ANGULO * BUTTERMILK CHANNEL * WWW.BUTTERMILKCHANNELNYC.COM

2 **P**

SERVES 4

1 small bone-in leg of lamb,
    about 5 pounds
Olive oil
Salt
8 anchovy fillets
4 garlic cloves
2 lamb bellies (also called
    lamb flaps and work a little
    like bacon but from lamb)
12 slices olive bread
2 tablespoons fresh rosemary,
    chopped
½ cup Lemony Aïoli
    (recipe follows)
2 bunches arugula
1 lemon
Salt
8 oven-dried Roma tomato
    halves (or store-bought
    sun-dried tomatoes)

"BUTTERMILK Channel" is the name of the tidal channel between Brooklyn and Governors Island. According to some, the phrase comes from the days when Brooklyn farmers used to drive their cattle to the island to graze at low tide. Others claim that it refers to a boat crossing so rough the milk on board was practically churned. One thing people seem to agree on: Chef Ryan Angulo's sure touch—he spins comfort food into something fresh, refined, and still familiar—has turned Buttermilk into not just a mainstay for those living in Brooklyn's Carroll Gardens (we've heard friends use words like "obsessed"), but also a draw for diners from all the boroughs.

Angulo's Lamb Club Sandwich couldn't be a better reflection of the laid-back/refined tone his restaurant sets. "This sandwich is one I daydream about all the time," he said. "I think about it every time a loaf of olive bread arrives or when I take a sizzling leg of lamb out of the oven."

* * *

Preheat the oven to 450°F. Rub the lamb leg with olive oil and salt. Place it on a roasting pan with a roasting rack, and make about 16 small incisions all over the lamb with a pairing knife (each should be a small pocket). Cut the anchovy fillets in half and the garlic cloves into quarters. Place a piece of anchovy and a piece of garlic in each pocket. Roast the lamb leg in the oven for 25 minutes; this will create a nice crust. Lower the oven temperature to 325°F and continue to roast for another 30 minutes. Don't discard the pan drippings. Let the lamb rest for 10 minutes before carving.

Bring the oven temperature up to 400°F. Rub the lamb belly flap with olive oil and salt and, when the oven is heated, roast it (on the same pan or a new one) until it's brown and crispy, about 20 minutes. Again, save the drippings.

Brush each slice of olive bread with olive oil and toast them all together. Mix the rosemary into the aioli. Cut the lamb belly into strips, and slice the lamb leg into thin pieces. Toss the arugula with a squeeze of lemon, a little olive oil, and salt. Spread about a tablespoon of aïoli onto each of 4 bread slices and then pile each of those high with the lamb leg slices and drizzle with reserved pan drippings. Top that with another slice of toasted olive bread. On each top slice of bread, spread another layer of aïoli and cover that with arugula, 2 oven-dried tomato halves, and some of the crispy lamb belly. Finish with a final slice of toasted olive bread and press down to secure.

NOTE: To make oven-dried tomatoes, preheat the oven to 200°F. Halve as many Roma tomatoes as you want to make and toss them with olive oil and salt. Place them cutside up on a baking sheet with a wire rack and cook in a 200°F oven for about 8 minutes. Remove from oven and reserve.

LEMONY AÏOLI

MAKES ABOUT 2¼ CUPS

1 tablespoon whole grain mustard

1 garlic clove

3 egg yolks

½ teaspoon salt

¼ cup lemon juice

2 cups canola oil

Put the mustard, garlic, egg yolks, salt, and lemon juice in a food processor and mix for 10 seconds. With the processor still running, slowly drizzle in the oil until it's incorporated. Adjust the seasoning to taste.

Salame Ala Diavola

NICK ANDERER ✳ MAIALINO ✳ WWW.MAIALINONYC.COM

1 **P**

SERVES 4

8 tablespoons olive oil

8 tablespoons red wine
vinegar

6 tablespoon green olives,
chopped (Castelvetranois a
good variety if you can
find it)

2 tablespoons or more
chopped Pickled Peppers,
plus 4 tablespoon of the
pickling liquid (recipe
follows)

4 (5 × 5-inch) pieces pizza
bianca or rosemary
focaccia, split in half

Small handful arugula

12 thin slices provolone cheese

8 thin slices prosciutto

8 thin slices mortadella

FOR restaurateur Danny Meyer, creating Maialino was no small order. The spot was to be in Ian Schrager's impeccable Gramercy Park Hotel—facing the elegant downtown park itself. Expectations were high, and the last eatery in the location had failed. Meyer did have a strong advantage—through his company Union Square Hospitality Group, he owned a number of successful restaurants in the neighborhood. He knew the crowd: sophisticated diners looking for high quality and low pretension. Therefore, to helm the kitchen, Meyer tapped Nick Anderer, the longtime sous chef at Meyer's Gramercy Tavern. Anderer (who's also worked at Mario Batali's Babbo) had developed his love of Italian food as a student at Columbia University, during which time he'd gone abroad for the art and instead fallen for the food.

And so, Maialino, a warm and inviting Roman-style trattoria, was born. The critics loved it. Anderer's refined approach to fresh ingredients plus his predilection for hearty meats and breads turned out home run after home run of dishes at once simple and absolutely satisfying.

As luck would have it, Anderer is a sandwich lover. At lunchtime, diners can settle in with the paper and the sun streaming through the large windows and watch new variations being cooked up before their eyes. At first glance, his pick for this book bears striking similarity to Anne Burrell's Spicy Ham, Mortadella and Provolone Sandwich (page 24). But, unlike Burrell's Panini, this one goes refreshingly unpressed. "This dish is, in all honesty, inspired by using leftovers," Anderer said. "The end pieces of prosciutto butts or any leftover Italian cold cuts find a home here. I've deliberately built the sandwich around a chunky Italian vinaigrette—spicy and acidic—that I just love. That makes the whole thing foolproof in that the bread and vinaigrette on their own would be a delicious snack. The meat and cheese (use them sparingly, and feel free to try other meats) are almost an afterthought. Less is always more with a good panino."

Mix the olive oil, vinegar, chopped olives, peppers, and pickling liquid. Spread that mixture on the inside of all the bread slices, reserving a little to toss with the arugula. Onto the bottom sandwich halves, alternate layers of cheese and meat. Top each sandwich off with arugula, and close with the top half of bread. Slice in half or serve as one whole square.

PICKLED PEPPERS

20 hot cherry peppers
Olive oil, to taste
5 cups Champagne vinegar
1 cup water
4 tablespoons kosher salt
3 tablespoons sugar
2 garlic cloves
1 tablespoon black
   peppercorns
2 sprigs thyme
1 bay leaf

Preheat oven to 500°F. Slit the peppers lengthwise but leave whole overall. Put them on a baking sheet. Lightly dress the peppers in olive oil and roast them in the oven for 10 minutes, or until slightly softened. Combine the vinegar, water, salt, sugar, cloves, peppercorns, thyme, and bay leaf together in a pot and bring it all to a boil on the burner. Pour the mixture over the peppers. Let cool, uncovered, at room temperature. Store in the refrigerator until ready to use.

PIEDMONTESE ROAST BEEF WITH PICKLED RAMP AÏOLI ON FOCACCIA

MICHAEL ANTHONY ✳ GRAMERCY TAVERN ✳ WWW.GRAMERCYTAVERN.COM

2 **P** **H**

SINCE 1994, the ceaselessly popular Gramercy Tavern—just around the corner from the Union Square Greenmarket—has been in the business of delivering experiences that are at once casual and breathtakingly extraordinary. The rooms are aglow with golden light and, no matter the season, filled with giant blossom branches—apple, cherry, pussy willow. (Around the holidays, giant handmade ornaments hang from the vaulted ceilings.) Throughout the space, there's a hum of absolute contentment.

It's hard to imagine a chef better suited to this environment—or, more specifically, better able to deliver on its promises—than award-winning Chef Michael Anthony. Having trained in Paris, worked at top New York kitchens such as Daniel and March, Anthony spent four years as executive chef at Blue Hill at Stone Barns in upstate New York, he's passionate about creating unforgettable meals that are elegant and sustainable.

Anthony said he chose this roast beef—a popular favorite—because it's such a strong reflection of these two forces. "There's always a combination of thrift, intrigue, and conscientiousness that goes in to the food that we serve," he explained. "The aim is to develop food that's delicious, healthful, and responsible. In this dish, we've used a cut of meat that's low in fat. Many cooking techniques can dry it out, so it's sometimes overlooked and goes to waste. Here, we've kept the moisture in and created some incredible complements to the flavor. The result is a less fatty, hugely satisfying beef sandwich."

SERVES 5

1½ tablespoons
  grapeseed oil
2½ pounds beef eye round
Salt
Black pepper
1 thyme sprig
1 rosemary sprig
1½ garlic cloves, crushed
10 slices focaccia
4 tablespoons Pickled Ramp
  Aïoli (recipes follow)
Small handful arugula

NOTE: Red meat is a rich source of iron and vitamin B, which help sustain energy and maintain nerve and cognitive health.

Preheat the oven to 300°F.

Heat the grapeseed oil in a large pan over medium-high heat. Season the beef heavily with salt and pepper, and sear it intensely on all sides to form a crust, being careful not to burn it. Place the beef in a roasting pan with the thyme, rosemary, and garlic, and slow roast for approximately 1 hour. When it's done (it should be a light pink inside), place it on a rack and cool to room temperature before slicing thinly.

Toast the focaccia. Layer approximately 5 paper-thin slices of roast beef on each of half of the bread pieces. Spread a tablespoon of the aïoli across the meat and top with a pinch of baby arugula lettuce. Cover each with the second piece of toasted bread and enjoy.

PICKLED RAMPS

3 cups sugar

3 cups water

2 quarts plus 1 cup rice wine vinegar

½ cup salt

¼ teaspoon mustard seeds

¼ teaspoon black peppercorns

¼ teaspoon fennel seeds

¼ teaspoon coriander seeds

6 cups ramps, trimmed

Mix the sugar, water, vinegar, salt, mustard seeds, peppercorns, fennel, and coriander together in a pot and bring to a boil on the burner. Remove the mixture from the heat, strain, and—when cool—add the ramps. Chill in the refrigerator.

PICKLED RAMP AÏOLI

⅛ cup white balsamic vinegar

1 egg yolk

1 cup grapeseed oil

1 cup olive oil

1 ½ teaspoons salt

¼ teaspoon white pepper

½ cup chopped Pickled Ramps

Stir the vinegar into the egg yolk and progressively whisk in the grapeseed and olive oils to form a light, mayonnaise-like sauce. Season with salt and white pepper and then fold in the chopped pickled ramps.

LAMB SANDWICH WITH HOMEMADE HUMMUS

SAUL BOLTON ∗ SAUL, THE VANDERBILT ∗ WWW.SAULRESTAURANT.COM

WWW.THEVANDERBILTNYC.COM

2 **H** STAY LIGHT ON THE HUMMUS AND MAYONNAISE.

WHEN Saul and Lisa Bolton opened Saul, in Brooklyn's Boerum Hill more than ten years ago, it might have seemed an odd choice for a chef who'd had a successful career at high-end standouts like Le Bernardin and Bouley. At the time, Smith Street in Brooklyn was hardly a dining destination. But the Boltons knew there was potential to develop, and the price was right. This was a place they could build something uniquely theirs.

The idea, it turns out, had a lot going for it. Bolton's expert cooking got early raves, and Saul became the first Brooklyn restaurant to receive a coveted Michelin star (business instantly went up by 25 percent). In 2009 history repeated itself, and the Boltons opened The Vanderbilt—this time in up-and-coming Prospect Heights.

Here, Bolton shares a sandwich that, like much of his menu, he's infused with a hearty dose of his surroundings. "The Boerum Hill neighborhood has the largest Yemeni population in the States, and out of love and respect I incorporate elements into my cooking," he said.

"I really love this particular sandwich because it reflects a taste, style, and feel which speaks to my cooking, to my feeling of place and to my history. As a kid my parents spoke a lot about Middle Eastern culture and made quite a bit of Middle Eastern-inspired dishes. They met and fell in love in Iran in the early 1960s. Thinking about all that, I've created something that has sweet, salty, earthy, meaty thing going on with a measure of acid, crunchy, juicy, and herbal. It covers all the bases—it makes complete eating sense."

LAMB

2 pounds lamb shoulder
Salt and pepper
6 tablespoons olive oil
1 medium onion, chopped
1 medium carrot, chopped
1 celery stalk, chopped
6 garlic cloves, crushed
1 jalapeño pepper, sliced
½ cup cilantro stems, chopped
1 tablespoon coriander seeds,
  toasted and ground
1 tablespoon cumin seeds,
  toasted and ground
1 tablespoon fennel seeds,
  toasted and ground
1 teaspoon ground cinnamon
2 cups chicken stock

SANDWICH

Harissa Mayonnaise (recipe
  follows)
4 (6-inch) rolls, opened
  lengthwise (do not cut in
  half; leave a hinge)
Hummus (recipe follows)
Pickled Turnips (recipe follows)
½ cup mint leaves
½ cup cilantro leaves
Lamb
2 cups shredded romaine
  lettuce
1 large carrot, shredded
  (about 1 cup)
Olive oil
Lemon juice

For the Lamb: Preheat oven to 300°F. Season the lamb with salt and pepper to taste. Heat the olive oil in a large saucepan over medium-high heat. Carefully add the lamb shoulder. Brown the shoulder well on both sides (about 8 minutes total), and move the lamb to a plate.

Combine the onion, carrot, celery, garlic, jalapeño, and cilantro stems to the saucepan. Cook until soft and sweet and then add the coriander, cumin, fennel, and cinnamon to the softened vegetables and cook while stirring for about 2 minutes or until fragrant. Mix in the chicken stock, and scrape the saucepan, making sure to loosen any particles that may be adhering to the bottom. Pour the vegetables into a large casserole dish. Add the lamb, cover lightly with aluminum foil, and roast in the oven until fork-tender, about 2 hours.

When the lamb is done, carefully remove it from the casserole and place it on a plate. Drain the cooking liquid through a strainer into a bowl, and skim off any excess fat. Remove the bones, excess fat, and gristle from the shoulder.

Add the lamb to the bowl with the cooking liquid and pull apart any big chunks using two dinner forks. The meat should absorb most of the cooking liquid. Season with salt and pepper, and cover and set aside until needed. The meat can be prepared several days ahead and kept in the refrigerator.

For the Sandwiches: Spread the Harissa Mayonnaise on one half of each roll and the hummus on other half (you can do this to personal taste). Layer the turnips down the length of one side of the sandwich, overlapping as you go.

Mix half the mint and half the cilantro with the lamb. Save the rest for seasoning. Divide the lamb between the rolls, pressing it in against the turnip side. In a bowl, toss the lettuce and carrots with the remaining cilantro and mint. Add a little olive oil and lemon juice to taste. Divide the lettuce and carrot mixture among the rolls and serve.

HUMMUS

½ (15-ounce) can chickpeas,
    drained and rinsed
⅛ cup water
3 tablespoons lemon juice
1 tablespoon tahini
1 garlic clove
2 tablespoons olive oil
Salt

Combine the chickpeas, water, lemon juice, tahini, and garlic in a food processor and blend until smooth. Stir in olive oil by hand and add salt to taste.

HARISSA MAYONNAISE

3 tablespoons harissa
6 tablespoons mayonnaise
2 tablespoons chopped
    cilantro
Squeeze lemon juice
Olive oil
Salt

Combine in a small bowl the harissa, mayonnaise, cilantro, lemon juice, and enough oil to make a spreadable consistency; mix well with a wooden spoon. Add salt to taste.

NOTE: Harissa is a North African chili sauce available at grocery stores or online.

PICKLED TURNIPS

2 cups water
1 cup white wine vinegar
2 tablespoons sugar
3 tablespoons salt
4 medium turnips, peeled and
    thinly sliced

Combine the water, vinegar, sugar, and salt in a saucepan over medium-high heat. Bring to a simmer. Place the turnips in a one-quart container and pour the liquid over them to cover. Chill overnight.

"Tartiflette" Grilled Cheese Sandwich

TERRANCE BRENNAN ✳ ARTISANAL FROMAGERIE, BISTRO & WINE BAR ✳ PICHOLINE

WWW.ARTISANALBISTRO.COM ✳ WWW.PICHOLINENYC.COM

1 **P**

SERVES 4

1 pound Yukon Gold potatoes, peeled and sliced into ⅛-inch rounds

1 tablespoon extra virgin olive oil

8 slices apple-smoked bacon (about 6 ounces), cut into ½-inch cubes

8 slices country bread, ¼ inch thick

14 ounces Reblochon, divided

Salt and pepper

3 tablespoons butter, at room temperature

AS recently as the 1990s, cheese was no big deal. There was Munster, mozzarella, and cheddar, and maybe—if you were lucky—goat's cheese. People did not "jones" for cheese.

Then along came Terrance Brennan. The tall, affable Virginia native had trained at the legendary Le Moulin de Mougins, on the French Riviera, and worked in renowned kitchens throughout Europe. In 1993, he opened Picholine and introduced the traditional cheese course—along with runny, stinky cheeses such as the one used in this recipe—to New York City diners. Ten years later, he founded Artisanal Fromagerie, which includes custom cheese caves for aging cheese, a restaurant, and a cheese retail operation.

Tartiflettes, a specialty of Haute-Savoie, are typically served casserole-style. "An authentic tartiflette is crunchy and crusty," said Brennan. He offers a sandwich version below.

✳ ✳ ✳

Preheat the oven to 350°F. Place the sliced potatoes in a bowl. Cover with water. Set aside.

In a sauté pan over medium heat, add the oil and the bacon. Cook the bacon until crispy, about 3 minutes. Turn off the heat. Drain the potatoes, and add them to the pan. Season with salt and pepper to taste. Toss the mixture until the potatoes are nicely coated. Transfer the bacon and potato mixture to a baking pan small enough to layer the potatoes ½ inch high, and level (for even cooking). Cover the pan with aluminum foil. Bake until the potatoes are tender, about 35 minutes. Remove the pan, and let cool.

Lay out 4 slices of the bread. Top with even portions of the Reblochon cheese. Add the bacon and potato mixture. Cover the sandwiches with the remaining 4 slices of the bread. Set a large sauté pan over medium heat. Brush both sides of each sandwich with butter. Place them into the pan. Cook each side until the cheese has melted, 3 to 4 minutes per side. While cooking, flatten the sandwiches using a spatula. Cut each sandwich in half and serve.

NOTE: If you can't find Reblochon, suitable substitutes include prefe de nos montagnes or Italian Robiola. Waxy cheeses such as Gruyère won't do, nor will oozy cheeses such as ripe Camembert or triple-crème Brie.

Sausage and Peppers Hero

JOEY CAMPANARO * THE LITTLE OWL * WWW.THELITTLEOWLNYC.COM

1 **P** **H** CHOOSE A LEAN CHICKEN, TURKEY, OR SEAFOOD SAUSAGE.

SERVES 4

1 pound sweet Italian sausage

1 garlic clove, chopped

½ white onion, sliced

2 red peppers, sliced

2 (28-ounce) cans whole
   peeled tomatoes, drained

4 slices provolone cheese

3 basil leaves, torn

8 slices Italian bread, toasted

THE West Village is full of tiny, beloved restaurants, but few have as broad and intense a following as this twenty-eight-seat corner spot, cozy on the inside with ceilings of gold-painted stamped tin and flowers expertly arranged. When Frank Bruni reviewed the restaurant for *The New York Times*, he remarked on its "irresistible earnestness and exuberance," a theme he was able to trace right back to Chef Joey Campanaro's cooking.

Born into a large and food-loving Philadelphia Italian family, Campanaro has built a small, carefully crafted menu that, like any good family recipe collection, is heavy on near-addictive favorites. Campanaro, who first gained recognition cooking for ingredient-conscious chefs such as Jonathan Waxman, seems especially adept at the art of making great ideas and combinations appear personal, effortless, and entirely delicious.

Case-in-point: this Sausage and Peppers Hero. "The sandwich is a take on one that I would take to school for my brown-bag lunch. I think I even got teased for it," Campanaro said. "But I loved the satisfying taste of the sausage and the sweetness of the peppers and onions so much I didn't care. The sharp provolone balances the richness of the sandwich. Also, the fact that it's made on Italian bread maintains the integrity of the sandwich. It holds up to the rich, flavorful moisture."

* * *

Crumble the sausage and brown in a skillet over medium heat. Once browned, add the garlic, onion, peppers, tomatoes, and torn basil leaves. Cook for a minimum of 45 minutes at medium-low heat. For each sandwich, add the cheese to the toasted Italian bread and pile the sausage mixture on top. Cut to the desired size.

PATTY MELT MADAME

JOHN FRASER ✳ DOVETAIL ✳ WWW.DOVETAILNYC.COM

❷

SERVES 4

3 plum tomatoes, sliced

3 tablespoons olive oil,
    divided

Salt and pepper

1⅓ pounds ground veal

⅓ pound ground beef

3 tablespoons Worcestershire
    sauce

1 tablespoon garlic powder

1 tablespoon onion powder

5 eggs, divided

Salt and white pepper

Tabasco

4 thick slices provolone cheese

1 Spanish onion, sliced

4 brioche rolls, halved
    lengthwise and toasted

Honey Mustard Vinaigrette
    (recipe follows)

12 parsley sprigs, chopped

BRICK columns, wooden panels, and floor-to-ceiling windows draw clean, vertical lines to accompany one of the most surprising food experiences in New York: a minimalist haven on the Upper West Side, serving some of the city's most critically (and popularly) acclaimed prix fixe menus.

For weekend brunch, Chef John Fraser created this sandwich; an upscale burger crossed with a Croque Madame. "Veal is more subtle in flavor than beef. Its leanness allows for the full expression of the fattier ingredients, such as egg and cheese," he said. The Patty Melt is easy, toothsome, and messy: have plenty of (linen) napkins on hand.

✳ ✳ ✳

Preheat the oven to 300°F. Place the sliced tomatoes on a baking sheet. Drizzle with 1 tablespoon of the olive oil and salt and pepper to taste. Roast until oven-dried, about 2 hours.

Thoroughly combine the ground meat, Worcestershire, garlic powder, onion powder, and 1 egg. Add salt, pepper, and Tabasco to taste. Form into four patties. Wrap each patty in plastic wrap. Chill for at least 30 minutes.

Place 2 teaspoons of the olive oil in a skillet over high heat. Add 1 veal patty and sear until medium rare, about 4 minutes. Flip the patty. Top with 1 slice of the provolone, and continue to sear until the cheese is melted and the desired doneness reached. Transfer to a paper towel–lined platter. Repeat with the remaining patties.

In a nonstick skillet, add 1 teaspoon of the oil over medium heat. When hot, cook the remaining 4 eggs until the bottom of the whites are set, about 3 minutes; then flip and cook until the whites on the other side are set, about 1 minute. You may need to cook these in batches. In a separate pan, heat the remaining tablespoon of oil over medium heat. Add the onion and cook, stirring occasionally, for about 3 minutes, or until caramelized.

To build the sandwiches, brush each toasted brioche roll side with the Honey Mustard Vinaigrette. Place a few slices of the oven-dried tomatoes on each roll bottom. Add a veal patty. Add an egg. Carefully top with the caramelized onions and parsley. Gently close the sandwiches. Serve warm.

HONEY MUSTARD VINAIGRETTE

MAKES ENOUGH FOR 4 SANDWICHES

1 cup Dijon mustard
2 tablespoons whole grain mustard
¼ cup grapeseed oil
2 tablespoons honey
3 tablespoons red wine vinegar
Salt

Combine the mustards, oil, honey, and vinegar. Season with salt to taste. Chill until ready to use.

WIENER SCHNITZEL SANDWICH

KURT GUTENBRUNNER

BLAUE GANS, CAFÉ KRISTALL, CAFÉ SALARSKY, THE UPHOLSTERY SORE, WALLSÉ * WWW.WALLSE.COM

② **P**

SERVES 4

¾ **pound veal top round**
Salt and white pepper
1 cup flour
2 eggs
3 tablespoons heavy cream
1½ cups unseasoned
   breadcrumbs
2 cups vegetable oil
4 tablespoons unsalted butter
4 Kaiser rolls, split lengthwise
½ cup mayonnaise
8 sweet pickle slices
1 small red onion, sliced
   thinly
4 Bibb lettuce leaves
Lemon wedges, for serving
4 teaspoons lingonberry
   preserves, for serving

K URT Gutenbrunner is considered by some to be the father of New York's modern Austrian cuisine. When he opened Wallsé in the West Village observers wondered whether the restaurant's white-tablecloth ambiance, Austrian wine list, and pricey schnitzels would be greeted with ridicule or joy. Customers rejoiced, and soon, the tastiness and elegance of Austrian cuisine caught on in New York.

A decade after the success of Wallsé, Gutenbrunner has branched into Austrian gastropub (Blaue Gans), museum café (Café Sabarsky), and tasting room (Upholstery Store). His schnitzel—the foundation for this classic sandwich—is still the finest in town, with a billowy, golden brown crust.

"Schnitzel is deceptively difficult to make. Use the freshest veal you can find, and make it thin and tender. While frying, keep moving the frying pan, so you get an airy and delicious schnitzel," said Gutenbrunner.

* * *

Remove all veal membrane. Cut the veal into four equal pieces. One at a time, place the scallopines in a thick plastic bag. Pound with a mallet until uniformly thin. Place the veal on a large platter. Season both sides with salt and pepper to taste.

Place the flour in a wide, shallow bowl. Place the eggs and cream in a similar bowl and whisk to combine. Beat to blend. Place the breadcrumbs in a third bowl. Arrange the bowls near the stove, along with a platter lined with paper towels.

Heat the oil in a deep skillet or sauté pan over high heat. When it's hot but not smoking, add the butter. Lower the heat to medium. Dust a veal cutlet with the flour. Dip the cutlet in the egg, turning to coat. Dip it in the breadcrumbs, coating well. Shake off any excess. Add the cutlet to the skillet. Fry for about 1 minute; the oil should turn frothy. While frying, gently move the pan in a circular motion on the burner. When the breading turns golden brown, turn the cutlet. Cook for another minute. Transfer the cutlet to the paper towel–lined platter.

Repeat with the remaining veal. Adjust the heat so that the breading cooks gradually and evenly without burning.

Toast the rolls. Spread the mayonnaise on each side. Place the drained schnitzels on top of the bottom half. Add the pickles, onions, and Bibb lettuce. Close the rolls. Serve with lemon wedges and lingonberry preserves.

MEATLOAF SANDWICH

CAL ELLIOTT ✳ RYE ✳ WWW.RYERESTAURANT.COM

3 **P**

SERVES 4

12 ounces bacon (8 to 10
    slices)
2 tablespoons olive, canola,
    or grapeseed oil
½ pound portobello
    mushrooms, finely chopped
1 large Spanish onion, finely
    chopped
3 garlic cloves, finely chopped
2 shallots, finely chopped
2 leeks (whites only), finely
    chopped
1 tablespoon unsalted butter
½ pound ground veal
½ pound ground pork
½ pound lean ground beef
½ pound duck breast, finely
    chopped
2 eggs
2 cups breadcrumbs

WHEN thinking of accompaniments for a stiff rye-based cocktail, meatloaf isn't the first dish that comes to mind. But that changed for New Yorkers when Chef Cal Elliott opened Rye, an unmarked, understated, well-reviewed restaurant on a quiet street in a Brooklyn enclave, and the pairing of a good rye old-fashioned with Elliott's signature meatloaf sandwich became a local legend.

For years, Elliott had been co-executive chef of nearby Dumont, so well known for its burgers that it opened another outlet (Dumont Burger) to meet demand. "The last thing I wanted to do was offer just another Williamsburg burger," said Elliott. So he took popular roast meats (veal, pork, short ribs, and duck), hearty vegetables (portobello mushrooms, leeks), sauces (homemade barbecue sauce, horseradish dressing), and sides (frizzled onions, salad) and fashioned this rich, multifarious sandwich. The most difficult part of this recipe is the chopping, so use a food processor, mandoline, or any other helpful tool in your arsenal. The components (Fried Onions, Onion Jam) are optional.

✳ ✳ ✳

Preheat the oven to 425°F. Position a rack in the middle of the oven.

Place the bacon in a heavy-bottomed pan. Fry over medium heat until crispy, about 5 minutes. Drain on paper towels. Discard all but ¼ cup of bacon grease. Add the oil and the mushrooms, onions, garlic, shallots, and leeks. Sauté until soft, about 8 minutes. Drain thoroughly in large colander. Cool for 2 hours.

Grease a 9-inch baking dish with the butter. When the vegetables are cool, add them to a large mixing bowl. Add the veal, pork beef, duck breast, eggs, breadcrumbs, ketchup, honey, mustard, Worcestershire sauce, and salt. Combine all the ingredients thoroughly—this is best done with your hands. Transfer the meat into the baking dish, and shape into a loaf. Place the dish on the middle rack of the oven. Bake for 1 hour.

Cut the meatloaf into 2-inch slices. If using the onion jam, spread it on each roll bottom. Add a slice of meatloaf. Add pickles and (if using) fried onions. Spread each roll top with the horseradish dressing. Close the rolls and serve.

1 ½ cups ketchup

1 tablespoon honey

1 tablespoon Dijon mustard

1 tablespoon Worcestershire sauce

1 tablespoon salt, or to taste

Onion Jam, optional (recipe follows)

4 (6-inch) hero rolls, split lengthwise

Dill pickles

Fried Onions, optional (recipe follows)

Creamy Horseradish Dressing (recipe follows)

NOTE: To avoid sogginess, pack components separately.

ONION JAM

MAKES ABOUT 3 CUPS

2 tablespoons unsalted butter

4 Spanish onions, thinly sliced

⅓ cup sugar

¼ cup sherry vinegar

¼ cup balsamic vinegar

Salt and pepper

Melt the butter in a heavy-bottomed pot. Cook the onions on medium heat until soft and brown, about 15 minutes. Add the sugar. Cook for another 5 minutes. Add the vinegars and cook until reduced until the liquid is cooked off, about 40 minutes. Season with salt and pepper to taste.

CREAMY HORSERADISH DRESSING

MAKES UP TO 3 CUPS

2 eggs, separated
5 garlic cloves
3 tablespoons whole grain
mustard
2 tablespoons fresh lemon
juice
2 tablespoons sherry vinegar
Salt and pepper
3 tablespoons grated fresh
horseradish
Oil
1 to 2 cups heavy cream

Separate the eggs, reserving the whites for another use. Combine the egg yolks, garlic, mustard, lemon juice, and vinegar in a blender. Season with salt and pepper to taste. Blend slowly. Add the oil in a steady stream, until completely incorporated. Repeat with the cream.

FRIED ONIONS

MAKES ABOUT 2 CUPS

2 Spanish onions, halved and
sliced thinly
1 quart (4 cups) buttermilk
2 cups all-purpose flour
3 cups canola or peanut oil
Salt and pepper

Soak the onions in the buttermilk for 15 to 20 minutes. Dredge the onions in the flour and shake off any excess. Place the oil in a frying pan over high heat. Add the onions in batches, and fry until golden brown. Season with salt and pepper to taste.

AUSSIE STEAK, EGG, AND BACON

CRAIG HOPSON ✳ LE CIRQUE ✳ WWW.LECIRQUE.COM

2

SINCE 1974, the name "Le Cirque" has had a glittering status—lavish, costly, and high-society. The restaurant helped launch the careers of top chefs, among them Daniel Boulud and Jacques Torres. Owner Sirio Maccioni's uncanny ability to keep his flagship right at the center of things has been tirelessly documented. Got a good table at Le Cirque? Even today, the implication is that you've got something special going on.

Now in its third powerhouse location—in Midtown's Bloomberg Tower—the kitchen is run (ironically, maybe) by a laid-back surf-loving Australian. Classically trained, Craig Hopson has a knack for elevating what we know and like almost effortlessly. His is food that's familiar, made much, much better.

Here, Hopson's Aussie Steak, Egg, and Bacon Sandwich reflects just that. "This sandwich reminds me of growing up in Australia, where it's a favorite lunch-time sandwich in pubs and cafés," he said. "It's very easy and for me has the taste of an Aussie Barbecue. Of course, with my line of work, I luxe it up a bit and add truffle mayonnaise, which adds a refined and unexpected touch. But if you're at home, you can definitely just take some mayonnaise from that jar in the fridge."

✳ ✳ ✳

Heat a small sauté pan and add half the oil. Sauté the onion over medium heat. Add salt to taste, reduce the heat to medium low, and cook until the onion is caramelized.

Heat the remaining tablespoon of oil in a large sauté pan over medium heat. Add the eggs and cook for about 2 minutes. Flip carefully when the white starts to look solid and a film forms over the yolk. Keep the yolk intact. Remove the eggs after 30 seconds.

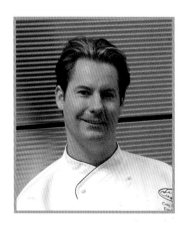

SERVES 4

2 tablespoons canola oil, divided

1 large white onion, finely sliced

Salt

4 eggs

12 slices smoked bacon

4 (3-ounce) sirloin steaks, pounded ¼-inch thick

8 slices country-style bread

Truffle Mayonnaise (recipe follows)

1 large tomato, sliced

4 leaves iceberg lettuce

Add the bacon, and cook until browned and slightly crisp, about 7 minutes, flipping once. Remove the bacon, and add the steaks to the pan and cook until medium rare (at least 5 minutes on each side).

Toast the bread. Spread the truffle mayonnaise on one side of each piece. Build each sandwich by starting with the steaks on the bottom piece of bread and then layering with the tomato, bacon, egg, lettuce, and onion. Add the top slice, press firmly, cut in half, and serve.

NOTE: For added texture within the sandwich, Hopson suggests switching up the egg and bacon steps. "Frying your egg straight in the leftover bacon fat in the same pan will get the edges of the eggs extra crispy," he said.

TRUFFLE MAYONNAISE

MAKES 1¼ CUPS

2 eggs, separated
1 tablespoon red wine vinegar
1 cup grapeseed oil
2 tablespoons black truffle paste
Salt and pepper

Because of its mild, neutral taste, you'll often see grapeseed oil in recipes for mayonnaise and salad dressings. The oil itself is high in antioxidants (among them, it contains resveratrol, the "magic" ingredient in red wine) and has half the saturated fat of olive oil.

* * *

Whisk the egg yolks in a bowl (reserving the whites for another use). Pour in the vinegar and combine well. Add the grapeseed oil while whisking, drop by drop at first and then in a steady stream until the mixture is thick. When the oil is incorporated, whisk in the truffle paste. Add salt and pepper to taste.

DOWNTOWN BOLLITO
(BEEF BRISKET WITH SALSA VERDE AND PICKLED RED ONIONS)

ERIC KLEINMAN * 'INOTECA * WWW.INOTECANYC.COM

3 **P** **H** **M** 4 TO 6 HOURS

SERVES 4

4 cups diced red onions
2 cups diced carrots
2 cups diced celery
½ bunch thyme
¼ cup peppercorns
5 bay leaves
1 cup white wine
2 pounds Brisket, brined
   overnight (recipe follows)
4 ciabatta rolls
Arugula Salad (optional;
   recipe follows)
Salsa Verde (recipe follows)
Pickled Red Onion (recipe
   follows)

IN the late 1990s, Jason and Jennifer Denton opened 'ino, a tiny restaurant in the West Village. Inspired by a trip they took to Italy, they went heavy on the panini on the menu. It's hard to tell which one New Yorkers fell for more—the pressed sandwich or the Dentons, who went on to partner and collaborate with Mario Batali on Lupa, where they first brought on Chef Eric Kleinman. In 2003, Jason, his brother Joe, and Eric partnered to open 'inoteca on New York's Lower East Side.

The neighborhood—for generations a slightly rough cross-road of Latin, Asian, and Jewish cultures, among others—was rapidly becoming a coveted destination thanks to affordable rent, both for residents and storefronts. 'Inoteca, with its inventive interpretations of rustic Italian fare, replicated 'ino's success in spades. Now with other outposts across the city, its nuanced and carefully built dishes (in a past professional life Kleinman studied engineering) are still going strong. Here, Kleinman breaks down one of his own all-time favorites. "Inspired by the classic bollito misto from Florence, our interpretation utilizes only beef brisket as opposed to the mix of meats in the classic sandwich," Kleinman said. "I often prepare this with Wagyu beef, adding depth of flavor and tenderness. The optional fresh salad on the side represents a deconstructed version of the classic salsa verde utilized in the dish."

* * *

Sweat the onions, carrots, and celery in a pot on medium heat for about 15 minutes; they should be cooked but not brown. Tie the thyme, peppercorns, and bay leaves in a cheesecloth pouch. Add the cheesecloth to the vegetables. Cook for 10 minutes.

Preheat the oven to 300°F. Then, add the wine and cook until almost all of the liquid has cooked into the vegetables. Finally, add the brisket, cover with water, and bring to a boil. As the mixture hits boil; turn it down to a simmer. Cover and put the pot in the oven. Cook for 4 to 6 hours, or until the brisket is so tender it looks like it's just about to fall apart. At that point, remove the brisket from the liquid and let it cool until you can cut it with a sharp knife without having it fall into pieces.

Cut each ciabatta in half. For each, hollow out the bottom part and stuff it with cooked vegetables. Put all eight of the bread halves on a baking sheet and toast them in the oven until they're lightly brown.

Slice the brisket across the grain (this minimizes stringiness), pile some of it on each bottom half of bread, and top with the arugula salad. On each top half, spread the salsa verde and cover with the pickled onions. Put the halves together and serve.

SALSA VERDE   SERVES 4

1 bunch parsley, leaves only
1 bunch basil, leaves only
1 bunch mint, leaves only
Olive oil
Salt and Pepper

Bring a pot of water to a boil over high heat. Blanch the parsley, basil, and mint separately for about 30 seconds each. Remove the herbs and dry them on a paper towel and then put them all in the blender. With the blender running, add just enough extra virgin olive oil to form a spreadable paste; focus on keeping the amount as low as possible to keep the spread from tasting too greasy. Add salt and pepper to taste.

NOTE: "To preserve the herbs' color, 'ice shock' them right after blanching," said Kleinman. "Keep a bowl of ice with just enough water to cover it, and as you remove each herb, plunge it into the bowl. This instantly stops the cooking process." You can use this technique for any vegetables.

PICKLED ONIONS   SERVES 4

2 red onions
Salt
1 cup red wine vinegar
Pepper

Slice the onions into rings. (The recipe works equally well with thick or thin rings, so make them according to your own preference). After they are sliced, combine the onions with the salt and vinegar in a bowl; the onions should be barely covered. Finish with pepper to taste. Let marinate 30 minutes to overnight.

ARUGULA SALAD

⅛ cup chopped parsley
⅛ cup chopped basil
⅛ cup chopped mint
⅓ cup arugula
Olive oil
Lemon
Freshly grated horseradish
Salt and pepper

Mix the parsley, basil, mint, and arugula together in a bowl. Dress with olive oil, lemon, horseradish, and salt and pepper to taste.

GRILLED CHEESE, WEST VILLAGE STYLE
MURRAY'S OLD SKOOL PLAYA AND BLEEKER STREET CLASSIC

ROB KAUFELT AND THE STAFF OF MURRAY'S KITCHEN

MURRAY'S CHEESE SHOP ✳ WWW.MURRAYSCHEESE.COM

HARD, soft, semi-soft, gooey, crumbly, not to mention nutty, sweet, earthy, grassy, buttery, toothsome—when it comes to cheese, the sheer number of textures and flavors can be as baffling as they are mouthwatering. At Murray's Cheese, a West Village fixture since the 1940s, you'll find three hundred to choose from. And, yes, the staff will gladly let you taste every single one.

The original Murray Greenberg, the story goes, was a radical left-leaning Jewish Spanish Civil War veteran with an eye for the bottom line. The store really took shape when it was bought in 1991 by Rob Kaufelt, a specialty shop entrepreneur living in the neighborhood. As clients and staff grew, so did the platform. Murray's now offers about as many cheese classes as there are cheeses. And if you think they are missing one, there is a suggestion form on their website. The test kitchens are home to many a grilled-cheese innovation. Here, the Murray's team has worked up two original grilled cheese recipes, presented with commentary from Kaufelt himself.

OLD SKOOL PLAYA

1 **P**

12 slices thick smoky bacon

8 slices white Pullman bread

Butter

12 ounces sharp cheddar
(such as Grafton
Village 1 Year Aged),
shredded or sliced

½ medium tomato, sliced
(about 8 slices)

For this one, we decided to go retro and resurrected the classic grilled cheese: That means lots of butter, a flat-top griddle, and loaf bread with a few simple ingredients. We tested a bunch of sandwiches, and leading the charge was Old Skool Playa (think "player," not a Mexican beach) with aged New York State cheddar and thick and incredibly smoky bacon.

* * *

Heat a skillet over medium-low heat and cook the bacon to desired degree of doneness; drain.

Preheat the broiler. Butter the bottoms of each piece of bread and evenly distribute the cheese across all eight pieces. Put thee pieces of bacon on top of each of half of the bread slices.

Place the bread on a baking sheet and toast until they're golden brown. (Note: If the bread is toasting faster than the cheese is melting, simply lower the heat.) Remove from oven, add 2 tomato slices to each cheese-and-bacon slice, and close all the sandwiches.

NOTE: Cheese sandwiches have obviously been around for quite some time, but actually melting cheese on bread didn't really take off until the 1920s, when cheap bread and processed cheese became widely available. The most common version was, actually, open-faced. The closed sandwich only became popular in the 1960s.

BLEECKER STREET CLASSIC

1 **P**

8 small loaves ciabatta, or
   any roll-style bread
12 ounces fresh mozzarella,
   thinly sliced
12 ounces hard salami, sliced
Basil
½ (or more) medium tomato,
   sliced (8 slices)
Extra virgin olive oil
Balsamic vinegar

Watch out, oenophiles. "Turophile" refers to a lover of cheese. The prefix is derived from "tyro"—the Greek word for cheese. Murray's started making panini (we like to think of them as gooey pressed sandwiches) back in the '90s, *way* before they were cool. The basics are still the best, we say. Our Bleecker Street Classic takes our top-selling cheese (a locally made mozzarella), and smashes it deep into the bread. Add a drizzle of balsamic, basil, and tomatoes and you've got something as amazing as it is easy.

* * *

Preheat a panini press at medium heat. Cut open each ciabatta. For each sandwich, put the cheese on both sides of the bread and evenly distribute the salami, basil to taste, and tomato among the sandwiches. Top with a little bit of oil and vinegar. Grill until the cheese melts and the bread is toasty.

NOTE: If you don't have a panini press, you can also preheat a nonstick pan or skillet on the burner and use that as your makeshift press; in another pan, you'll heat the sandwich, pressing down on it with the preheated one

PANINO WITH PORCHETTA AND BROCCOLI RABE

TONY AND MARISA MAY, OWNERS ✳ SD26 ✳ WWW.SD26NY.COM

1 **P** **H**

HAVING first managed and eventually owned New York's venerable Rainbow Room, restaurateur Tony May had a high bar to meet when he opened San Domenico in 1986. For twenty-two years, the Central Park South restaurant stood for authentic upscale Italian fare. May even wrote one of the leading culinary textbooks on the cuisine, and San Domenico itself was one of only twenty-four restaurants worldwide to receive the Italian government's *Insegna del Ristorante Italiano*, an award denoting the finest Italian restaurants outside of Italy. Arguably, what made the restaurant even more special was the fact that May's daughter, Marisa, joined him in the venture. Having practically grown up in restaurants, Marisa slipped into the role of general manager with such upbeat charm and ease that she soon earned the nickname "bossina" or "little boss."

In 2009, the Mays gave San Domenico a facelift, moving it downtown, making the decor more modern, and renaming it SD26. The delectable food and Marisa's warm welcome, however, remained exactly the same. For the book, Marissa (who co-owns the new restaurant) took the reins to pick out a sandwich very much in line with the transporting experience the restaurant strives to deliver. "This recipe is one of many that remind me of my childhood summers in Capri and Naples with my family," she said. "We would make panino con porchetta and broccoli rabe, and other panini, to have as a fresh snack, with Coca-Cola as a kid and red wine as I got older, when we would spend the days sailing and swimming on the Amalfi coast. Even to this day, the scent of garlic, rosemary, and olive oil together reminds me of those summers."

Bring a large pot of salted water to a boil over high heat. Clean the broccoli rabe by washing it and peeling the ends and add it to the boiling water. Cook until the broccoli rabe is softened, but still firm (it's going to be cooked again). Remove it from the boiling water and quickly submerge it into a bowl of ice water. Once it's completely chilled, remove it and pat dry with a paper towel.

Heat the oil in a sauté pan over medium heat and add the garlic. When the garlic is lightly brown, add the red pepper flakes and the broccoli rabe. Sauté until tender and heated through. Season with salt and pepper to taste.

Drizzle all the bread slices with olive oil and toast them until they're lightly brown. Distribute the broccoli rabe across four slices of bread and top each with four slices of porchetta. Season with salt and pepper to taste, and place the second piece of bread on top of the meat to finish the sandwich.

SERVES 4

1 pound broccoli rabe
Olive oil
2 garlic cloves
1 teaspoon crushed red
     pepper flakes
Salt and pepper
8 slices country bread
16 thin slices of porcetta

NOTE: Sometimes referred to as rapini or broccolini, broccoli rabe is one-stop shopping for nutrients. It is high in vitamins A, C, and K, as well as potassium, calcium, iron, and folic acid.

PRESSED TURKEY, RICOTTA, AND CHERRY CHUTNEY ON BRIOCHE

SHANNA PACIFICO * BACK FORTY * WWW.BACKFORTYNYC.COM

1 **P** **H** RICOTTA'S CONSIDERED TO BE A COMPARATIVELY LOW-FAT CHEESE.
IT CAN ALSO BE PURCHASED AS LOW-FAT OR PART-SKIM.

SERVES 4

8 slices brioche
8 tablespoons smoked ricotta
8 to 12 slices turkey breast
8 (or more) tablespoons
    Dried Cherry Chutney
    (recipe follows)
Butter

SOME days—okay, many days—life can get so fast that the only conceivable remedy is a good meal, preferably somewhere pleasant, where time doesn't matter. Back Forty, the casual (think lots of wood and a garden) East Village sister restaurant to Chef Peter Hoffman's Savoy, is just that. It's the kind of place you'll see people nestled into when it rains, or spread out at the bar on a summer Sunday afternoon. Like Savoy, Back Forty is committed to organic food, but here the menu's smaller—more beer-and-a-burger in the most mouthwatering of ways.

Chef de cuisine Shanna Pacifico—who's cooked here since the 2007 opening—has a passion for sourcing and preparing organic meat, which she often butchers herself. She's tireless about flavor and quality, something that comes across strongly in her spin on a simple turkey sandwich: "My pressed turkey sandwich is a great representation of Back Forty's style. I took a classic American sandwich and gave the flavors more depth by using smoky ricotta. By adding the dried cherry compote, I gave it some of that familiar coziness that I usually only experience around Thanksgiving."

* * *

For each sandwich, slather the brioche slices with the ricotta and then add the turkey and chutney and close it up. Toast on a griddle pan with a touch of butter until it's warmed and the cheese melts.

DRIED CHERRY CHUTNEY

SERVES 4 PLUS

1 small red onion, diced
1 celery stalk, diced
2 garlic cloves, minced
Pinch of nutmeg
Pinch of cardamom
Pinch of allspice
1 cup chopped dried cherries
¼ cup brown sugar
¼ cup red wine vinegar
¼ cup apple bourbon
Salt

Sweat the onion, celery, garlic, nutmeg, cardamon, and allspice together until the vegetables are soft and translucent. Add the dried cherries, sugar, and vinegar, bring to a boil, and allow the liquid to almost reduce all the way (it will thicken considerably). Pour in the bourbon and season with salt. Let the mixture boil so it can reduce again to remove the alcohol. If the chutney seems at all dry, add a little water until it is spreadable.

NOTE: Cherries—and all dark fruits and berries—are rich in anthocyanins, a class of polyphenol antioxidants thought to be especially potent in helping to reduce inflammation and preventing cancer.

CHICKEN SOUVLAKI

MICHAEL PSILAKIS ∗ FISH TAG, KEFI ∗ WWW.KEFIRESTAURANT.COM

3 **P** **M** 2 DAYS

SERVES 4

1 pound boneless,
   skinless chicken breast
   (about 4 single breasts)
Souvlaki Brine (recipe follows)
Marinade (recipe follows)
Sea salt and cracked black
   pepper
½ cup Ladolemono (recipe
   follows)
4 pita bread rounds
Extra virgin olive oil
8 tablespoons Tsatziki (recipe
   follows)
½ recipe Greek Salad (recipe
   follows)

As a boy, Michael Psilakis watched as his parents, immigrants from Greece, turned their suburban backyard into a lamb roasting pit. While hardly bacchanalian (this was, after all, Long Island), the events made a lasting impression.

In 2001, he owned a restaurant called Ecco, yet Psilakis was not a chef. Fortune (and the Greek gods) was smiling when Psilakis showed up at work one day and found himself three cooks short. He went into the kitchen and fell in love with cooking.

At Kefi, Psilakis' tender grilled octopus, garlicky gyros, glistening lamb, and baked pastas are meticulously classic and authentic. Yet there's something deeply revelatory about the cooking: The meat is juicier, the salads brighter, the sauces more evocative. This tender souvlaki—complex but worthwhile—provides a glimpse into the methods of this award-winning chef.

"I can't emphasize enough the importance of brining lean meats and poultry. With meat that does not have a lot of fat, we brine to make it tender and juicy. You have to plan ahead . . . , but the payoff is truly fantastic. Give it twelve hours in the brine. If you have to choose [between brining and marinating], brining is more important," said Chef Psilakis.

∗ ∗ ∗

Cut the chicken into large (1½- to 2-inch) chunks. Place the chicken in the brine. Cover and refrigerate overnight.

Remove the chicken from the brine. Rinse under cool running water. Pat dry with a paper towel. Thread the chicken onto four wooden skewers. Immerse the skewers in the marinade. Cover with plastic wrap, pressing the plastic onto the meat to eliminate air. Refrigerate for at least 4 hours (preferably overnight).

Remove the skewers from the refrigerator and let stand at room temperature for 20 to 30 minutes. Preheat a charcoal or gas grill, or ridged cast-iron grill pan. Season the chicken lightly with salt and pepper to taste. Grill the chicken until firm and char-marked on all sides, about 6 minutes. Transfer to a resting platter. Dress with Ladolemono.

Brush extra virgin olive oil over the pita rounds, season with salt and pepper to taste, and grill until char-marked on both sides. Smear 2 tablespoons of the Tsatziki in the center of each pita round. Push the chicken off the skewer on top of the Tsatziki. Top with even portions of Greek Salad. Pull the sides of the pita up to meet in the center, like a taco. Wrap and secure it with a wide strip of parchment paper.

NOTE: Kefi, Greek for the state of bliss that accompanies a bacchanalian celebration, is encouraged during a meal at its namesake restaurant. It doesn't hurt that the restaurant—adorned with over-sized Greek pottery and seafaring accessories—serves a New York first: shots of *ouzo*, Greece's powerful, licorice-like spirit.

SOUVLAKI BRINE

1 quart cold water
¼ cup kosher salt
¼ cup granulated sugar
1 cup distilled white vinegar

The molecular structure of tendons and proteins are tightly coiled in lean meat, said Chef Psilakis. Brine encourages the proteins to uncoil, so that cooked chicken, for example, remains juicy. If more brine is required to cover the chicken, increase the quantity of the brine, but keep the ratios consistent: one quart water to a quarter cup of salt.

* * *

In a plastic or ceramic bowl, combine the water, salt, sugar, and vinegar. Stir until the salt and sugar are dissolved, about 2 minutes.

LADOLEMONO

3 tablespoons fresh lemon
   juice
2 teaspoons Dijon mustard
2 teaspoons dry Greek
   oregano
½ teaspoon kosher salt
Cracked black pepper
⅓ cup extra virgin olive oil

In a bowl, combine the lemon juice, mustard, oregano, salt, and a generous grinding of pepper. Whisk to blend mixture completely and, whisking all the time, drizzle in the olive oil. Whisk or shake in a jar before using.

MARINADE

1 cup extra virgin olive oil

3 garlic cloves, smashed and
    chopped

3 to 4 thyme sprigs

2 dried bay leaves

2 rosemary sprigs

2 shallots, sliced

Kosher salt and cracked black
    pepper

In a deep baking dish or roasting pan, combine the olive oil, garlic, thyme, bay leaves, rosemary, and shallots. Season with salt and pepper to taste.

TSATZIKI

1 English cucumber, peeled

10 garlic cloves, smashed and
    finely chopped

1 cup distilled white vinegar

4 shallots, thickly sliced

1 cup small, picked sprigs dill

2½ cups strained or Greek
    yogurt, or labne spread

2 tablespoons extra virgin
    olive oil

2 tablespoons fresh lemon
    juice

Kosher salt and cracked black
    pepper

Quarter the cucumber lengthwise and trim off the triangular wedge of seeds. Cut the cucumber into a very small, even dice. Transfer it to a mixing bowl.

In a food processor, combine the garlic, vinegar, shallots, and dill. Pulse until finely chopped, but not puréed. Add the mixture to the cucumbers. Add the yogurt. Fold together with a rubber spatula. Add the olive oil and lemon juice. Season with the salt and pepper to taste.

Tsatziki can be stored in a covered, clean jar in the refrigerator for up to one week.

GREEK SALAD

½ small Spanish or sweet
 onion, thickly sliced

Extra virgin olive oil

Kosher salt and cracked
 black pepper

¼ iceberg lettuce head, sliced
 paper thin

1½ pounds whole trimmed
 bulbs of fennel, thinly
 sliced crosswise

1 small roasted red bell
 pepper, cut into strips

6 cherry or grape tomatoes,
 halved

½ English cucumber, peeled,
 halved, deseeded, and
 thickly sliced

2 scallions, thinly sliced

½ red onion, thinly sliced

2 tablespoons roughly
 chopped dill

2 tablespoons roughly
 chopped parsley

1 teaspoon dry Greek oregano

12 mixed olives, brined
 and/or oil-cured, pitted
 and halved

4 whole caperberries

2 tablespoons crumbled feta
 cheese

1 pepperoncini, thinly sliced

Brush the Spanish or sweet onion slices with a little olive oil. Season with salt and pepper to taste. On a grill or griddle, or in a cast-iron skillet, grill the onion until tender. Separate into rings. Combine the lettuce, fennel, roasted pepper, tomatoes, cucumber, scallions, red onion, dill, parsley, oregano, olives, and caperberries. Toss with clean hands. When ready to use, add the feta and pepperoncini.

MEDITERRANEAN GRILLED CHICKEN SANDWICH

ELISA SARNO ✳ BISTRO DE LA GARE ✳ WWW.BISTRODELAGARENYC.COM

1 **P** **H** **M** 1 DAY

SERVES 2

½ cup extra virgin olive oil

¼ cup lemon juice (about 2 lemons)

¼ cup white wine

2 rosemary sprigs, chopped

4 thyme sprigs, chopped

¼ teaspoon crushed red pepper flakes

2 garlic cloves, grated with a microplane

1 cup wild arugula

2 boneless, skinless chicken breasts (preferably organic), about 11 ounces

Salt and pepper

½ recipe Roasted Peppers, Zucchini, and Eggplant (recipe follows)

½ recipe Marinated Mushrooms (recipe follows)

4 (7-inch) pieces focaccia bread

WHEN Babbo alum Elisa Sarno opened Bistro de la Gare with fellow chef Maryann Terillo, it was a breath of fresh air. The place—a fun, breezy venture between lifelong friends—was billed as a "casual" white-tablecloth eatery, and it featured Mediterranean flavors and ingredients with an American twist.

This sandwich is a case in point. On the Bistro menu, it's actually a salad. But we liked its simplicity and unusual flair (the mushrooms are tinged with orange zest), and asked Chef Sarno to adapt it for us as a sandwich. It oozes—literally!—with the goodness of the Mediterranean.

"We wanted our grilled chicken salad to be a little different from the ones we had seen, and also kind of light. This one involves no butter or frying," said Chef Sarno.

✳ ✳ ✳

Combine the oil, lemon juice, wine, rosemary, thyme, red pepper, and garlic to make a marinade. If the chicken breasts are more than 2 inches thick, butterfly them (halve lengthwise, leaving a connector intact). Place the chicken in a tight-fitting container. Pour the marinade over it. Marinate for 4 hours, or overnight in the refrigerator. Broil the chicken under a high flame until done, 8 to 10 minutes.

Place a layer of the roasted vegetables on 2 pieces of the focaccia. Add 1 chicken breast on each piece. Add a layer of mushrooms. Top with the remaining pieces of focaccia and serve.

ROASTED PEPPERS, ZUCCHINI, AND EGGPLANT

1 zucchini, sliced into ½-inch rounds

1 Japanese eggplant, sliced into ½-inch rounds

5 tablespoons extra virgin olive oil, divided

3 assorted bell peppers (red, yellow, and orange)

Salt and pepper

Preheat the oven to 475°F.

Toss the zucchini and the eggplant rounds with 4 tablespoons of the oil. Rub the whole peppers with the remaining tablespoon of oil. Salt and pepper the vegetables to taste. Place them in a baking dish. Roast until soft, about 30 minutes. Remove from the oven and let cool.

Slice the peppers in half. Remove the seeds and peel off the skin before using.

MARINATED MUSHROOMS

¾ cup plus 2 tablespoons extra virgin olive oil, divided

¼ cup white wine

¼ cup white wine vinegar

Zest of 1 lemon

Zest of 1 orange

1 rosemary sprig

1 thyme sprig

¼ teaspoon crushed red pepper flakes

1 garlic clove, sliced

Salt and pepper

1 pound fresh wild mushrooms (preferably shiitake, cremini, portobello), cleaned

Combine the ¾ cup of the oil, wine, vinegar, lemon and orange zest, rosemary, thyme, pepper flakes, and garlic in a saucepan. Season with salt and pepper to taste. Bring to a boil over high heat. Lower the heat to medium low, and simmer for about 5 minutes. Set aside.

Heat a sauté pan. Add the remaining 2 tablespoons of olive oil. Sauté the mushrooms quickly; they should remain firm. Place the mushrooms in a bowl. Cover with the vinegar and citrus mixture and allow to marinate for at least 30 minutes.

DUCK CLUB SANDWICH

BRUCE AND ERIC BROMBERG ✳ BLUE RIBBON BAKERY ✳ WWW.BLUERIBBONRESTAURANTS.COM

1 **P** **M** 1 DAY

**MAKES 4
SANDWICHES**

4 (8-ounce) Muscovy duck
　breasts
Kosher salt and freshly
　ground black pepper
½ cup Olive Oil Mayonnaise
　(recipe follows) or regular
　mayonnaise
12 slices Raisin Walnut Bread
　(recipe follows) or other
　raisin bread, toasted
4 tablespoons crumbled
　cooked bacon (from 4 slices)
2 cups shredded iceberg
　lettuce
2 small tomatoes, thinly sliced
1 small red onion, thinly sliced

IMAGINE the delight of the brothers Bromberg. New Jersey-raised Eric and Bruce had both trained at the Cordon Bleu, in Paris. As cooks, they'd traveled through France and seen the massive wood-fired hearths in which some French still bake bread and roast meats. But here was one that hailed back to the 1860s, and it was in Soho, just blocks from the spot where the Brombergs' original Blue Ribbon had taken Sullivan Street by storm a few years earlier. Best of all, it had not—like similarly idle ovens—crumbled into dust.

That was in 1995. After four years of careful restoration, Blue Ribbon Bakery opened. Today, it thrives, based on the products of the original, 16 × 12-foot oven, such as this classic French recipe.

"Using succulent duck breast really elevates the humble turkey club to a more regal level. Add in the sweetness of the raisin bread, the crispiness of the bacon, and a dollop of creamy mayo, and you've got a club sandwich that brings others to shame. We serve it with chips, for a homey touch," said Eric Bromberg.

✳ ✳ ✳

Preheat the oven to 400°F.

Using a sharp knife, score the fat of the duck breasts, taking care not to cut through to the meat. Season the duck generously with salt and pepper. Heat a large skillet over medium-high heat until hot. Sear the duck breasts, skin side down, until the skin browns and fat is rendered, about 8 minutes. Transfer the duck, skin side up, to a rimmed baking sheet.

Roast the duck until a thermometer inserted into the thickest part of the duck registers 140°F (the duck will continue to cook as it cools), about 15 minutes. Remove from the oven. Once cool, slice very thinly against the grain.

To assemble the sandwich, spread 1 tablespoon mayonnaise on each of 4 slices of toast, and sprinkle with half of the bacon. Divide the lettuce evenly among the bread slices, and top each with half of the duck slices. Top with a second layer of toast. Spread the remaining mayonnaise over the slices. Sprinkle with the remaining bacon. Top with tomato slices, red onion, and the remaining duck. Cover the sandwiches with the remaining slices of toast, cut into quarters, and serve.

RAISIN WALNUT BREAD

MAKES 1 (9 x 4-INCH) LOAF

1⅛ teaspoons active dry yeast or 2 ounces fresh yeast
3 large eggs, lightly beaten
⅓ cup granulated sugar
¼ cup packed dark brown sugar
¼ cup honey
5¾ cups bread flour
2 teaspoons kosher salt
1½ teaspoons ground cinnamon
8 tablespoons (1 stick) unsalted butter, room temperature, cubed
2 cups raisins
½ cup chopped walnuts

In the bowl of an electric mixer fitted with the hook attachment, combine the yeast with 1½ cups lukewarm water. Let the mixture stand at room temperature until it starts to foam, about 10 minutes.

Add the eggs, both sugars, and honey and mix for several seconds to combine. Add the flour gradually, mixing on medium speed until the dough starts to come together. Sprinkle in the salt and cinnamon and continue mixing.

Add the butter, cube by cube, and continue mixing. Once the butter has fully incorporated into the dough, about 10 minutes, add the raisins and walnuts and mix until combined.

Lightly grease with nonstick cooking spray. Shape the dough into a loose ball and place it in the bowl. Grease plastic wrap with nonstick cooking spray and cover the dough loosely. Allow the dough to rise until doubled in size, 1½ to 2 hours.

Preheat oven to 375°F. Lightly grease a 9 x 4-inch loaf pan.

Punch down the dough, form it into a loaf, and place it in the prepared pan. Cover it loosely with the plastic and let it rest until puffed up to the edge on the pan, about 30 minutes. Uncover and bake for 50 minutes to 1 hour, or until the top is a dark golden brown and the loaf sounds hollow when tapped. Allow the bread to cool in the pan for 5 minutes before turning out onto a wire cooling rack.

OLIVE OIL MAYONNAISE

1½ teaspoons red wine
   vinegar
¼ teaspoon kosher salt
1 large egg
1 large egg yolk
2 teaspoons Dijon mustard
¾ cup extra-virgin olive oil
½ cup extra-virgin olive oil
Freshly ground black pepper

In a large bowl, whisk together the vinegar and salt until the salt dissolves. Whisk in the egg, egg yolk, and mustard until fully combined. Whisking constantly and vigorously, very slowly drizzle in the oils until the mixture is fully emulsified and thickened. Season with pepper to taste.

YaGLama SanDWicH

ORHAN YEGEN * SIP SAK * WWW.SIP-SAK.COM

1

AT the heart of this unassuming restaurant is a chef widely credited with popularizing Turkish food in New York City. Orhan Yegen has helmed or cooked at five of the most prominent, and pioneering, Turkish restaurants in Manhattan.

This traditional Turkish dish is a ten-layer sandwich that alternates pitas with spiced ground meat and yogurt sauce, said Yegen. The recipe isn't difficult to make, but in the interests of forming a more cohesive, on-the-go sandwich, we modified his recipe into a sort of Turkish "sloppy Joe"—messy, rustic, comforting, and delicious.

* * *

Place the oil in a sauté pan over medium heat. When the oil is hot, add the meat and stir constantly until brown, about 3 minutes. Add the onions, bell peppers, garlic, and butter. Cook until the onions are translucent, 8 to 10 minutes. Add the tomato paste, tomatoes, parsley, and black pepper. Cook for 5 minutes, and remove from heat. Season with salt to taste.

Place two pitas on a platter, and microwave on high for 30 seconds. Repeat with the remaining pitas. Place one pita on a dinner plate. Add meat mixture, and then yogurt sauce to taste. Top with second pita, and enjoy.

SERVES 4

2 tablespoons vegetable or olive oil

1 pound ground lamb (you may substitute beef, although lamb is preferred)

2 small onions, minced

2 medium (or 1 large) red bell peppers, minced

2 to 3 garlic cloves, mashed and roughly chopped

4 tablespoons unsalted butter

2 tablespoons tomato paste

2 vine-ripened tomatoes, chopped

1 cup minced fresh parsley

½ teaspoon black pepper

Kosher salt

8 small pitas, about 4 inches in diameter (preferably whole wheat)

Yogurt Sauce (recipe follows)

YOGURT SAUCE

MAKES ABOUT ¾ CUP

¾ cup plain yogurt
2 garlic cloves, minced
Salt

Combine the yogurt and garlic. Season with salt to taste.

GRILLED HANGER STEAK AND MINT PESTO SANDWICH

MANUEL "MEMO" TREVIÑO * TRAVERTINE * WWW.TRAVERTINENYC.COM

② **Ⓟ**

SERVES 4

**3 to 4 pounds hanger steak
(or skirt steak)**
1 cup olive oil
12 garlic cloves, crushed
4 rosemary sprigs
Salt and pepper
Mint Pesto (recipe follows)
**4 ciabatta rolls, 4-inch sections
baguette, or 8 slices
country bread, toasted**
8 ounces Gorgonzola cheese
**Caramelized Onions (recipe
follows)**
2 pears, thinly sliced

NOTE: "Ciabatta bread is fantastic for a picnic. You can build the sandwich in plastic wrap. The bread absorbs moisture, and by the time you're ready to eat it, it's softened, but not soggy," said Chef Treviño.

T HE stone entryway of Travertine is a welcome surprise on the long approach to the Williamsburg Bridge. This portion of an otherwise hip neighborhood retains an industrial feel. Then, one comes across a marble step and massive wooden door and spots the hip downtown patrons walking in and out.

Part of the draw is a menu that's as intense as it is Italian. For example, this sandwich hits all the flavor receptors, said Chef "Memo" Treviño, formerly of Le Cirque 2000, Babbo, B. R. Guest, and *Top Chef* season 4. "The pears balance the salt of the cheese and the savoriness of the steak. Caramelized onions transmit sweet receptors. Mint pesto gives a little bit of extra fat to dress the bread (i.e. give it moisture), and the freshness of mint enhances the meat," he said. The components give it a gender-neutral appeal. "I find that men tend to order this sandwich, but I'm pleasantly surprised when I stick my head into the dining room and there's a table full of women eating it," he said.

* * *

Place the steak in a container or dish. Add the olive oil, garlic, and rosemary. Season with salt and pepper to taste. Cover tightly, and refrigerate overnight.

Remove the steak from the refrigerator while you preheat a grill. When the grill is hot, grill the steak on one side until lightly charred, 4 to 5 minutes. Turn and grill the other side for about 3 minutes. Allow the meat to rest for a few minutes. Slice thinly. Season with salt and pepper to taste.

Spread the Mint Pesto on each roll or slice of bread. Place 2 ounces of Gorgonzola cheese in each roll. Add the caramelized onions. Using a toaster oven, toast the bread until the Gorgonzola melts. Add the pears and sliced steak. Close the sandwiches and serve.

MINT PESTO

2 bunches fresh mint, leaves
   picked
½ cup pine nuts
1 garlic clove
1 teaspoon salt
1 cup extra virgin olive oil
½ cup grated Pecorino
   Romano cheese
Black pepper
Chili flakes

Place the mint, pine nuts, garlic, and salt into a food processor or blender. Chop or blend on medium speed. While blending, drizzle in the olive oil and add the cheese. Season with the pepper and chili flakes to taste.

CARAMELIZED ONIONS

2 onions, thinly sliced
Olive oil

Pan-fry the onions with the olive oil on low heat until soft and brown, about 8 minutes.

PROSCIUTTO, GRILLED FENNEL, AND PEAR SANDWICH

JASON ZUKAS * CHARLES * WWW.RESTAURANTCHARLES.COM

❶ Ⓗ

SERVES 4

1 fennel bulb, thinly sliced

Salt and fresh-cracked black pepper

Extra virgin olive oil

8 slices country bread, focaccia, challah, or brioche

8 ounces arugula (about 6 cups)

6 ounces prosciutto di Parma, sliced thin (12 slices)

2 Bosc pears, thinly sliced

Gorgonzola Aïoli (recipe follows)

THIS West Village restaurant made a splash when it opened in 2008, specifically because it dared to pull a non-splash. With its windows papered over and its entrance still marked with the name of the previous restaurant, Charles "quietly" slid into business.

The result? Trend-seekers reveled and lunged for hard-to-get reservations. Those not in-the-know either seethed or simply shrugged. Frank Bruni at *The New York Times* wrote a bemused review. Now that Charles has a new chef—Jason Zukas, a Tom Valenti alum and winner of the Food Network show *Chopped*—things have quieted down. The windows are now bare, the right sign is up, and everyday people can come and dine normally on the light New American menu.

Likewise, Zukas' sandwich is part splashy and part understated. True to Zukas' half-Sicilian heritage, the main ingredients are Mediterranean. Grilled fennel, prosciutto, and Gorgonzola are arranged on a spring-fresh bed of arugula and pear, making it at once crunchy and smoky, salty and sweet. Featuring fennel in a sandwich was natural for the chef. "I grew up with fennel," he said. "At the end of a meal, we always ate it raw with fruit and nuts to help us digest. Sometimes we widen the hollow of the stalks, and use them—like straws—to sip wine."

* * *

Season the fennel with salt and pepper to taste. Drizzle with the extra virgin olive oil. Grill or sauté the fennel until charred and softened. Drizzle one side of each bread slice with extra virgin olive oil, and grill until toasted. Lay down 4 slices of bread, toasted side up. Line each slice with the arugula, prosciutto, fennel, and pear. Spread the remaining four slices of bread with the aïoli. Top the sandwiches and serve.

GORGONZOLA AÏOLI

2 garlic cloves
1 large egg, separated
½ teaspoon Dijon mustard
¼ cup olive oil
2 teaspoons fresh lemon juice
    (just under ½ lemon)
1 tablespoon creamy
    Gorgonzola
Salt and pepper

Place the garlic in a food processor or blender and pulse a few times. Add the egg yolk and the mustard. Turn the processor or blender to high, and add the oil slowly until emulsified. Add the lemon juice and the Gorgonzola. Taste and season sparingly (the Gorgonzola might lend enough salt). Add a few drops of water until creamy.

Chapter 5

THE HAUTE SANDWICH

* * *

IF NEW YORK IS THE ULTIMATE CHOOSE-YOUR-OWN-ADVENTURE CITY, IT GOES without saying that restaurants are a big part of what's getting you there. Against the dense background of brick and concrete, each door opens up to an entirely different set of tastes, colors, and experiences. The talent is high, the competition sometimes fierce, and the rewards rich.

Historians have traced New York's top-tier culinary scene back to the early nineteenth century, when pubs and boarding houses slowly started giving way to places like Delmonico's. Having evolved from a small downtown room with wooden chairs to the city's first venerable dining destination, the restaurant's lavishly prepared Parisian fare is largely credited with redefining the way New Yorkers ate out. Restaurants became curators of new tastes, precious ingredients, and exciting flavor combinations.

By the 1960s, when the Four Seasons rose to prominence as "the place" to power lunch, dining out had evolved into an event. Value and meaning were added to an occasion—be it a deal struck or a tryst sealed—based on the spectacle of the meal, from food and wine to the service and overall presentation.

With the ante going ever higher, it was just a matter of time before the chefs themselves became the draw. Today, chefs from Daniel Boulud to Jean-Georges Vongerichten have become celebrities in their own right. And it's not always what they can do with a truffle that's of interest—it's how they can elevate any ingredient combination.

That's right where the New York sandwich fits in. With just a few ingredients, top chefs can really show their mettle. How do you meet those high expectations with just, say, bread and ham and cheese? Or make a classic soar with just one significant change, reinterpretation or addition? Be it pork belly pastrami, an Indo-British spin on simple tea sandwiches, or a simple croque monsieur perfected with years of practice, a New York haute sandwich is always in a league of its own.

* * *

RED FIFE BRIOCHE WITH EGG, SPECK, AND GREENS MARMALADE

DAN BARBER ✳ BLUE HILL, BLUE HILL AT STONE BARNS ✳ WWW.BLUEHILLFARM.COM

③

IN May 2009, Chef Dan Barber was named one of *Time* magazine's 100 most influential people of the year; later that month, the James Beard Foundation awarded him its top chef award. For an activist chef who's also on the advisory board of Harvard Medical School's Center for Health and the Global Environment, has spoken at the prestigious TED conference, and has had his writing broadly published and anthologized, you could call them fitting tributes.

Classically trained in France, California, and New York, Barber always had a passion for where ingredients come from. Already in the 1990s, he was cooking for friends and family on a farm (called Blue Hill) in Massachusetts. By 2000—long before the local food movement took off—he was ready to take those farm-to-table sensibilities to the Manhattan food scene. He opened the elegant West Village restaurant Blue Hill, a restaurant devoted to food that's both well chosen and well prepared, and was met with nothing short of rave reviews.

In 2004, Barber took that concept back to the farm, launching a hugely successful public experiment. Blue Hill at Stone Barns in upstate New York is a way for diners to experience Barber's cooking right at the source. Here, diners can see how ingredients are grown and, ideally, make a connection to their environment.

Of this selection Dan Barber said: "Dream Breakfast: buttery brioche, runny egg, smoky speck. At Blue Hill at Stone Barns, our pastry chef, Alex Grunert, makes a whole wheat brioche with red fife flour that I wake up thinking about. If we're talking really dreamy, the egg is from pastured chickens at Blue Hill Farm in Great Barrington, Massachusetts, where Sean Stanton raises eggs with yolks the color of noonday sun. And the speck would be by Adam Kaye, our master curer in the Blue Hill kitchen, whose work is astounding. But really, the combination is what's key: salt, protein, and fat. Heaven."

Poach the eggs for 6 minutes in boiling water. Remove with a slotted spoon. Drain on paper towels.

Meanwhile, toast the brioche. Add a drizzle of extra-virgin olive oil to a nonstick skillet over low heat. Gently heat the speck for 4 seconds in the pan. Dry, and then wrap one slice of speck around each egg. Spread one side of each brioche toast with 1 tablespoon of Greens Marmalade. Top with speck-wrapped egg and serve immediately.

SERVES 6

6 eggs
6 slices Red Fife Brioche (recipe follows)
Extra virgin olive oil
6 thin slices speck (or substitute fine-quality prosciutto)
6 tablespoons Greens Marmalade

GREENS MARMALADE

MAKES ABOUT 1 CUP

2 quarts washed mixed greens like spinach or romaine, lightly packed
2 tablespoons diced mixed pickles (pickled cauliflower, pickled fennel, capers, lemon confit, black olives)
Juice of ¼ lemon
1 teaspoon pickled mustard seeds or whole-grain mustard
½ tablespoon chopped mixed herbs (such as basil, tarragon, and chives)
Salt and pepper

Blanch the greens in a large saucepan of boiling, salted water for 1 to 2 minutes or until wilted. Drain and refresh in a bowl of cold iced water. Press the greens into a colander to remove excess liquid. Let drain, preferably overnight, in the refrigerator. (You can use a bowl to weigh down the greens.) You should have about 1 cup of greens.

Cut the cooked greens into chiffonade or ribbons. Combine the greens with the pickles, lemon juice, pickled mustard seeds, and fresh herbs in a saucepan over low heat. Add cooked greens until you reach a marmalade consistency. Season with salt and pepper to taste.

RED FIFE BRIOCHE

DOUGH STARTER

½ cup red fife flour
¼ cold water
¼ teaspoon grams salt
¼ teaspoon fresh yeast

DOUGH

4½ teaspoons fresh yeast
⅛ cup water
3⅔ cups red fife flour
1 cup unbleached all-purpose
    flour
2 teaspoons salt
½ cup sugar
Dough starter (see above)
7 large eggs
¾ pound (3 sticks) butter,
    chilled (not straight from
    the refrigerator; it should
    be slightly softened), cut
    into small cubes

Day One: Make the starter. Combine the flour, water, salt and fresh yeast. Cover with plastic wrap and let rest overnight at room temperature.

Day Two: Make the dough. Dissolve the yeast in water. In a large standing mixer fitted with a dough hook, mix the yeast, red fife flour, all purpose flour, salt, sugar, and dough starter. Add the cold eggs, one by one. Add butter pieces one by one and mix until dough gets a silken texture. Cover dough with plastic wrap and let rise in the refrigerator overnight.

Day Three: Brush the loaf pans with clarified butter. Cut the dough into 4 equal pieces; dust the surface lightly with red fife flour, and shape. Place the dough in molds. Cover with plastic wrap and let rise (preferably in a warm, humid place) for 30 minutes. Preheat the oven to 350°F.

Bake for 25 to 30 minutes, until loaves are golden brown and sound hollow when tapped. (The internal temperature should be at least 200°F.) Let rest for 5 minutes, and then transfer the loaves to wire racks. Allow them to cool to room temperature before slicing.

CROQUE MONSIEUR

DANIEL BOULUD * DANIEL, CAFÉ BOULUD, DB BISTRO MODERNE, BAR BOULUD, DBGB
WWW.DANIELNYC.COM
❷

ON a pristine Upper East Side address sits Daniel. There's a grandness about even the awning—like there's something incredibly special inside. And, indeed, from the lighting to the perfectly executed dishes, everything about a dinner with Chef Daniel Boulud plays out as though the experience was made with precisely you in mind.

There's a reason Boulud's restaurants—which also include Café Boulud farther north, DB Bistro Moderne in Midtown, Bar Boulud on the Upper West, and now the cheekily named DBGB in the East Village—keep raking in the awards. There's such a superb attention to detail, from the way Boulud experiments with flavors to how he creates dishes, that once you arrive (or, in this case, try the recipe), your whole experience melts into one flawlessly orchestrated meal.

This is something Chef Boulud underscores well in describing the croque monsieur he picked out for the book. "Even the simplest dish can be sublime when you pour plenty of care and the best ingredients into it," he said. "To some a croque monsieur may be just a glorified hot ham and cheese. But to those who know better, it is layers of a toasted, melting, oozing, satisfying platonic ideal of a sandwich laced with taste memories."

"At the restaurant, we have a few tips to make sure the sandwich is perfectly constructed," said Damian Sansonetti, executive chef at Bar Boulud, where the sandwich is a brunch-time favorite. "Take the time to pre-toast the bread very lightly, 10 to 15 minutes in a 300°F oven should do the trick. It gives the bread just enough firmness so that the béchamel won't seep in and make it soggy. Also, weight the sandwiches for a few hours before baking. Line them up on a cookie tray, place another tray on top and then place a weight on top of that. This extra step assures the sandwich won't fall apart in either the baking or the eating."

For the Béchamel Sauce: In a small saucepan over low heat, melt the butter and whisk in the flour until blended but not colored. Gradually whisk in the milk and cook, stirring constantly, until thickened, about 10 minutes. Season to taste with the nutmeg, salt, and pepper. Set aside. (This may be made up to 24 hours ahead of time and stored, refrigerated, with a layer of plastic wrap placed directly on the surface of the sauce. Gently reheat before serving.)

For the sandwiches: Preheat the oven to 400°F. Line a baking sheet with parchment paper and brush it with melted butter.

On a work surface, place the bread slices in a single layer and spread each one evenly to the edges with béchamel. (Store any extra béchamel sauce in the refrigerator; it's great with eggs and will keep for about a week.) Divide the ham among four of the slices, trimming it if necessary so it's within ¼ inch of the edges of the bread. Top all eight slices with equal amounts of cheese, spreading it evenly to within ¼ inch of edges. Place the four bread slices with béchamel and cheese, cheese side up, on top of slices layered with ham.

Transfer the sandwiches, cheese side up, onto the baking sheet. Bake until the grated cheese topping is melted and golden brown, 10 to 15 minutes. Serve immediately.

SERVES 4

BÉCHAMEL SAUCE

3 tablespoons unsalted butter
¼ cup all-purpose flour
3 cups whole milk
Freshly grated nutmeg
Salt
Freshly ground white pepper

SANDWICH

2 tablespoons unsalted butter, melted
8 slices high quality Pullman loaf bread, sliced ⅓- to ½-inch thick, very lightly toasted
Béchamel Sauce
12 ounces thickly sliced high-quality ham (Jambon de Paris is a good choice)
10 ounces Gruyère cheese, coarsely grated

NOTE: This popular French ham-and-cheese made its first documented appearance on a French café menu in 1910. Its literary debut was a big one—in 1918, Proust himself wrote about it in volume two of *In Search of Lost Time*.

CROQUE MADAME

NICOLAS CANTREL * BISTROT BAGATELLE * WWW.BISTROTBAGATELLE.COM

②

FOR the past decade or so, the Meatpacking District has been a nightlife mainstay. Restaurants, bars, and nightclubs (not to mention designer boutiques and hotels) have supplanted the slaughterhouses to create a meat market of a whole different sort. Bistrot Bagatelle—chic, French, and brimming with pretty people—first made waves for its endless celebration; the cork-popping revelry never seemed to stop (probably a welcome escape for more than one laid-off investment banker). But once journalists had exhausted the "endless party" angle, another angle started to emerge—the food was exceptionally good. On her blog, veteran food critic Gael Greene called her experience "oddly charming."

Chef Nicolas Cantrel first trained in Alain Ducasse's restaurant empire in France. In New York he worked for Daniel Boulud. Now at Bagatelle, he delivers just the kind of rich and delicious French food you'd expect from a true haute Parisian bistro. Cantrel's croque madame is a perfect example. "To me, food should be simple and comforting," he explained. "When I thought about brunch items for the Bistrot Bagatelle menu, one of the first things that came to mind was a croque madame. It's absolutely delicious and with its ham, egg, and creamy melted cheese, it's a perfect brunch item. By preparing it using truffle butter, crème fraîche, and quail eggs I was able to make it more refined, yet still quintessentially French, which is exactly what Bistrot Bagatelle is all about."

SERVES 4

3 tablespoons truffle butter,
divided (you can make
it at home by blending
truffle oil or truffle salt with
regular unsalted butter)
8 slices white bread
16 slices Swiss cheese
16 slices boiled ham
4 teaspoons crème frâiche
4 quail eggs (you may
substitute 4 regular eggs)
Fleur de sel or kosher salt
Black pepper

NOTE: Quail egg shells are harder than chicken eggs. Cantrel recommends cracking them open by giving them a quick strike with the blade of a sharp knife. Once the shell is split, separate the halves.

Preheat the oven to 400°F. Butter all eight pieces of bread on just one side, reserving about half the butter for later use. Flip half the slices so the buttered side faces down, and cover each with three slices of the cheese. Place 2 slices of the ham over the cheese, and put the top slice of the bread over the ham, buttered side up. Grill the sandwiches in a griddle or on a heavy-bottomed pan over medium-high heat for about 3 minutes per side. Set them on serving plates. Spread a thin layer of crème frâiche on top of each sandwich, and finish with the last slice of Swiss cheese. Heat the sandwiches in the oven until the cheese has melted.

In a nonstick skillet, melt the remaining butter over medium-high heat, until it starts to bubble. Pour 1 egg at a time into the pan, being careful not to break the yolks. Sprinkle the eggs with fleur de sel to taste. Cook each egg sunny side up, about 3 minutes. Center a fried egg over each of the grilled sandwiches and sprinkle with pepper to taste.

EXOTIC TEA TRIO
CORONATION CHICKEN, PETIT PLOUGHMAN, AND CILANTRO-CURED SALMON WITH COCONUT LABNE

BRAD FARMERIE ✳ DOUBLE CROWN, PUBLIC

WWW.DOUBLECROWN-NYC.COM ✳ WWW.PUBLIC-NYC.COM

HERE'S the AvroKo story: Four designers come together, collaborate, and execute restaurant concepts so original and transporting, you feel like you stepped into a wormhole and came out in an alternate—much prettier—universe. The downtown eateries Public (with its secret-box-like annex The Monday Room) and Double Crown (inspired by Britain's nineteenth-century colonial collisions in Southeast Asia) are beautiful examples.

And thanks to the cuisine of Chef Brad Farmerie, who helms the kitchens of both, those examples extend well into the kitchen. Each menu is eclectic, original, and still perfectly suited to the space and theme. The outcome is like reading—or tasting—a travel adventure book.

For this book, Farmerie's put together a trio of Indo-British tea sandwiches. The Indian twists on familiar concepts make these recipes especially fresh and up-to-date, as they add depth and complexity of flavor. To each, he's added his own notes and reflections.

NOTE: "Labne is a thickened yogurt that takes on the consistency of cream cheese, yet has the fresh acidity that is often lacking there," said Farmerie. "It is simple to make and is a great base for any flavor that you choose. (Although after you taste the coconut labne in the recipe on page 112, you might look no further for inspiration!)"

CORONATION CHICKEN
WITH TOASTED ALMONDS AND MANGO CHUTNEY

SERVES 4

1 **P**

CORONATION
CHICKEN SALAD

2 cups chicken stock*
1 large chicken breast, skin
    off and seasoned with salt
    and pepper
¾ cup mayonnaise
¼ cup crème fraîche
¼ cup golden raisins
¼ cup lightly toasted almond
    slices
2 celery stalks, peeled and
    finely diced
1½ tablespoons curry powder
¼ teaspoon sea salt

SANDWICHES

Coronation Chicken Salad
8 slices white bread
Watercress
Finely shaved fresh fennel
    (optional)
Olive oil
Mango Chutney

Coronation chicken was a mild addiction of mine when I was living in London. It's derivative of a dish composed by Constance Spry, the Martha Stewart of mid-century England, for the coronation of Queen Elizabeth II in 1953. She envisioned a chicken dish using the "exotic" spices of India as the highlight of the celebration. This lightly curry-spiced chicken salad gets a lively lift from sweet-sour mango chutney and crunchy almonds.

* * *

For the Coronation Chicken Salad: Place the chicken stock (or seasoned water substitute) in a saucepan and bring to a boil. Put the chicken breast in the pot, and lower the heat to a light simmer. Poach the chicken breast in the stock until completely cooked; then take the pot off the heat and allow it to the chicken to cool in the liquid. Once cooled, dice the chicken and combine with the mayonnaise, crème fraîche, raisins, almonds, celery, curry, and salt.

For the sandwiches: Divide the Coronation Chicken Salad among four slices of bread. Lightly dress the watercress and shaved fennel (if using it) with olive oil and place this on top of the chicken mixture. Spread a thin layer of mango chutney on the other four slices of bread and place each on top of a salad slice to make a sandwich. Slice off the crusts, and cut into quarters or sixths, or any other desired shape and serve.

*NOTE: You can substitute salted water with bay leaf and thyme if chicken stock is unavailable.

PETIT PLOUGHMAN

1 **P** **H** OMIT THE CHEESE

PICCALILLI

1 cauliflower head, cut into
  very small florets
2 Spanish onions, finely diced
8 shallots, finely diced
2 tablespoons salt
1 cucumber, peeled, seeded,
  and finely diced
2 cups high-quality white
  wine vinegar
1 cup cider vinegar
½ teaspoon dried chile flakes
1½ cups superfine or castor
  sugar*
½ cup yellow mustard
  powder
3 tablespoons turmeric
3 tablespoons corn flour

SANDWICHES

Butter
8 slices whole wheat bread
4 slices aged British cheddar
  or Lancashire cheese
Watercress, baby spinach, or
  other greens
Salt

In the United Kingdom, the Ploughman's lunch is a rustic indulgence of salty British cheddar cheese, Branston Pickle, and some bread.

* * *

For the Piccalilli: Combine the cauliflower, onions, shallots, and salt in a mixing bowl and refrigerate for several hours, preferably overnight.

Rinse the vegetables in a colander under cold water. Allow the vegetables to drain thoroughly and then place them in a mixing bowl. Add the cucumber and set aside.

Combine the vinegars in a saucepan over medium heat. Add the chile flakes, sugar, mustard powder, and turmeric and bring to a simmer. Mix the corn flour with ¼ cup of water and whisk that into the vinegar mixture. Reduce the heat and continue to cook at a simmer for 5 minutes. When done, pour the vegetables into the mixture and take off the heat. Allow to cool.

For the sandwiches: Spread a thin layer of butter on all the bread slices. Cover each of the four bread slices with a slice of cheese, top the cheese with the piccalilli, and finish with a very fine layer of your choice of greens. Place the buttered bread on top and press lightly to make the sandwich stick together, slice off the crusts, and cut into quarters, sixths, or any other desired shape.

*NOTE: You can create your own superfine sugar by putting granulated sugar in a food processor for about a minute.

CILANTRO-CURED SALMON
WITH COCONUT LABNE

SERVES 4

1 **P** **H** USE NON-FAT GREEK YOGURT.

M REFRIGERATE THE LABNE FOR 12 HOURS. IF YOU OPT FOR THE HOME-CURED
SALMON, IT WILL NEED TO MARINATE FOR FIVE DAYS.

COCONUT LABNE

1 cup Greek yogurt
3 tablespoons Thai coconut
     cream powder

SANDWICHES

8 pieces rye or pumpernickel
     bread
Coconut Labne
1 pound salmon fillet, skin on
     and bones removed
¼ cup sugar plus ¼ cup salt,
     mixed
½ cup chopped parsley
½ cup chopped cilantro
1 spring onion, chopped
½ teaspoon toasted fennel
     seeds, lightly crushed
½ teaspoon coriander seeds,
     lightly crushed
Zest of ½ lemon
Extra virgin olive oil
Black pepper
1 English cucumber, peeled,
     seeded, and thinly sliced
Cilantro (optional)

This sandwich is a great unexpectedly Asian twist on the traditional smoked salmon with cream cheese. The flavors are really layered; salmon and coriander mix with nuances of coconut and the crunch of cucumber. The look may be familiar, but the taste is modern and memorable. I recommend that you try to cure your own fish because the flavor will be more interesting than the store-bought variety. But if you don't want to go through the trouble (or you haven't planned five days ahead) gravlax or smoked salmon are fantastic substitutes.

* * *

For the coconut labne: Thoroughly combine the yogurt and the coconut cream powder in a mixing bowl. Line a colander or sieve with cheesecloth or a clean towel and pour the mixture in. Place the sieve or colander over a bowl to catch any of the moisture that drains out and store in the refrigerator for 12 hours.

Remove the labne from the towel, place in an airtight container, and refrigerate until needed.

For the sandwiches: Lightly score (cut) the salmon on the skin side at 1 inch intervals. Spread the salmon with a thin layer of sugar and salt on both sides, using about 2 tablespoons of the mixture. Place the parsley, cilantro, onion, fennel seeds, grated lemon, and remaining sugar and salt in a nonreactive bowl and mix thoroughly. Let the mix sit for 15 minutes. (This will let it become wet and pliable.) Cover the flesh side of the salmon with half of the mixture, and place the remainder of the mixture in a plastic container and put the salmon, skin side down, on top. Refrigerate for five days, flipping each day to ensure that the fish "cures" evenly. After five days, remove all of the marinade and pat dry. Just before serving, slice the salmon as thinly as possible.

Lightly spread the top and bottom piece of bread with the coconut labne. Place thinly sliced salmon onto the labne, drizzle with olive oil, and season with a little freshly ground black pepper. Put one layer of thin slices of cucumber and some cilantro on the salmon. Place the top piece of bread on the sandwich, trim off the crusts, and cut into quarters, sixths, or any other desired shape.

WELSH RAREBIT WITH MARROW CRUST

PAUL LIEBRANDT ✳ CORTON ✳ WWW.CORTONNYC.COM

❸

THE British chef Paul Liebrandt had his work cut out for him. Having replaced venerated, longtime predecessor Montrachet, his new restaurant Corton, a collaboration with Montrachet owner Drew Nieporent, had to prove itself in Tribeca's booming scene.

Kudos soon poured in, securing the talent of Liebrandt, who had worked with the U.K.'s Marco Pierre White, Paris' Pierre Gagnaire, and New York's David Bouley. He created this simple, fancy sandwich for our book.

"Welsh rarebit is a classic cheese and tomato sandwich with gratineed cheese," he said, adding that he ate it a lot as a kid. This upscale variation uses Comte instead of cheddar, and incorporates bone marrow for the crust.

✳ ✳ ✳

Halve the veal pipes lengthwise. Soak in cold water overnight in the refrigerator.

The next day, put the marrow pipes in a pot with the chicken stock. Warm over low heat until just before a simmer. Remove the pot from the heat and allow it to come to room temperature. Remove the cooked marrow from the bones. Discard the stock.

In a large skillet, lightly brown the butter over medium-high heat, about 3 minutes. Allow to cool. Combine the butter cheese, brioche crumbs, and salt and pepper to taste in a food processor and blend to form a paste. Spread the paste between 2 parchment paper sheets on a very flat sheet pan and cover with plastic wrap. Freeze overnight. Slice into 3-inch squares.

Preheat the oven broiler. Slice brioche into four 3-inch squares. Add a tomato slice to the two of the slices. Top with a 3-inch square of marrow crust. Sprinkle with fleur de sel and green peppercorns to taste. Place the remaining two slices on top. Broil on high until lightly browned, about 2 minutes.

SERVES 2

1 pound 3-inch veal marrow bone pipes (ask your local butcher for pipe-cut marrow bones)
4 cups chicken stock
1 cup unsalted butter
2 cups grated Comte cheese
1 cup brioche crumbs (crumble day-old brioche bread)
Salt and white pepper
Toasted brioche
1 heirloom tomato, sliced
Fleur de sel and green peppercorns (available at gourmet grocers)

PORK BELLY PASTRAMI ON SEEDED RYE BAGUETTE

CHRISTOPHER LEE ✳ AUREOLE ✳ WWW.CHARLIEPALMER.COM

2 **P** **M** SMOKE 6 HOURS; COOK 6 HOURS

SERVES 4

1 cup salt
2 pounds pork belly
1 cup pastrami spice
   seasoning (available online
   and in grocery stores)
1 seeded rye or plain
   baguette
Coleslaw (recipes follows)
Russian Dressing (recipe
   follows)
4 slices Raclette cheese,
   approximately 6 × 2 inches

SINCE its 1988 opening, Chef Charlie Palmer's Aureole has had a dazzling top-tier reputation. Palmer has often said that Aureole was his original "dream restaurant" and, indeed, he's worked tirelessly to keep it in line with his own sensibilities, from complex dishes in a luxe Upper East Side townhouse to what the restaurant is today—more familiar cuisine in a larger, approachable Midtown space. What hasn't changed is the ambition.

Chef Christopher Lee, the 2005 recipient of the James Beard Foundation's Rising Star Chef of the Year award, steers the kitchen. He's known for his unerring ability to take something familiar and add to it a whole new dimension—a variation you didn't know existed, but you're pretty sure should. Case in point, the Pork Belly Pastrami he's developed for the book. (One look at the recipe and you'll see why this particular pork belly pastrami is a perfect match for the haute section.) "I love pork for its flavor and versatility, so it made sense to me to use it to reinterpret the traditional pastrami," he explained. "Since pastrami is normally made with a fatty piece of beef brisket, subbing in pork belly, in my opinion, tastes even better. In addition, pork belly loves to be smoked, slow cooked, and spiced. Serving it in this format is a perfect fit."

✳ ✳ ✳

Bring a gallon of water to a boil and add the salt. Once the salt dissolves, cool the brine. Then, pour the brine into a large dish and place the pork belly into the brine. Brine the pork belly for 6 hours in the refrigerator.

After 6 hours, remove the pork belly and rinse well under cold water. Pat the pork belly dry and then coat with the pastrami spice. In a smoker or covered grill, smoke the pork for 1 hour using hickory wood chips at 225°F. After smoking, place it in a pan with a rack and pour about 2 cups of water into the pan. Cover with foil and cook at 275°F for 6 hours. Once the pork belly is fork-tender, remove. Press the belly between two pans and cool. When cool, cut into 6 × 2-inch pieces.

For each sandwich, put the pork belly on the bottom slice of bread and top with the coleslaw. Spread the Russian dressing on the top piece of bread and add a cheese slice. Assemble each sandwich and eat as-is, or toast in the oven until the cheese just begins to melt.

NOTE: Raclette is a mild, semi-hard cow's milk cheese that's especially good for melting.

COLESLAW

SERVES 4 PLUS

1 cup heavy cream
½ cup water
½ cup white wine vinegar
1 teaspoon ground caraway seeds
Salt
1 head green cabbage
1 carrot

Place the heavy cream, water, vinegar, caraway seeds, and salt to taste in a pot and bring to a boil. Meanwhile, finely julienne the cabbage and carrot. Once the mixture comes to a boil, pour over the cabbage and carrots. Cover with plastic wrap and let cool on the counter. After about 30 minutes, poke three holes into the plastic and place into the refrigerator until serving.

RUSSIAN DRESSING

MAKES ¾ CUP

½ cup mayonnaise
¼ cup ketchup
2 tablespoons minced cornichons
2 teaspoons lemon juice
Zest of 1 lemon
2 tablespoons chopped parsley
Salt and pepper

Place the mayonnaise, ketchup, cornichons, lemon juice, lemon zest, parsley, and salt and pepper to taste into a bowl and mix well. Reserve until serving.

Lamb Pastrami Sandwich
with Spaghetti Squash Sauerkraut

STEPHEN LEWANDOWSKI ✳ TRIBECA GRILL ✳ WWW.MYRIADRESTAURANTGROUP.COM

3   **P**   **M** 3 TO 7 DAYS

I N the early 1990s, the neighborhood surrounding Tribeca Grill was but a desolate wasteland full of vacant warehouses, graffiti, and a smattering of pioneering artists. Then, the visionary investors in this restaurant—including Robert De Niro, Bill Murray, Mikhail Baryshnikov, Sean Penn, and Christopher Walken—saw what Tribeca would turn into: a high-end residential community in which warehouses become lofts and their owners are drawn to eat upscale comfort food with Italian leanings and a consistent movie star following.

Fast forward to 2010. The graffiti is gone. The warehouses are some of New York's priciest homes. The movie stars—mostly on the A-list—remain. The Grill's 200-seat space, housed in a 1905 coffee warehouse, still bustles nightly, as diners are drawn indeed to Chef Stephen Lewandowski's upscale comfort menu.

Take this signature sandwich. Added to the menu seven years ago, this pastrami riffs on a tried-and-true New York deli tradition. In place of beef, the chef uses lamb. He brines it for three (or more) days, cures it with a dry rub, and then slow roasts it. The result is salty and distinctive and can be served warm or cold. The topper is another homage—this time to the chef's Polish heritage ("I'm 100 percent Polish, married to a second-generation Pole," he said): a sauerkraut made, not with the traditional cabbage, but with sweet, delicate strands of spaghetti squash. The addition of kielbasa completes the analogy. "We make food intriguing, not intimidating," said the chef.

Place the lamb in a deep container. Add the salt and the water. Refrigerate for 3 to 7 days.

Preheat the oven to 200°F. Remove the lamb from the brine. Pat it dry.

Grind the paprika, coriander seeds, brown sugar, peppercorns, mustard seed, and garlic in a spice or coffee grinder. Mix well. Coat it thoroughly with the dry rub, and place it on a rack with a sheet pan underneath. Roast the lamb until the meat's internal temperature is 125°F, about 2 to 3 hours. Remove and let rest. The Lamb Pastrami can be stored in an airtight container in the refrigerated for up to five days.

Preheat the broiler. Spread 4 slices of the bread with half of the mustard. Top each with 2 slices of the cheese. Place them one at a time under the broiler until the cheese is melted, about 30 seconds. Remove the bread from the broiler. Divide the sliced pastrami and sauerkraut among the sandwiches. Spread the remaining slices of the bread with the remaining mustard. Close the sandwiches, slice them in half, and serve with the Spaghetti Squash Sauerkraut.

SERVES 4

- **1 top round lamb roast (about 2 pounds)**
- **1 cup kosher salt**
- **½ gallon cold water**
- **4 tablespoons paprika**
- **3 tablespoons coriander seeds**
- **3 tablespoons brown sugar**
- **1 tablespoon black peppercorns**
- **1 tablespoon white peppercorns**
- **2 tablespoons mustard seed**
- **1 tablespoon chopped garlic**
- **8 slices country rye bread**
- **4 tablespoons whole-grain mustard**
- **8 slices Swiss cheese**
- **Spaghetti Squash Sauerkraut (recipe follows)**

SPAGHETTI SQUASH SAUERKRAUT

MAKES ABOUT 3 CUPS

- **1 spaghetti squash**
- **1 cup diced kielbasa**
- **½ cup sugar**
- **½ cup white wine vinegar**

Preheat the oven to 350°F. Halve the squash lengthwise. Scoop out the seeds and pulp. Place the halves face down on a sheet pan. Bake until tender, about 1 hour. When the squash is cool enough to handle, use a fork to scrape out the flesh, which will resemble long strands of spaghetti. Place the flesh in a saucepan. Add the kielbasa, sugar, and vinegar. Simmer over medium-low heat for 20 to 30 minutes.

ROASTED LOIN OF PORK BANANA BREAD SANDWICH
WITH FRUIT CHUTNEY AND GREEN PLANTAIN CHIPS

JULIAN NICCOLINI, CO-OWNER ✳ THE FOUR SEASONS

WWW.FOURSEASONSRESTAURANT.COM

2 **H**

FEW restaurants anywhere in the world have gotten as much ink as the legendary Four Seasons in the Seagram Building on 52nd and Park. Since 1959, its iconic Mies van der Rohe Grill Room and Pool Room have played host to just about every scene imaginable—from lunches among the country's most powerful and intriguing people (the Dalai Lama goes, as does Henry Kissinger) to frequent celebrity sightings (Madonna and Martha Stewart are both fans). And, yes, every so often somebody gets overexcited and jumps into the pool.

Owned for decades by business partners Alex Von Bidder and Julian Niccolini, this original three-martini lunch spot still has, in its way, the power to give even the most jaded New Yorkers that sense of glittering, big-ticket glamour. From tender cuts of meat to buttery lobsters, the menu is an exercise in indulgence. For this book, Niccolini has worked with the chefs to develop a sandwich that captures the restaurant's "of course you can" attitude. "We wanted to make something truly spectacular and extraordinary, and so, of course, we thought of combining savory and sweet. The banana bread, even by itself, has those qualities—steaming it adds a depth of taste to it—but then adding so many more layers of those flavors with pork meat and the chutney turns this into something incredibly sexy—satisfying and original."

SPICED PORK

½ **tablespoon roughly chopped cilantro**
2½ **tablespoons chopped garlic**
4 **tablespoons ketchup**
2 **tablespoons oyster sauce**
3 **tablespoons ketjup manis (a sweet Indonesian soy sauce)**
1 **tablespoon honey**
2 **cinnamon sticks**
½ **teaspoon black pepper**
¾ **cup grenadine**
Juice of ½ lime
2 **pounds pork loin**
1 **tablespoon olive oil**

SANDWICHES

Fruit Chutney (recipe follows)
Banana Bread (recipe follows)
4 **Romaine lettuce leaves**
Spiced Pork
1 **red onion, sliced**

NOTE: For an easy side dish, julienne 3 green plantains and fry them in ¼ inch of oil until they're golden brown and crisp. Remove them from the oil, season with salt and pepper, and place on paper towels.

For the Spiced Pork: In a mixing bowl, combine the cilantro, garlic, ketchup, oyster sauce, ketjup manis, honey, cinnamon, black pepper, grenadine, and lime juice. Place pork loin in the marinade and refrigerate, preferably overnight.

Preheat the oven to 350°F. Remove the pork loin from the marinade and roast in a large sauté pan with olive oil over high heat to sear and caramelize the meat on both sides, about 5 to 7 minutes. Place the pork loin in the oven and roast until the internal temperature of the pork reaches 160°F, about 1½ hours. Remove from oven and let the meat rest for about 10 minutes before slicing.

For the Sandwiches: For each sandwich, spread a layer of fruit chutney on the banana bread. Top with the lettuce and the pork, and garnish with a few slices of onion.

FRUIT CHUTNEY

2¼ cups lime juice
1¼ cups pineapple juice
6 tablespoons rice vinegar
6 tablespoons mirin or sherry
1½ cups sweet chili sauce
1 tablespoon curry powder
1 tablespoon turmeric
¼ cup sugar
⅓ cup brown sugar
2 tablespoons minced fresh
   ginger
1 teaspoon minced fresh garlic
5 tablespoons cornstarch
¾ cup black raisins
½ cup chopped red onion
⅔ cup chopped red bell
   pepper
4 cups diced fresh pineapple
   (you can substitute canned)
4 cups diced ripe mango
Chopped cilantro (optional)
Scallions (optional)

Combine the lime juice, pineapple juice, vinegar, mirin, and chili sauce in a large sauce pot. Bring to a simmer over medium heat. Add the curry powder, turmeric, sugars, ginger, and garlic. Mix well and cook until the mixture has reduced by half, about 20 minutes. In a bowl, mix the cornstarch with 6 tablespoons of water, making sure that there are no lumps. Add the cornstarch slurry to the pot. This will thicken the chutney. Add the raisins, onion, pepper, and pineapple. Cook the chutney until the pineapples are translucent but not overcooked. Remove the mixture from the heat, and fold in the mango. You can also add chopped cilantro and scallions to taste before serving.

BANANA BREAD

4 ripe bananas (mashed
   together)
1 cup rice flour
1 cup potato starch
1¼ cups unsweetened coconut
   milk
1 tablespoon sugar
1 teaspoon salt
1 tablespoon unsweetened
   shredded coconut

Preheat the oven to 350°F. Combine the bananas, rice flour, potato starch, coconut milk, sugar, salt, and coconut. Pour the mixture into a greased 9-inch bread pan and cover with aluminum foil. Put the bread pan into a larger pan with sides. Fill the large pan with enough water to come half way up the bread pan. Bake for 55 minutes or until the bread is sticky, but firm. Let the bread cool before removing from the pan and then cut into slices for the sandwich.

Classic New York Cheesesteak Sandwich

CHEF WILLIAM OLIVA ∗ DELMONICO'S ∗ WWW.DELMONICOSNY.COM

2

SERVES 4

4 mini baguettes, or 2 large
    baguettes, cut into
    6-inch segments

24 ounces filet mignon, cut
    into 2 × ½-inch pieces

Salt and pepper

1 tablespoon butter

½ cup thinly sliced white
    onion

¾ cup olive oil

6 ounces classic demi-glace*

1 pound Vermont cheddar
    cheese, grated

*NOTE: You can buy demi-glace at most specialty food stores.

OPENED in 1837, this Financial District restaurant was a pioneer of continental cuisine. In a city of restaurants offering bland flavors and boiled preparations, Delmonico's presented bright flavors and innovative creations, many of which made their debut here. Thus, eggs Benedict, lobster Newburg and baked Alaska (a crowning glory here) were introduced to the dining public.

Now gorgeously updated, the dining rooms at Delmonico's are still steeped in Old World touches, as on a cruise liner from a bygone era.

Velvety and tender, this sandwich is one of the simplest, most understated luxuries in this cookbook. As befits a steakhouse in New York City, the sandwich uses the high-quality tips of fine filet mignon. At home, buy regular filet mignon and julienne it into small pieces. It's expensive but simple, and your family will love you.

* * *

Preheat oven to 350°F. Place the baguettes on a baking sheet and warm for 5 minutes. (To keep the bread moist, add a pan of water to the oven.) Remove.

Season the filet mignon with salt and pepper to taste. Heat the butter in a pan over medium heat. When frothy, add the onions and sauté until translucent and then set aside.

Add the olive oil to the hot pan. When oil begins to smoke, add the filet mignon to the pan and sear until medium rare, about 2 minutes.

Add the sautéed onions, demi-glace, and cheese. When the cheese melts, which should take less than a minute, remove from heat immediately. Fill the baguettes with the meat. Slice the sandwiches, and serve immediately.

SMOKED BRISKET WITH CHEESE AND SMOKED CHILI JAM

ZAKARY PELACCIO ✳ FATTY CRAB, FATTY 'CUE

WWW.FATTYCRAB.COM ✳ WWW.FATTYCUE.COM

3 **M** SMOKE 12 TO 14 HOURS

SOMETIMES, it's the unexpected that works out best. Like, say, leaving your high-end chef job to write and produce for the Food Network plus start a successful kitchen software company—then leaving those ventures to open an incredibly popular Brooklyn joint, only to ultimately wind up cooking some very bold Malaysian food in the West Village. While you're at it, expand to the Upper West Side; then try something in Willliamsburg, Brooklyn. Barbecue, maybe. Hey, why not?

There is, of course, much more to Chef Zakary Pelaccio's meteor-like string of successes—he's trained at the French Culinary Institute and in the kitchens of Kuala Lumpur and Chiang Mai. And over the years, he's been mindful about using all his skills. For the book, he chose a brisket that reflects what really happens when he puts that process to work. "The smoked brisket sandwich came about when I was playing around with ideas for Fatty 'Cue," said Pelaccio. "I love American brisket, so I wanted to see what would happen if I ramped up the savory and added some Eastern flavors. Could I make the tastes bolder and deeper? Yes. It's definitely a classic on crack."

For the Dry Rub: In a spice grinder, grind the chiles, lime zest, and peppercorns to a fine powder. Transfer to a bowl and mix with the salt.

For the Paste: Combine the palm sugar, fish sauce, garlic, shallots, ginger, and coconut milk in a food processor and purée until thick. The paste should not be completely smooth, but the bits and lumps should be rather small. Place in a bowl and set aside.

For the Brisket: Massage well all of the dry rub into the brisket so it really penetrates. This should be done in a deep-sided container large enough to accommodate the brisket and any errant rub. Make sure to coat the brisket thoroughly with the salt as well. Rub the paste over the seasoned brisket, again using all of the mixture. Cover the container and refrigerate for 24 to 48 hours.

Preheat a smoker to 200°F. Remove the brisket from the container and put it in the smoker. Discard any additional paste. Smoke the brisket for 12 to 14 hours. Pay attention to the smoker's temperature. At 10 hours, check the beef with a skewer. It should be met with very little resistance. If it's still tough, let it cook another hour before testing it again.

Remove the brisket from the smoker using large, flat spatulas. Let the meat sit untouched for at least 20 minutes to give the brisket some time to allow the juices to re-absorb into it. Carve against the grain into ¼-inch slices. Toss the brisket with the Tomato Chili Jam and set aside.

For the sandwiches: Preheat the oven to broil. Slice the baguette pieces lengthwise ¾ of the way through and open for sandwich filling. Smear the inside of the seeded baguette with aïoli on both sides, and add a generous amount of the jam-tossed brisket, so the sandwich is brimming. Top the stuffed baguette with the sliced cheese and place on a tray. Slide the tray into the oven and broil until the cheese starts to bubble. Remove from the broiler and serve immediately.

SERVES 9

DRY RUB
1 pint dried red chiles
Zest of 4 limes
2 cups black peppercorns
1 to 1½ cups kosher salt

PASTE
**½ round palm sugar
    (or substitute ½ cup
    brown sugar)**
¼ cup fish sauce
20 garlic cloves
10 small shallots
2 inches young ginger
¼ cup coconut milk

BRISKET
1 whole untrimmed brisket
Dry Rub
Paste
**Tomato Chili Jam (recipe
    follows), or another spicy
    jam of your choosing**

SANDWICHES
**3 seeded baguettes, cut into 3
    pieces**
Aïoli (recipe follows)
Brisket
**16 ounces Fior di latte cheese
    or provolone, sliced**

TOMATO CHILI JAM

¼ cup whole canned tomatoes

2 tablespoons oil (such as canola, peanut, olive oil blend, or grapeseed)

3 shallots (1 cup), sliced

1 bulb of garlic (½ cup), sliced

2 long red chiles, sliced

1 piece galangal root, sliced (a Thai ingredient; ginger is about the closest approximation)

1 tablespoon dried prawns

½ teaspoon belacan (a Malay version of shrimp paste), toasted

1 ounce palm sugar round, broken into small pieces (or substitute ¼ cup brown sugar)

2 tablespoons tamarind paste

3 teaspoons fish sauce

Preheat a smoker to 200°F. Purée the tomatoes in a blender until they're smooth. Cook the purée in a saucepan over medium-low heat until reduced to a paste, about 20 minutes. Smear the paste onto a parchment paper–lined baking sheet. Put the baking sheet in the smoker and smoke for about 3 hours. Remove the baking sheet from the smoker, scrape the smoked paste into a bowl, and cover with a damp towel.

In a deep-sided sauté pan, heat the oil over medium heat. Add the shallots, garlic, chile, galangal root, and prawns to the pan and sauté until they become soft and fragrant. Remove the sautéed vegetables from the pan and transfer them to a food processor. Grind the sautéed mixture into a smooth paste and return to the pan to sauté again over medium heat.

Add the belacan, sugar, tamarind, and fish sauce. Cook gently until all the ingredients have been incorporated. Then remove the mixture from the heat and cool. When the paste has cooled, fold it into the smoked tomato paste until it's completely incorporated.

AÏOLI

1 egg yolk

2 small garlic cloves, minced

2 cups grapeseed oil

1 teaspoon Japanese rice vinegar

1 teaspoon lime juice

Kosher salt

Put the egg yolk and garlic in the bowl of a food processor and pulse until smooth. Slowly add the oil while the machine is running, until the aïoli has emulsified. Add the vinegar, lime juice, and salt to taste and pulse to combine.

BBQ DUCK CONFIT SANDWICH

RYAN TATE ✳ SAVOY ✳ WWW.SAVOYNYC.COM

2 **P** **M** MARINATE OVERNIGHT AND COOK 5 HOURS

MORE than twenty years ago, Chef Peter Hoffman and his wife, pastry chef Susan Rosenfeld, opened a restaurant on a dingy Soho corner—Prince and Crosby. Meticulously, the couple transformed the storefront into an intimate bi-level restaurant with fireplaces on each floor, reflective of the 1830s townhouse's roots. In the kitchen, Hoffman—a New Jersey native who studied biology and animal science in college—set about creating a crave-worthy menu to really highlight the flavors, smells, and colors of organic, seasonal, and market-fresh food.

From the start, Savoy soared among critics and diners alike. Because he adopted green cooking early, Hoffman has become a bit of a poster child for the movement. He has spent fifteen years on the advisory board of the city's greenmarkets (he still visits on his bike, after dropping his two children off at school), and he was recently named one of *Organic Style's* fifty top environmental crusaders.

Savoy has often been called "intelligent," and you can see why: To this day, the kitchen brims with the rich tastes of fresh spices (not to mention sweet honey, some grown on NYC roofs in hives owned by the restaurant), organic meats, and in-season vegetables. The fitting together of tastes and their stories makes for a compelling narrative, perfect conversation fodder for a fascinating meal. Here, Ryan Tate, Savoy's chef de cuisine, shares a sandwich reflective of the restaurant's style and technique. It's a spin-off of his and Hoffman's signature dish, a crisp melt-in-your-mouth salted and baked duck. Said Tate, "The main reason I love this sandwich is because barbecue confit of duck combines the rich tradition of the French kitchen with a beloved American comfort food. The duck really adds new, rich layers of taste to the barbecue."

CURED DUCK

2 cups kosher salt
⅔ cup sugar
2 tablespoons black peppercorns
1 teaspoon whole cloves
1 teaspoon whole allspice
Peel of 1 orange
6 duck legs
4 cups rendered duck fat

SANDWICHES

1 teaspoon grapeseed oil
Cured Duck
2 tablespoons BBQ Sauce (recipe follows)
4 brioche buns, toasted
Coleslaw (recipe follows)
BBQ Potato Chips (recipe follows; optional)

NOTE: At 420°F, grapeseed oil also has a higher smoking point (the temperature at which the substance starts to break down) than most other oils. Studies show that the higher an oil's smoking point, the less of it is absorbed into any food it happens to be cooking, making grapeseed a healthy cooking and frying alternative.

NOTE: Unlike butter, duck fat is quite high in monounsaturated fats, which are thought to combat heart disease. Duck meat itself is also a good source of iron, all the B vitamins, and protein.

For the cured duck: Blend together the salt, sugar, peppercorns, cloves, allspice, and orange. Liberally apply the mixture over the duck legs and massage it in a bit. Let sit in the refrigerator overnight.

Preheat the oven to 250°F. Wash the legs in cool, running water, pat them dry, and place them in an oven-safe dish, at least 4 inches tall. Heat the duck fat in a heavy-bottomed skillet until the fat is completely melted and warm. Pour the fat over the legs and cover the pan with foil. The legs must be completely submerged in order to cook properly. Place the pan in the oven for about 5 hours, or until the meat separates easily from the bone. Remove and allow to cool. Once the legs are cool enough to handle, but still warm, remove them from the fat. Gently remove all bones from each leg (there are 3 bones) and refrigerate.

For the sandwiches: Place a large skillet over a medium flame. Add the grapeseed oil. When the pan is sufficiently hot, place the boneless legs skin side down in the hot skillet. Allow to cook for about 3 to 4 minutes over medium heat, shaking the pan occasionally to prevent the duck from sticking. Remove the legs from the pan; the skin should be very crispy. Roughly chop them and mix with the BBQ sauce. Evenly distribute between 4 toasted brioche buns and top with coleslaw. Serve with potato chips, if desired.

BBQ SAUCE

¼ cup canola oil

4 garlic cloves, sliced

2 onions, sliced

44 ounces ketchup (about 1 bottle)

1½ tablespoons ground chipotle

1½ tablespoons ground coriander

½ tablespoon ground allspice

1 tablespoon paprika

½ tablespoon smoked paprika

½ tablespoon ground mustard seeds

½ cup brown sugar

½ cup cider vinegar

½ cup molasses

Salt and pepper to taste

Heat the canola oil in a pan. Add the garlic and onions and cook until translucent. Combine the ketchup, chipotle, coriander, allspice, paprikas, mustard seeds, brown sugar, cider vinegar, molasses, and salt and pepper in the pan and reduce by half. Purée in a blender and pass through a course strainer.

BBQ POTATO CHIPS

2 potatoes

2 quarts (8 cups) canola oil

2 tablespoons smoked paprika

2 teaspoons salt

1 teaspoon brown sugar

½ teaspoon ginger powder

½ teaspoon ground chipotle (optional)

Slice raw potatoes very thinly on a mandoline directly into cold water. In a heavy-bottomed pot, heat the oil to 300°F. Combine the paprika, salt, brown sugar, giner powder, and chipotle pepper to make a barbecue spice. Working in batches, fry the potatoes until golden. Season immediately with the barbecue spice.

COLESLAW

½ green cabbage head
1 carrot
1 small red onion
4 tablespoons rice wine
     vinegar
3 teaspoons salt
2 teaspoons sugar

Cut the green cabbage into ¼-inch strips, grate the carrot on the medium hole of a box grater, and thinly slice the red onion. Mix the cabbage, carrot, onion, vinegar, salt, and sugar together and let stand for at least one hour, stirring occasionally.

HOT and CRISPY Tuna

JEAN-GEORGES VONGERITCHEN

ABC KITCHEN, JEAN-GEORGES, JOJO, THE MARK, MATSUGEN, MERCER KITCHEN, PERRY STREET, SPICE MARKET

WWW.JEAN-GEORGES.COM

1 P H

I T'S hard to imagine the New York culinary map without a few very pronounced dots labeled "JG." Since 1986, when at just twenty-nine he earned a coveted four stars from *The New York Times*, Chef Jean George Vongerichten has been defining the city's restaurant landscape with one iconic restaurant after the next.

In 1991, Jo Jo, his first solo venture, made then-*New York Times* critic Ruth Reichl write, "his cuisine took my breath away." Jean-Georges, his Upper East Side namesake, is one of just seven New York restaurants to be awarded four stars by *The New York Times*. Mercer Kitchen, in Soho's Mercer Hotel, and Spice Market both remain celebrity haunts years after opening—a tall order in a finicky city. Perry Street, an ingredient-centric restaurant on the westernmost side of New York's downtown Meatpacking district now features his son (a rising chef in his own right) at the helm, and a menu recognized for its innovation as much as its stunning views and décor. And the list goes on.

Over the course of his career, Vongerichen has cultivated a reputation for clean, smart cooking. He has a penchant for Asian touches—he's widely credited with pioneering some high-end fusion techniques—and has a valuable and innate ability to reduce a recipe to its essence. This tuna sandwich, which he put together specifically for the book couldn't be a better reflection of his sensibility: "I love this sandwich because you can cook it up quickly, and it's an unexpected take on a classic tuna sandwich," he said. "The different textures, the warm bread with the rare tuna in the middle, everything's a delicious surprise."

With a rolling pin, flatten each slice of bread until ¼ inch thick. Trim the tuna, and cut into fourths, so that each piece will fit on a slice of bread with a ¼-inch border around the tuna. Brush half the bread slices, right to the edges, with egg yolk. Place a slice of tuna in the center of each bread slice and season lightly with salt and pepper to taste. Cover each with another slice of bread. Press the edges together to make a package; the egg will help seal the edges.

In a small sauté pan, heat about 2 tablespoons olive oil until hot. Add the first sandwich and cook over medium-high heat until golden brown on both sides, about 1 minute per side for rare tuna, 2 minutes per side for medium. Transfer to a paper towel–lined plate. Repeat to cook all the sandwiches. Cut the sandwiches into quarters and serve immediately.

SERVES 4

8 slices white sandwich bread, crusts trimmed
12 ounces fresh tuna (sliced about 1 inch thick)
4 egg yolks, beaten with 4 tablespoon of water
Salt and freshly ground pepper
8 tablespoons extra virgin olive oil, divided

Salmon Croquette on a Hamburger Bun
with Vinegar Slaw

DAVID WALTUCK ✳ CHANTERELLE

1 **P** **H**

SERVES 4

2 salmon fillets, skinned and
   cut into 2-inch pieces
1 cup dry breadcrumbs
½ cup heavy cream
¼ cup finely chopped shallots
1 garlic clove, finely chopped
2 tablespoons mixed chopped
   fresh herbs (choose
   3 or so, such as parsley,
   dill, chervil, or tarragon)
2 tablespoons Dijon mustard
2 large eggs
2 tablespoons lemon juice
¼ teaspoon Tabasco sauce
Salt and pepper
All-purpose flour
½ cup canola oil
2 tablespoons unsalted butter
4 hamburger buns
Tartar Sauce (recipe follows)
Vinegar Slaw (recipe follows)

IN 1979, twenty-four-year-old David Waltuck and his wife, Karen, opened a tiny restaurant on Grand Street in Soho. On staff were just two waiters and a dishwasher. A mere six weeks into the run—on New Year's Eve—he was on the cover of *New York Magazine*. Five years later, Chanterelle was awarded four stars in *The New York Times*.

For nearly thirty years, Chanterelle (which eventually expanded and relocated to Tribeca) set the bar with critics and diners for what it means to be a downtown Manhattan restaurant: casual, yet an epicenter of sophistication and taste. The spot became so popular with artists, among them Cy Twombly, Robert Mapplethorpe, and Keith Haring, that the Waltucks started letting them design menu covers, a tradition that spawned an astounding collection and continued until the restaurant closed in fall 2009.

The Waltucks say they chose the name Chanterelle to sound French, yet not at all pretentious. It's hard to imagine a better metaphor for this chef's now-legendary style: simultaneously transporting and deeply satisfying. Seasonal ingredients get close attention and flavors—be they from a market green or a fresh piece of fish—are treated with care and attention. For this book, Waltuck thought about the ease, convenience, and deliciousness people look for in sandwiches, and chose a recipe his whole restaurant had loved. "Although my ideal of a restaurant staff meal is one eaten calmly, seated at the table, sometimes this is not possible," he said. "The Salmon Croquettes, always a Chanterelle staff meal favorite and always served with Tartar Sauce, attain perfection served as a sandwich and allow those who have the time to sit and savor, and those who don't to still have the full experience."

Grind the salmon through the medium blade of a meat grinder into a large bowl. Add the breadcrumbs, cream, shallots, garlic, herbs, mustard, eggs, lemon juice, Tabasco, and salt and pepper to taste. Mix well, and form into 6 burger-like patties. Spread about ½ cup flour on a plate and dip the croquettes to coat on both sides.

Heat the oil in a large heavy skillet over medium heat. Add butter to the oil, and as soon as it has melted, add the salmon croquettes. Fry them until they're golden brown on the outside (3 to 5 minutes per side). Drain on paper towels, and serve on toasted hamburger buns topped with tartar sauce and coleslaw.

NOTE: Salmon is especially high in omega-3 fatty acids, which are thought to play a role in areas as wide-ranging as weight loss, heart health, cancer prevention, and mood improvement. According to one study in *The American Journal of Clinical Nutrition*, adults who ate omega-3-rich fish and meat a few days a week were nearly 20 percent less likely to develop dementia than those who consumed none of either.

TARTAR SAUCE

MAKES ABOUT 1 ⅓ CUP

1 cup mayonnaise
3 tablespoons sweet relish
3 tablespoons bottled white
   horseradish (measured
   after draining)
½ teaspoon sherry vinegar
½ teaspoon Worcestershire
   sauce

Combine the mayonnaise, relish, white horseradish, sherry vinegar, and Worcestershire in a small bowl. Whisk until well blended.

VINEGAR SLAW

MAKES ABOUT 7 CUPS

1 cup cider vinegar
¼ cup sugar
½ teaspoon salt
5 cups shredded savoy or
   green cabbage
1 red bell pepper, stemmed,
   seeded, and julienned
1 carrot, peeled and grated

Combine vinegar, sugar, and salt in a bowl. Whisk until they're blended and the sugar and salt are dissolved. Add the remaining ingredients and toss well. Allow to marinate at least 2 hours or overnight. Drain before serving.

Chapter 6

THE VEGETARIAN SANDWICH

* * *

NEW YORK MAY FEEL AS FAR AWAY FROM NATURE AS YOU CAN GET, BUT WHEN it comes to farm-fresh ingredients, the city couldn't be better positioned. For one thing, it's surrounded by fertile agricultural land, extending up through New England and down to Pennsylvania. Stop by, say, the Union Square Farmers' Market and you'll see it all in action—from the bearded Amish farmers selling cheese to macrobiotic produce stands. It's a mish-mash of eccentric, passionate, and eclectic vendors perfectly appropriate to the city.

Not only does having such a pick of artisanal cheeses and seasonal fruits and vegetables open up an incredible range of flavor combinations for chefs, but for diners, also, that access is becoming priceless. Thanks to writers and activists such as Michael Pollan, New Yorkers' interest in clean, healthy living couldn't be growing faster or stronger.

Case-in-point: Thirty years ago, Woody Allen spoofed the West Coast health-food craze in *Annie Hall*. Today, New Yorkers are eating such words, having discovered their own delectable interpretation. Where a food comes from is now a topic of interest, often outlined in detail on menus or when waiters describe specials. Sometimes, its origins are even closer than you think—many restaurants source from urban rooftop gardens.

All this has moved New York dining toward a pared-down, ingredient-focused approach to food. Whether it's richly marinated mushrooms served up on fresh-baked bread or thick slices of farmstead mozzarella matched with heirloom tomatoes and hearty country rolls, sandwiches have been reborn as a sure way to let flavors speak for themselves. Moreover, in recent years, limiting meat intake has become important to many New Yorkers. Where vegetarian restaurants and menu choices were once a rarity, they now proliferate—fighting for the attention of diners, who're gladly reaping the spoils.

* * *

HaRD-BOILED EGG SanDWICH

COSME AGUILAR ∗ BAR HENRY ∗ WWW.BARHENRY.COM

1 **H** CUT DOWN ON FAT AND CHOLESTEROL BY MAKING THE SANDWICH WITH EGG WHITES ONLY (ADD AN EXTRA EGG PER PERSON TO THE RECIPE).

SERVES 4

8 eggs
1 small bunch basil
1 garlic clove
4 teaspoons extra virgin olive oil
Salt and pepper
1 small zucchini
1 small carrot
1 tomato
1 baguette
Mayonnaise

IN France, they talk about "mon oncle d'amerique," a reference to a fictional rich American uncle who'll someday swoop in with riches galore. In New York, restaurateurs Winston Kulok and his wife, Carole Bergman Kulok, brought that image to life a little when they opened Bar Henry, the plush complement to their West Village restaurant Cafe Henri, a few blocks away.

Both restaurants share the same mascot—a drunken Maltese patterned after the owners' (presumably sober) dog named, of course, Henry. Both spots have also perfected that cozy, comfortably worn-in feeling one might expect of Village mainstays: the neighborhood living room that's just asking you to come in for a bite and maybe a glass of wine. Yet, like that American uncle, Bar Henry's mobilized upward, fulfilled some ambition while still keeping diners in the family. It has a pricier wine list, for example, complete with a well-regarded sommelier (John Slover, whose list has won raves from the wine critics). But it also lets diners purchase just half of a full bottle—what's left gets sold by the glass.

The same is true of the menu—simple and refined. Food you might ask the butler for in that living room of yours. The egg preparations, in particular, are a draw, having been written up in nearly every review. Like everything here, their story has a very personal, familial touch: "I originally came up with the sandwich because my brother, who's also a chef, loves eating eggs for their health benefits," said Aguilar. "He would always order omelets, which I really see as a breakfast food. I wanted to give him something that was still simple, but that could pass for any meal. To get him to switch, I also had to make it extremely delicious."

Boil the eggs in water for 10 minutes. When they've cooled, peel and slice them lengthwise. Mash the basil and garlic clove with the olive oil and salt and pepper to taste to make a pesto. Julienne the zucchini and carrot, and thinly slice the tomato. Cut the baguette in half, spreading mayonnaise on one slice of the bread and pesto on the other slice. Place the sliced tomato, eggs, carrot, and zucchini within the slices of bread.

NOTE: Who says you can't have wine with egg salad? For this sandwich, Bar Henry's Wine Director recommends a barrel-aged Verdicchio, an Italian white known for its light acidic flavor.

Quinoa Salad Sandwich

SCOTT ANNAND ✳ DEAN & DELUCA ✳ WWW.DEANDELUCA.COM

1 **P** **H**

SERVES 1

1 teaspoon olive oil

1 small zucchini, cut into
  ½-inch dice

1 cup water

Dash of salt

½ cup quinoa

1 tablespoon toasted pumpkin
  seeds

½ cup chopped spinach

2 scallions, minced

1 tablespoon dried
  cranberries

1 tablespoon blanched
  almonds

1 tablespoon pine nuts

1 tablespoon golden raisins

2 tablespoons extra virgin
  olive oil

2 tablespoons sherry vinegar

White pepper

1 whole wheat pita

IT'S hard to believe that Dean & DeLuca, now a household name, was launched as recently as 1988. The flagship store of the upscale retail food chain remains in its light and lovely home on Prince Street, in Manhattan's Soho, but other stores are as far-flung as Napa Valley, Kuwait, and Tokyo.

"We like to have a good balance of everything in the prepared food case. People are more health conscious, and the quinoa salad is very popular, [so] it goes over very well. It's light and flavorful," said Chef Annand. We add the salad to a pita for a healthy sandwich.

* * *

Add the olive oil to a skillet over medium heat. Sauté the zucchini until soft and buttery, about 3 minutes. In a saucepan, bring the water and the salt to a boil over high heat. Add the quinoa. Cover and reduce the heat to low. Simmer for 15 minutes. Remove from the heat, and let stand until the water is absorbed, about 15 minutes. Transfer the quinoa to a large bowl. Add the zucchini, toasted pumpkin seeds, spinach, scallions, cranberries, almonds, pine nuts, and raisins. In a separate bowl, whisk together the oil and vinegar. Season with salt and pepper to taste. Pour the dressing over the quinoa salad. Toss to coat. Open the pita and add the quinoa salad.

EGGS ROTHKO

GEORGE WELD AND MELISSA BENAVIDEZ * EGG * WWW.PIGANDEGG.COM

2

HOW apt that a child of the south (Virginia and the Carolinas) who craved pancakes for dinner came up with the idea of a brunch-only spot. Together with Chef Melissa Benavidez, owner of an all-natural burger and hot dog joint in Williamsburg, George Weld opened this tiny, breakfast-centric shop in Williamsburg, and named it Egg.

Right away, Egg took off. The eponymous eggs were farm fresh, the biscuits crisp and buttery, the grits cheesy, and the Kentucky country ham rightly salty. At noon, the place stopped serving. The price of success? Egg is now open for lunch and dinner, too, with meal-appropriate menus that offer far more than pancakes.

Elsewhere, sandwiches that form vessels for fried eggs make references to nature, such as toads in the hole, or bird's nests. Egg's version is special: It references Chef Benavidez's world-famous great uncle, the artist Mark Rothko. "The sandwich sort of looked Rothkoesque when the yolk broke through. I figured I'd give it a more conventional name when I reprinted the menu for the first time, but by then it caught on, and I was stuck with it," said Chef Weld, adding that it's one of the top-selling items on his (breakfast) menu.

* * *

Heat a skillet or griddle. Place 1 tablespoon of the butter in the skillet. When the butter is melted, add the bread slices. Toast briefly (about 1 minute). Turn heat off. Preheat the broiler.

Using a cookie cutter or a drinking glass rim, cut a hole in the middle of each slice of bread. Discard the excess bread. Turn the heat back on, and add 1 teaspoon of the butter in each hole. Add a carefully cracked egg. Cook until the bottoms of the whites are set and the bread is golden, about 2 minutes. Carefully flip each bread slice over. Cook until the egg white is completely set, about 30 seconds to 1 minute. Remove from the heat.

Place the bread onto a baking pan. Sprinkle ½ cup of the grated cheese on each slice. Slide the pan under the broiler. Melt the cheese, about 1 minute. The white should be set, and the yolk runny. Serve.

SERVES 2

- 1 tablespoon plus 2 teaspoons unsalted butter
- 2 (1-inch) slices rich bread (preferably brioche or challah)
- 2 eggs
- 1 cup grated cheese (preferably aged Cheddar, Taleggio or Gruyère)

NOTE: The first time we made this sandwich, the egg fell out of the hole when we flipped it. To avoid this, first, use a nonstick pan. Second, don't skip placing extra butter in each brioche hole. Third, flip quickly and confidently. If you're still wary, you can just skip the flipping altogether. Cook the egg for a minute longer on that first side, lighten up on the cheese over the egg (you'll need the heat of the broiler to reach the top of the white), then put it under the broiler.

FARMHOUSE LENTIL SANDWICH

WHITNEY AYCOCK ✳ COUNTER ✳ WWW.COUNTERNYC.COM

1 **P** **H** CUT DOWN ON FAT BY HALVING THE AMOUNT OF OLIVE OIL.

SERVES 4

⅛ cup toasted walnuts

1½ cups dried French lentils

½ onion, chopped

1 bay leaf, preferably fresh

⅛ teaspoon paprika

⅛ teaspoon cayenne pepper

Salt

Pepper

½ bunch fresh parsley, chopped

2 tablespoons chopped fresh
   thyme

¼ cup olive oil

4 bread rolls (such as
   ciabatta), sliced in half

Mayonnaise (preferably
   vegan)

1 head arugula, just a few
   leaves

1 red onion, thinly sliced

1 tomato, sliced

THE East Village wouldn't be the East Village without a bit of counterculture, and the aptly named Counter is certainly one restaurant that fits the bill. An organic cocktail and wine bar slash vegetarian bistro, it's one of those places that is as it does. Owner Deborah Gavito launched her career selling organic baked goods in the nearby Union Square Greenmarket, and here, she's just as hands-on: Herbs are grown on her nearby roof, for example. There's a kids menu (Gavito is an enthusiastic vegetarian mom). And the food—it's the kind of mouthwatering, comfort-inducing stuff you'd want to eat whether or not you're vegetarian.

Much of this is thanks to Whitney Aycock, whose Southern roots (he even went to cooking school in North Carolina) shine through in his ability to work savory wonders with vegetables and legumes. Here in New York, he's furthered those sensibilities, applying his skills in some unexpected ways: "I think the Farmhouse Sandwich came about because of my love affair with bánh mì," he said. "The lentils, of course, take the place of the pâté and are the heart and soul of the sandwich. By no means are they the same, but there's something about the textures and the powerful flavor that really resonate. It's an extremely satisfying combination of flavors."

✳ ✳ ✳

Preheat oven to 350°F. Place the walnuts on a baking sheet and toast in the oven for about 8 minutes. In a pot, combine the lentils, onion, bay leaf, paprika, cayenne pepper, and salt and pepper to taste. Fill with just enough water to cover the lentils. Bring the water to a boil; then reduce to a simmer, cooking until the lentils are soft, about 35 minutes. Drain any remaining water.

In a blender or food processor, blend the lentils with the walnuts and parsley and thyme, seasoning with salt and pepper to taste. Reduce the blending speed to the slowest setting and gradually add the olive oil. Refrigerate the finished mixture for at least 30 minutes to let cool and marinate.

Lay out all the bread roll halves, and spread a layer of lentil purée on each. Follow with a thin layer of mayonnaise, also on each. Reserve the remainder of the purée as a salad. On the just bottom halves, add arugula, onion, and tomato to taste. Close the sandwiches and brush them with olive oil. Place the sandwiches in the oven and toast them for 10 to 15 minutes.

NOTE: If you like your onions on the sweeter side, you can sweat them in a pan (frying them until they're clear) for about 5 minutes before cooking them with the lentils.

NOTE: To keep your sandwich bottom from getting soggy, always put the wetter ingredients—like tomatoes—closer to the top of the stack and start with the dryer ones, such as lettuce.

Mozzarella in Corozza

MARIO BATALI

NYC RESTAURANTS: BABBO, BAR JAMON, CASA MONO, DEL POSTO, EATALY, ESCA, LUPA, OTTO, SPOTTED PIG

MARIOBATALI.COM

❶

SERVES 4

8 slices American-style
  sandwich bread, crusts
  removed

1 pound fresh mozzarella
  di bufala, cut into four
  4 × 3-inch chunks

7 eggs, 3 of them separated

1 cup whole milk

1 teaspoon chopped fresh
  thyme

1 teaspoon kosher salt

2 tablespoons extra-virgin
  olive oil, divided

2 tablespoons unsalted butter

SUPER chef Mario Batali needs no introduction. The flame-haired, rosy-cheeked, orange-clogged chef is larger than life, and he's ubiquitous—in the media, the airwaves, and his quiver of restaurants in New York, Los Angeles, and Las Vegas (lately, he's also been making appearances in films and Nintendo games). Having worked his way up in kitchens from New Brunswick, New Jersey, to the U.K., Provence, Paris, and along the California coast, Batali formed a partnership with Joe Bastianich (son of Felidia's Lidia) here in New York. The successful Po (no longer part of the enterprise) led to the monumental Babbo Ristorante e Enoteca, still one of the most difficult reservations to obtain in this city after thirteen years.

The simple, elegant sandwich Chef Batali created for our book means mozzarella in a carriage.

"I love this recipe as a starter during holiday gatherings, but it's perfect for any occasion. The fresh Mozzarealla di Bufala is decadent and luxurious. The result is like grilled cheese sammies—elevated to art. When that hot lactic blast hits you right out of the pan, you can't imagine anything better," he said. Allow the sandwiches to soak up a good amount of the egg mixture so they ooze with richness, and serve while hot.

* * *

Top each of 4 slices of bread with a piece of mozzarella. Cover with the 4 remaining slices of bread to form sandwiches. Trim the bread to within ¼ inch of the cheese.

In a wide, shallow bowl, whisk the 4 whole eggs and 3 yolks together. (Reserve the whites for a healthy omelet.) Add the milk, thyme, and salt and whisk well. Dip the sandwiches into the egg mixture one by one to coat.

In a large nonstick sauté pan over medium high heat add 1 tablespoon of olive oil and wait until it's smoking. Add 1 tablespoon of the butter and cook until the sizzling subsides. Place 2 sandwiches in the pan and cook slowly until golden brown on the first side, about 2 minutes. Flip each sandwich and cook on the other side for 2 more minutes. Remove the sandwiches and set aside in a warm oven. Repeat the process with the remaining oil, butter, and sandwiches. Serve immediately.

EGG AND COOKED TOMATO BRUSCETTA

MARCO CANORA ✳ HEARTH, INSIEME, TERROIR

WWW.WINEISTERROIR.COM ✳ WWW.RESTAURANTHEARTH.COM

1 **P** **H**

SERVES 4

4 eggs, divided

¼ cup extra virgin olive oil

½ small garlic clove, thinly sliced

1 small pepperoncini, finely chopped

½ teaspoon dried Sicillian oregano, crumbled

1 (14-ounce) can whole peeled tomatoes

Kosher salt and freshly ground black pepper

2 tablespoons chopped fresh basil

4 slices toasted country bread

NO New York book would be complete without at least one East Village punk rock nod—and so we bring you Terrior Wine Bar. The story starts out civilized enough: Chef Marco Canora grew up cooking in the kitchens of his Tuscan mother and aunt. As an adult, he shot through the ranks at Gramercy Tavern, apprenticed in Italy, served as chef at Tom Colicchio's Craft (which won a James Beard Award during his tenure), and opened Craftbar, Colicchio's popular offshoot.

In late 2003, Canora struck out on his own. Hearth, his critically acclaimed East Village restaurant, became a destination for bold and simple ingredient-focused dishes. Insieme, an uptown counterpart, followed. Then, Canora, his wine director Paul Grieco, and partner Steven Solomon (a captain at Gramercy Tavern) decided to open a wine bar that pushed some boundaries. The space is jammed with lively punk references, and the aim is to really get at the origin and essence of the wines it serves up. That high-octane energy is just as evident in the menu—craveworthy, toothsome, and satisfying. And heavy on sandwiches, a feature that proved to be so popular Canora created an expanded selection for the bar's Tribeca offshoot. (Solomon now gleefully calls the original Terroir EVill.)

✳ ✳ ✳

Separate the eggs. Reserve each yolk in its shell and combine two of the whites in a cup. Set aside the two remaining whites for another use.

In a medium skillet, off the heat, combine the oil, garlic, pepperoncini, and oregano. Turn on the heat and infuse over medium flame until the garlic just begins to fry and the mixture becomes fragrant, about 2 minutes. Raise the heat to high. Using your hands, break 5 tomatoes into the skillet allowing the juices to fall into the pan.

Season lightly with salt and pepper to taste. Fry the tomatoes until they concentrate and no longer look watery, 2 to 3 minutes. Add the basil. Lower the heat to medium and stir the egg whites into the sauce. Cook just until the whites firm and the sauce thickens, about 1 minute.

Turn off the heat. Using the back of a spoon, make four indentations in the sauce, allowing space around each. Place an egg yolk in each indentation. Draw in the sauce from the edges of the pan mounding it evenly around each of the yolks. Cover the skillet and leave it on the stove with the heat off until the yolks are just warmed through and beginning to set, 3 minutes. Spoon a yolk with sauce onto each piece of toast and serve immediately.

Panini San Gimignano
Tuscan Pear, Cheese, and Prosciutto Sandwich

CESARE CASELLA ∗ SALUMERIA ROSI ∗ WWW.SALUMERIAROSI.COM

1 **P** **H** HALVE THE CHEESE AND CUT 40 CALORIES AND 3.5 GRAMS OF FAT.

WHEN Tuscan-born Chef Cesare Casella came to New York nearly twenty years ago to take over as the executive chef of Coco Pazzo—a glitzy, now-legendary 1990s restaurant—he'd already earned a Michelin star in Italy, as well as a bona-fide celebrity following long before that concept was as widespread as it is today. Not only did New Yorkers seem to like him just as much as the Europeans did, but Casella also had a knack for growing with the times. That same decade, he went on to help open Il Cantinori (a Carrie Bradshaw favorite on *Sex and the City*) and in the next, the approachable and elegant Beppe and Maremma—his first solo ventures.

Now, befitting the city's newfound passion for putting emphasis on the ingredients themselves and their origin, Casella has opened Salumeria Rosi, a restaurant-cum-provisions store comfortably nestled in the heart of New York's laid-back Upper West Side. In intent and design, the place is just like an Italian neighborhood shop, he's quick to point out. It's a fitting full circle for Casella, who, as the first-ever dean of the Italian Culinary Academy at the International Culinary Center (formerly the French Culinary Institute), is charged with bringing the tastes and flavors of Italian ingredients and techniques to scores of young chefs.

It's a mission he captures wholeheartedly in this sweet, salty, and rich melt. "This panini highlights some of my favorite parts of Italy, things that are very close to my heart," he said. "From the Tuscan hills, San Gimignano produces such wonderful prosciutti; in this case, one grilled with fresh herbs. Pears from the garden at my restaurant in Lucca always made their way into our kitchen somehow. And though Taleggio isn't Tuscan, it still is one of my favorite Italian cheeses."

SERVES 4

**8 slices Tuscan bread (a
   round, country-style loaf)**
12 ounces prosciutto
**½ to 1 pear, thinly sliced
   (whatever kind is in
   season)**
**6 ounces Taleggio DOP (a
   mild-flavored washed rind
   Italian cheese)**

NOTE: Though simple, this sandwich is rich in flavor. Chef Casella suggests keeping accompaniments light, such as a side of lightly dressed mesclun greens or a pickle.

For each sandwich, divide about a quarter of the total amount of meat evenly between two slices of bread. Place a few pear slices on one sandwich half. Remove the rind from the Taleggio DOP and make thin slices about ¼ inch thick. Cover the second half of each sandwich with cheese slices.

Preheat a panini press if you have one. If not, you can use a preheated nonstick pan or skillet. (You'll press it down onto the sandwich, creating a makeshift press.) Place the slices of bread together, and cook until golden brown.

PEPPERS AND EGGS SANDWICH

VINNIE DEFONTE * DEFONTE'S * WWW.DEFONTESOFBROOKLYN.COM

①

IN 1922, Nick Defonte bought an Italian-owned sandwich shop at the bustling pier in Red Hook, Brooklyn. Quickly, Defonte's made a name for its high-quality sandwiches and eye-popping portion sizes created for ravenous longshoremen.

Eighty years later, the family—now in its third generation—opened another outlet in Manhattan. Today, this old-school sandwich shop still stands apart: for its tongue-in-cheek names (we love the "Vinnie Barbaresco"), the massive combinations (fried eggplant with roast beef, fried eggplant with three types of ham), and the meticulous counters. Sure, the sandwiches can be eaten in one sitting—if you're starving. Case in point: There are four eggs in each serving in this recipe. Defonte's prepares them as an omelet, but we recommend scrambling them for ease and convenience.

* * *

Lay each hero roll on a plate. Add the 2 teaspoons of oil to a skillet. Add the onion and sweat until soft, about 3 minutes. Place the cooked onions and the raw peppers in a medium pot, and cover with water. Bring to a boil. Lower the heat, and cook until soft, about 8 minutes. Drain.

While the vegetables are cooking, whisk the eggs in a large mixing bowl, and season with salt and pepper to taste. Using the onion skillet, add 1 to 1½ teaspoons of oil (if necessary). When the skillet is hot, add a quarter of the beaten eggs, or about 4 eggs. After 2 minutes, add a quarter of the vegetables, season again, and scramble. Just before the mixture has reached desired doneness, add the mozzarella. Fill each hero roll with the scrambled egg. Cook the remaining 3 batches the same way.

SERVES 4

4 (10-inch) Italian hero loaves (or other large, soft roll), halved lengthwise

2 teaspoons plus 2 tablespoons vegetable oil

1 large Spanish onion, cut into 1-inch pieces

2 green bell peppers, quartered, deseeded, and diced

2 red bell peppers, quartered, deseeded, and diced

16 eggs, beaten

Salt and fresh-cracked black pepper, to taste

2 cups shredded whole-milk mozzarella (Defonte's uses Polly-O)

ISRAELI WORKINGMAN'S LUNCH

SNIR ENG-SALA ∗ COMMERCE ∗ WWW.COMMERCERESTAURANT.COM

1 **P** **H** **M** 1 DAY

SERVES 2

2 pitas (preferably the thick Israeli kind)
4 tablespoons Israeli Hummus (recipe follows), or fresh, store-bought hummus
Olive oil
Green Eggs (recipe follows)
Katan Katan (recipe follows)

AMIDST charming brownstones, the West Village's loveliest cobblestone street turns an elbow-like corner. In this corner sits Commerce, a restaurant whose quaint location doesn't hinder a full house nightly, and on weekends. The draw? Snir Eng-Sala's fresh breads and creative New American cooking.

On a brunch menu packed with eggs, pastries, and other popular New York breakfast items, one item stands out: a sandwich from the chef's native Israel. It meant a lot to Eng-Sala during the early part of his career, and nostalgia prompted him to add it. "I was working two jobs—as a chef in a catering company and a restaurant. In between, I'd go to a corner hummus shop—any one, since they all had it—and order this. It would tide me over for the rest of the day," said Eng-Sala. Aptly enough, he named this nourishing, balanced sandwich (now a Commerce bestseller) after its crucial role in those bygone days.

∗ ∗ ∗

Place each pita on a plate. To each, add a large dollop, or about 2 tablespoons, of hummus. Drizzle with olive oil, to taste. Add equal portions of the Green Eggs and the Katan Katan.

ISRAELI HUMMUS

2 cups small dried chickpeas
8 cups water
3 garlic cloves
½ tablespoon baking soda
Salt
1 cup tahini paste, plus ½ cup water
½ cup fresh lemon juice
3 tablespoons olive oil
Fresh-cracked black pepper

Soak the chickpeas in the water overnight. Drain the water.

Place the chickpeas in a pot, and cover with more water. Add the garlic, baking soda, and salt to taste. Bring to a boil. Turn the heat down, and simmer until the chickpeas are very soft, about 1 hour.

Purée the cooked chickpeas in a blender or food processor, adding water as needed until smooth. Season with salt and pepper to taste. In a separate bowl, mix the tahini paste with water until the paste turns white and the water is incorporated. Season the tahini with the lemon juice, olive oil, and salt and pepper. Add the tahini mixture to hummus, mixing well. Adjust the seasoning, and allow to cool before using or serving.

NOTE: To check doneness, Eng-Sala suggests using a time-tested Israeli method. "Take a chickpea out of the pot, and throw it at the wall. If it sticks, it's ready. If it doesn't, keep cooking."

GREEN EGGS

8 to 10 parsley sprigs (about ¼ bunch), stems removed and chopped
4 mint sprigs, stems removed and chopped
4 cilantro sprigs, stems removed and chopped
4 dill sprigs, stems removed and chopped
4 tarragon sprigs, stems removed and chopped
4 chive sprigs, chopped
2 tablespoons olive oil
2 eggs, whisked lightly
¼ cup lemon juice (about 2 lemons)
Salt and pepper

Combine the herbs. Place the olive oil in a skillet. Heat until hot, but not smoking. Add the eggs. As they begin to set, turn off the heat. Add the herbs and lemon juice and salt and pepper to taste.

KATAN KATAN
(ISRAELI CHOPPED SALAD)

2 Persian cucumbers,
  finely diced
1 ripe tomato, finely diced
½ medium onion, finely diced
4 parsley sprigs, chopped
4 mint sprigs, chopped
¼ cup fresh lemon juice
  (about 2 lemons)
½ cup olive oil
Salt and pepper

Toss the vegetables and herbs in a large mixing bowl. Dress salad with lemon juice and olive oil. Season with salt and pepper to taste.

TRIO OF SIMPLE BREAKFAST PITA SANDWICHES

ELIAS GHAFARY (OWNER) ✳ AL BUSTAN ✳ WWW.ALBUSTANNY.COM

❶ P Ⓗ

FOR seventeen years, Midtown's Al Bustan quietly produced some of New York's finest Lebanese food: bright tabbouleh, juicy shawarma, garlicky grilled prawns, and a rainbow of delicious meze. Recently, the restaurant moved into splashy (and sprawling) new digs, replete with crystal chandeliers and a cocktail lounge. Despite his extensive menu, owner Elias Ghafary gave us two off-the-menu sandwiches he remembers fondly from his childhood in Lebanon plus a third sandwich that he discovered fairly recently.

Every day, most people in Beirut eat either a zatar or a labne sandwich for breakfast, he said. "When we were kids, they used to tell us that a labne sandwich makes you strong, and a zatar sandwich makes your brain function better," he added, joking that he ate both with gusto. These minty, summertime sandwiches are deceptively flavorful—and a cinch to make.

The third sandwich, based on an Armenian dish called muhammara, was something that owner Ghafary discovered while catering an event at the Armenian church in Midtown Manhattan. A woman was breaking off bits of pita and dipping them into something bright red. He asked what it was, and she invited him to try it. The simple sandwich—a healthy mix of nuts, ground red pepper, and seasoning—delivers a surprisingly complex burst of flavor.

ZATAR SANDWICH

SERVES 1

2 tablespoons zatar (found in Middle Eastern grocery stores)

1 tablespoon olive oil

1 pita bread, warmed

½ ripe tomato, sliced

6 or 7 mint leaves

Salt

Combine the zatar with the olive oil to form a paste. Spread the paste on one half of the inside of the pita bread. Add the tomato slices. Add the mint leaves. Salt to taste. Roll the pita tightly and enjoy.

LABNE SANDWICH

1 container plain yogurt

1 pita, warmed

1 tablespoon chopped
scallions (about ½ scallion)

6 or 7 mint leaves

10 small green olives, pitted

Salt

Cut an 8-x-6-inch section of cheesecloth. Spoon the yogurt into the middle of the cheesecloth. Gather together the corners, and tie them tightly. Standing over a sink, wring the cheesecloth a few times with the yogurt inside. When the liquid starts to drip more slowly, place the cheesecloth sack into a colander or chinois. Put it into the refrigerator, with a bowl underneath. Strain overnight.

Cut open the sack. Spoon the thickened yogurt into a pita. Sprinkle in the chopped scallions. Add the mint leaves and olives, and season with salt to taste. Roll tightly and enjoy.

MUHAMMARA SANDWICH

2 to 3 large red bell peppers,
deseeded and roughly
chopped

1½ cups chopped walnuts
(raw)

2 tablespoons tomato paste

4 tablespoons pomegranate
molasses (available in
Middle Eastern grocery
stores)

1 tablespoon garlic powder

½ teaspoon cayenne pepper

½ tablespoon cumin

Salt

Plain breadcrumbs

4 pitas, warmed

Place the bell peppers in a blender or food processor and pulse until thoroughly ground. Spoon the peppers into a colander and drain. Place into a bowl. Add the walnuts, tomato paste, and pomegranate molasses. Mix well to combine. Add the garlic powder, cayenne, and cumin. Season with salt to taste. If the mixture is watery, add the breadcrumbs until the liquid is absorbed, but the consistency should still be moist. Divide the muhammara among the pitas and serve.

MUSHROOM SANDWICH

1 **P** **H**

NOTE: Research has found that Maitake mushrooms are particularly good at stimulating immune system cells in cancer patients as well as other anti-cancer activity in the body (in labs, they can make cell growth slow and even cause cancer cell death). More broadly, these, and all mushrooms, are a rich source of antioxidants.

IN November 2009, friends Christophe Hille, Nathan Foot, and Chris Ronis opened Northern Spy Food Co. on a cozy street in the East Village. Named after a kind of New York State apple, the establishment's mission is to pay tribute to the bounty of local ingredients to be found the Northeast and Mid-Atlantic regions. The restaurant became something of an instant classic. Go there in the afternoon and you'll see a seamless flow of neighbors wandering in and out, some stopping for a bite and a chat, others picking up savory delicacies from the counter or the attached store. At nighttime, the room is packed and aglow. There's something vital and organic about the mood; the restaurant has really become a source of nourishment in more ways than one.

Taste the food and it's easy to see why. Flavorful and fresh, each dish offers up a variety of textures and tastes, as conceived by partner Christophe Hille (who made waves at San Francisco's A16 and is now studying nutrition at New York University) and Executive Chef Nathan Foot (whose credits include San Francisco's Myth restaurant). You'll see their incredible teamwork in action in Nathan's description of how they came up with this mushroom sandwich, one of their most noted menu items: "We wanted to craft a flavorful, satisfying vegetarian sandwich that mirrored some of the experience of eating a meat-based sandwich, rather than what's frequently offered to vegetarians, which is essentially a salad in bread," he said.

"Mushrooms can provide a similar experience and are often described as 'meaty.' We decided to add olive-oil-poached potato because it helps add heft and a subtle flavor to the sandwich. We also added Cabot Clothbound cheddar because it complements the richness of the mushrooms and the creaminess of the potatoes, plus it has that slightly and funky quality that aged cheeses get. The sandwich is finished with arugula to balance everything with the bitter, fresh pepperiness of those salad greens."

Place the potatoes in a snug saucepot and cover with olive oil. Bring to a gentle simmer, cover and cook until potatoes can be easily pierced with a paring knife. Remove from the heat, pull out the potatoes with a slotted spoon and set aside to cool. Reserve the olive oil for future use. When fully cooled, cut the potatoes into ½-inch cubes.

Preheat the oven to 375°F. Tear the mushrooms into rough shreds. Toss in a bowl with olive oil just to coat lightly. Add the thyme sprigs and garlic and season with salt and pepper to taste. Place on a baking sheet and bake until well caramelized, 15 to 20 minutes. Remove from the oven and allow to cool.

To assemble the sandwiches, warm the baguette pieces in the low oven just to get them a bit crusty. Warm the mushrooms and diced potato in the oven as well. Divide the cheddar crumbles between the four baguettes, sprinkling along the interior. Divide the mushroom and potato mixture among the four baguettes and lay over the cheese.

Season the arugula greens with olive oil, lemon juice, and salt and pepper to taste. Top the sandwiches with the greens. Press the sandwiches down a touch to get the ingredients to hold snug, and then cut each sandwich in half across the middle.

SERVES 4

2 medium Yukon Gold potatoes
Olive oil
½ pound maitake mushrooms (also known as Hen of the Woods)
½ pound oyster mushrooms
3 sprigs thyme
2 garlic cloves, lightly crushed
Salt and freshly ground black pepper
4 (6-inch) pieces crusty baguette
½ pound crumbled cheddar (Northern Spy uses Cabot Clothbound)
4 small handfuls arugula greens
Lemon juice

GENERAL TSO'S FRIED TOFU SUB

TYLER KORD * NO. 7 SUB * WWW.NO7SUB.COM

1 **P**

BESIDES Tyler Kord, there are few New York chefs so freewheeling in their gift for global interpretation; a sandwich at No. 7 Sub is often a ticket around the world.

After two years as sous-chef at Jean-George Vongrichten's Perry Street, Kord opened his first sandwich shop in Fort Greene, Brooklyn. His combinations are born in a stream-of-conscious game of leapfrog.

"I start with an ingredient. I think about how I want to cook it and what goes well with it classically. Then I . . . swap out the classic ingredients for unusual ones with a similar flavor profile," said Chef Kord.

The process isn't novel, but Kord maximizes the level of daring and inventiveness. A prime (and wacky) example is No. 7's seasonal Braised Lamb Sandwich. Fixings include mint jelly (classic pairing with lamb), peanut butter (both a natural accompaniment for jelly and a nod to Thai peanut sauce, which, Kord points out, often accompanies southeast Asian curries made of lamb), and crunchy, cumin-loaded pappadam (cumin goes with lamb, he reasons, and pappadam is another snack from that part of the world).

This Fried Tofu Sub is a bestseller at No. 7's busy second location in Manhattan's Ace Hotel. The sauce began as two sauces for two different dishes and contained disparate flavors such as horseradish, fresh tarragon, and smoke. "One of my cooks would mix them and dip his French fries in it," said Chef Kord, adding that "combined, they make unicorns dance."

FRIED TOFU

1 (1-pound) block firm tofu
Salt
1 tablespoon sugar
1 tablespoon Spanish paprika
1½ teaspoons garlic powder
1½ teaspoons onion powder
3 tablespoons cornstarch
2 eggs, separated
2 cups panko breadcrumbs
4 cups canola, peanut, or
    other neutral oil

SANDWICHES

4 (6-inch) soft submarine
    rolls, sliced all the way
    through lengthwise
2½ cups Unicorn Sauce
    (recipe follows)
2 cups snow pea shoots,
    frisée, arugula, or other
    lightweight salad green
1½ carrots, julienned
Roasted Onions (recipe
    follows)
1 lime, cut into wedges

NOTE: Not only is tofu "cheap and vegetarian," said Chef Kord, "if treated properly, it can be totally triumphant… like a savory flan." Fried, he adds, it's crunchy, but retains "that custardy interior." One final note: Don't be afraid to add salt. "It will make everything taste awesomer."

For the fried tofu: Slice the tofu into planks about ½ inch thick. You should get a total of 8 planks. Salt both sides of each tofu piece to taste. Combine the dry spices, and sprinkle the mixture liberally over both sides of the tofu.

Whisk the cornstarch and egg whites together to create a thick, smooth paste. Place the panko breadcrumbs in a bowl. Place the seasoned tofu planks on your left, the cornstarch slurry in front of you, and the bowl of panko to the right of it, and a clean plate next to that.

One piece at a time, dip a tofu plank into the cornstarch slurry. Let it hang over the bowl for a few seconds, allowing excess slurry to run off. Dip it in the panko, rolling it around with your other hand. Be gentle. Place the breaded tofu plank on the empty plate. Repeat for the 7 remaining tofu planks. Heat the oil. Fry the tofu in small batches until brown, about 1½ to 2 minutes. Drain on paper towels. Salt to taste.

For the sandwich: Give the inside of each roll half a generous squirt of the Unicorn Sauce. Divide the greens evenly among the rolls. Add the carrots, roasted onions, fried tofu, and a little more of the sauce. Squirt some lime juice into each sub, or place a dish of lime wedges out for your guests. Cut the subs in half, and serve.

ROASTED ONIONS

1 medium yellow onion, sliced into thick rings
1 tablespoon olive oil
Salt

Preheat the oven to 400°F. Toss the onion rings with the olive oil. Salt to taste. Place the rings on a baking sheet and roast until brown.

UNICORN SAUCE

1 egg, separated
1 teaspoon salt, divided
1½ teaspoons apple cider
1½ teaspoons malt vinegar
½ jalapeño pepper, roughly chopped
½ cup sour pickles
10 to 12 fresh tarragon leaves
¼ teaspoon liquid smoke
¾ cup canola oil
½ 14-ounce can plum tomatoes
1 tablespoon plus 1½ teaspoons prepared horseradish
1 garlic clove
¼ teaspoon sesame oil
1 tablespoon white vinegar
1 tablespoon Sriracha
½ cup extra virgin olive oil
Kosher salt

Place the egg yolk, ½ teaspoon of the salt, apple cider, malt vinegar, jalapeño, pickles, tarragon, and liquid smoke into the bowl of a food processor (if you don't have a food processor, use a blender on low speed, so that the sauce remains chunky). Pulse until relatively smooth, but not puréed. Slowly drizzle in the canola oil until emulsified.

Place the canned tomatoes, horseradish, garlic, sesame oil, the other ½ teaspoon of salt, white vinegar, and Sriracha in a blender. Purée at medium speed. Slowly drizzle in the olive oil until emulsified. Combine the two sauces. Season with salt to taste.

Raw "Tuna" Salad Sandwich

SARMA MELNGAILIS * PURE FOOD AND WINE * WWW.ONELUCKYDUCK.COM/PUREFOODANDWINE/

2 **P** **H**

SERVES 4

"TUNA" SALAD

4 cups whole raw almonds

1½ cups finely diced celery

**2 medium yellow onions,
    diced very small**

1 garlic clove, minced

**1 cup parsley leaves, chopped
    small**

1 tablespoon capers

½ cup lemon juice

1 tablespoon sea salt

½ teaspoon cayenne pepper

THE raw vegan food movement has always been a bit of a tough sell. Why pay up for lettuce, vegetables, and a few nuts, you might wonder? Pure Food is one very inspired reason to wonder no more. Tucked into a corner of Manhattan's Gramercy Park, the downtown enclave near the Union Square Farmers' Market known for its picturesque streets and stately old buildings (with price points to match), the restaurant is set to impress before you even try the food. Deep reds and golden light fill the interior, while just behind the dining room you'll find a breathtaking garden space, done up with tea lights and strung lanterns. Come early, because it's always crowded.

Yes, you read right: Crowded, and not just with dedicated vegans or brave lovers of a good table. Couples, families, loud dinner parties—you'll see them all digging into hearty dishes, from lasagna-like creations to curries to "cheeses" made from nuts. One chef—a non-vegan—who'd worked at the restaurant said he'd especially enjoyed the experience because without meats and animal fats to lean on (bacon, butter, cheese—they're all pretty foolproof), he really had to elevate his game.

To thank for this is Sarma Melngailis—a onetime investment banker whose passion for food, especially the raw stuff, led her and a partner to open Pure in 2004. Just as Pure's honed an elegance that melts it into the prettiness of Gramercy, Sarma's melded her own experiences into the restaurant—living just across the street, she's brought her hands (for a time, she was the executive chef), her business acumen, and the highs and lows of her own life (she's extremely candid on the Pure Food blog) into the restaurant. For most diners who pass through Pure's door, raw food is something they'll try infrequently, but the flavors and the story that the restaurant infuses makes it an experience that's deliciously memorable. Here, Melngailis shares the inspiration behind one of her personal favorite comfort dishes. "At Pure Food and Wine we usually don't go out of our way to mimic meat or fish flavors, but I for one miss eating tuna sandwiches. My Chef de Cuisine uses seaweed to add an ocean flavor to a base of almonds and a creamy avocado pine nut mayo, with the familiar crunch of celery and onions," she said. "This is my favorite lunch when I'm really hungry and want more than just a salad."

* * *

For the "tuna" salad: Pulse the almonds in a food processor until they are broken down into very small pieces. Dice up the celery, onions, garlic, parsley, and capers. Add these to the almonds. Finish with the lemon juice, salt, and cayenne pepper.

For the mayonnaise: Blend the pine nuts, avocado, lemon juice, dulse seaweed, vinegar, sea salt, garlic, and nori seaweed in a high-speed blender, adding water as needed, until the mixture is smooth like mayonnaise.

For the sandwiches: Mix the mayonnaise into the salad until you reach your desired consistency. For each sandwich, cover 1 slice of bread with tomato and avocado. Drizzle with extra virgin olive oil and salt, if desired. Add a few pieces of the lettuce of your choice, and on top of that, add a scoop of "Tuna Salad," and garnish with capers if desired. Top with another piece of bread, and serve.

PINE NUT MAYONNAISE

- **1 cup pine nuts**
- **1 ripe avocado**
- **½ cup lemon juice**
- **1 very small handful dulse seaweed (an especially moist variety of seaweed)**
- **2 tablespoons apple cider vinegar**
- **1 teaspoon sea salt**
- **1 small garlic clove**
- **½ sheet nori seaweed**
- **Water as needed**

SANDWICHES

- **Pine Nut Mayonnaise**
- **"Tuna" Salad**
- **8 sliced manna bread (a thick and hearty sprouted grain bread cooked at low temperatures)**
- **1 tomato, sliced**
- **1 avocado, sliced**
- **Olive oil**
- **Salt**
- **Lettuce, just a few leaves**
- **Capers (optional)**

NOTE: Dulse seaweed has been a health food favorite for years. Found on coastline rocks, it's an especially rich source of fiber, protein, and vitamin B. Moreover, researchers are uncovering seaweed's power as a fat fighter. One British study found that it could induce the body to absorb up to 75 percent less fat.

COUNTRY-STYLE ITALIAN: BASIL, TOMATOES, GARLIC, AND OLIVE OIL

FORTUNATO NICOTRA ✳ FELIDIA ✳ WWW.FELIDIA-NYC.COM

1 **P** **H**

SERVES 4

1 loaf country bread,
   sliced into ½-inch-thick
   slices, or 1 baguette, sliced
   lengthwise
2 garlic cloves
3 to 4 tomatoes, preferably
   over-ripened
1 handful fresh basil
Extra virgin olive oil
Sea salt
Freshly ground black pepper

I N 1981, Lidia Bastianich opened a restaurant called Felidia on New York's Upper East Side. This was no small feat for a female chef at that time, and it was made more meaningful by the fact that the venture was financed and run by Bastianich herself, and her family. The restaurant rapidly won popular and critical acclaim—including three stars in *The New York Times*—and marked a decisive leap in Bastianich's culinary career, which would expand to TV, books, and, of course, involvement in a host of projects with her son Joseph (whose own ventures extend from wineries to a famed Mario Batali partnership in other landmark restaurants such as Babbo and Lupa).

Still, throughout, the hands-on, family side of Felidia is part of what's turned it into such a destination. Since 1996, close friend Fortunato Nicotra has been running the kitchen. Having emigrated from Italy with two Michelin-star restaurants already under his belt, he's seamlessly kept the restaurant both current and timeless, holding on to its three stars through two *Times* reviews.

Here, Nicotra shares that blend of the traditional and contemporary with a sandwich he says he also frequently makes at home. It's an easy way to merge the pungent flavors of Italy—think basil, olive oil, garlic, and tomatoes—with today's penchant for quality ingredients. "Simple to assemble, yet flavorful and delicious, I really find this to be the perfect base for any favorite cured meats, vegetables or cheeses. It's what I invariably come back to," Nicotra said. "Since there are so few ingredients, the secret here is freshness. I use over-ripened tomatoes and a handful of fresh basil sprigs from my garden."

Place the slices of bread onto a hot grill and toast until grill marks appear. Rub the garlic cloves over the grilled bread while it's still hot. Slice the tomatoes in half and rub atop the bread until all the juices and seeds cover it (the bread should appear almost soaked). Discard the tomato skins. Spread the basil leaves evenly on top of the bread, and drizzle with good extra virgin olive oil. Finish with a sprinkle of sea salt and freshly ground black pepper.

NOTE: For an even richer taste, Chef Nicotra suggests trying any one of these toppings (or several—serving a few of each for a lunch or dinner spread): prosciutto, mortadella, smoked salmon, mozzarella, or ricotta.

SPRING VEGETABLE SANDWICH

MICHAEL ROMANO * PUBLIC FARE, UNION SQUARE CAFÉ * WWW.USHGNYC.COM

1 **P** **H**

SERVES 4

6 ounces cherry tomatoes,
   halved
2 tablespoons extra virgin
   olive oil, divided
Kosher salt and black pepper
Dried oregano
½ cup fresh goat's cheese
½ cup fresh ricotta cheese
2 medium zucchini,
   sliced lengthwise and cut
   into 1-inch dice
2 garlic cloves
Dried parsley
4 soft ciabatta rolls, split
1 cup arugula

OPEN since 2009, Public Fare provides Central Park's outdoor theatergoers with better-than-usual sandwiches from Union Square Hospitality Group, Danny Meyer's popular restaurant empire. Among these is a creation by Michael Romano, president of culinary development for the Union Square Hospitality Group and founding chef of Union Square Café.

"I wanted [to make] something vegetarian. I was thinking about the richness of spreading bread with cream cheese. But for a sandwich I thought, why not use ricotta?"

Romano mixed fresh ricotta with Mita, a sheep's milk cheese that resembles fresh, soft goat's cheese (which we've substituted here). He added an abundance of sautéed zucchini ("The ricotta mixture binds to it like a creamy dip," he added), sweet oven-roasted tomatoes, arugula, and parsley. The result is moist, sweet, bitter, and explosively good.

* * *

Preheat the oven to 275°F. Place the tomatoes in a baking dish. Drizzle with 1 tablespoon of the olive oil. Season with salt, pepper, and oregano to taste. Roast for 45 to 60 minutes.

Combine the cheeses and mix thoroughly. Salt and pepper to taste. Heat a sauté pan over medium heat, and add the remaining tablespoon of olive oil. Add the zucchini and sweat. Season with salt and pepper to taste. Using a microplane, finely grate the garlic into the pan. Toss with more oregano and the parsley to taste. Spread the cheese mixture on the rolls. Add the arugula, zucchini, and then the tomatoes. Press down firmly, and serve.

ESSEX MARKET DUO
BEST-EVER MOZZARELLA AND GRILLED CHEESE WITH SPICY PICKLE

ANNE SAXELBY ∗ SAXELBY CHEESEMONGERS ∗ WWW.SAXELBYCHEESE.COM

IN 1940, Mayor Fiorello LaGuardia introduced the Essex Street Market on New York's Lower East Side—at that time a primarily Italian and Jewish neighborhood—in an effort to get pushcarts off the streets. Since then, the market's been reflective of the neighborhood's own evolution. In the 1950s there was an influx of Puerto Rican vendors. Through the 1970s and 1980s things fell apart a little when the area was notoriously rough. In the late 1990s they began to improve when a private investor bought the real estate and set about assembling a set of compelling, unique storefronts that would make Essex a destination, just in time for the neighborhood's fashion, food, and art renaissance.

Among the most written-about of the Essex store vendors is Anne Saxelby. A Midwestern artist-turned-cheese-obsessive, she started studying cheese almost as soon as she graduated from college, spending time working at Murray's Cheese in the West Village, and later at a farm in Vermont. There, Saxelby's enthusiasm really took focus, and she became passionate about American farmstead cheese, a product that's made on the same farm it's sourced. Such farms are dwindling in number, and Saxelby saw an opportunity to bring their wares to the growing food-interested population on the Lower East Side. This kind of introduction and cross-pollination of new communities was, of course, what the Lower East Side and Essex Market did best.

In 2006 Saxelby Cheesemongers opened, becoming the first cheese shop in the United States devoted solely to American farmstead cheese. Here, Saxelby—who herself has become something of a spokesperson for the farmstead cheese movement—shares two sandwiches that are especially well loved (we actually have a friend who's been known to call ahead for the mozzarella specifically so he's sure they'll save enough for him). Saxelby's commentary accompanies the recipes.

BEST-EVER MOZZARELLA SANDWICH

🅐 Ⓟ

4 ciabatta rolls
Olive oil
3 ounces fresh mozzarella
Sea salt (preferably Maldon)
Freshly ground pepper

I think this sandwich is amazing because of its simplicity. It totally highlights the quality of the ingredients, and gives you a great chance to appreciate the little things in life. In less than five minutes, you can have a totally satisfying lunch or a crowd pleaser for a party.

* * *

Slice the ciabatta and drizzle it liberally with olive oil. Slice the mozzarella into thin slices (about ¼- to ½-inch thick). For each sandwich, sprinkle the ciabatta with coarse sea salt and freshly ground black pepper. Layer the mozzarella on the bread and put the top on the sandwich. Your sandwich is served.

NOTE: "To get those little bursts of salinity in your sandwich, try a large grain salt, such as Maldon. It gives an unforgettable melt-in-your mouth extra to the finished product," said Saxelby

GRILLED CHEESE AND
SPICY PICKLE SANDWICH

① P

**12 ounces Pawlet cheese
(or fontina)**

4 spicy pickles

4 focaccia pockets

We came up with this sandwich originally because we were asked to participate in a festival called Pickle Day that takes place every September on the Lower East Side. I thought to myself, pickles and cheese? Why the heck not?! The spicy pickle used in this sandwich is clutch because it gives such an added punch of flavor. And after all, nothing says comfort food like a good grilled cheese. My grandma June taught me that way back when.

* * *

Preheat a panini press if you have one. If not, you can use two pre-heated nonstick pans or skillets. (You'll cook the sandwich in one and press down onto the sandwich with the other, creating a makeshift press.) Slice the cheese into slices about two to three times as thick as the slices you get from a deli counter. Slice the pickles into thin strips the long way. It's important not to have too many pickle-y chunks. Cut the focaccia pockets down the middle and evenly distribute the slices of cheese and the pickles inside.

Place the sandwich in the panini press or a pan over medium heat and toast (using the second pre-heated pan if you're doing the burner method) until the bread is golden brown. Flip and cook on the other side until the cheese is melted to the point of being gooey. Press down on the sandwich as you cook. Allow to cool for a minute or two before serving.

Chapter 7

THE ASIAN SANDWICH

‏✳ ✳ ✳

AS A RULE OF THUMB, BREAD IN ASIA IS A RARITY—AN IMPORTED PHENOMENON enjoying fad status in Tokyo and Taipei, but far less prevalent than rice, noodles, steamed buns, and assorted pancakes. The very idea of an Asian sandwich could have been a dubious, groan-worthy fusion. Then New Yorkers caught wind of something amazing.

It started with the Vietnamese bánh mì ("BUN-mee"). French Indochina had left its culinary imprint, in part with this eight-inch section of crackling baguette stuffed with meat (pâté, fish, or chicken), Vietnamese pickles, chopped chiles, mayonnaise, and leafy herbs. Until 2005 (or so) in New York, bánh mì was a little-known take-away prize available in the city's trio of Chinatowns. Then—forgive us—the cat(fish) got out of the bag(uette): New Yorkers caught wind of this spicy-sour-sweet concoction and became instantly addicted.

Fast forward to 2011: The wax paper–wrapped treat is synonymous with long lunch lines—and playful modernization. At Baoguette, Michael "Bao" Hyunh consistently sells out of the "Sloppy Bao," an overstuffed pork curry sandwich that offsets its punishing heat with slivers of young green mango. At Num Pang, modern Cambodian chef Ratha Chau plants Italian flair (meatballs, basil, tomato sauce, garlic butter) in his Spicy Veal Meatball Sandwich, in a nod to Italian-food-loving New York.

Soon, the humble pork bun elbowed its way into the mix, too. Outside of Chinatown, the steaming treat caught fire, filled with anything from pork belly to King Phojanokong's Filipino pulled pork adobo. Not to be outdone, Chinese restaurants upped the ante on their famous pancakes: flaky rounds wrapped with everything from beef slices to thin slivers of omelet. Ubiquitous in most of these recipes: handfuls of fresh herbs and pickled and crisp raw vegetables to balance the richness of the fillings.

These sandwiches will stretch your imagination—and your flavor pantry.

✳ ✳ ✳

HOISIN VEaL MEaTBaLL SaNDWICH

RATHA CHAU ✳ NUM PANG SANDWICH SHOP ✳ WWW.NUMPANGNYC.COM

❷

SERVES 4

- 1 pound ground veal (you may substitute ground chicken, beef, or pork)
- 1 cup hoisin sauce
- 1 basil sprig (preferably Thai), minced
- 2 tablespoons jasmine rice, cooked
- Salt and pepper
- 1 (24-ounce) can whole peeled tomatoes, drained and rinsed
- 2 tablespoons fish sauce
- 4 semolina baguettes, split in half lengthwise
- Garlic Butter (recipe follows)
- Spicy Mayo (recipe follows)
- 2 Kirby cucumbers, julienned
- Pickled Carrots (recipe follows)
- 1 bunch cilantro, washed and tender sprigs picked

HAVING grown up with the French influences of his native Cambodia, Ratha Chau rejoices in the common language of food. "We're not that different in how we eat. All of our cultures are tied somehow, in a weird way," he said. This fascination with global cuisine led Chau to open Kampuchea (the city's first modern Cambodian restaurant), and later, Num Pang, a tiny, bustling sandwich shop near NYU. Although Cambodia is at their core, both spots incorporate flavors, formats, and ingredients from elsewhere.

This recipe is a prime example. The French brought sandwiches, or num pang, to Cambodia. Both Italians and Cambodians enjoy meatballs. To moisten the meat, Chef Chau replaces breadcrumbs with a bit of cooked rice (if you don't have any on hand, he suggests buying a bowl of jasmine from your neighborhood Asian restaurant). Basil, semolina bread, garlic butter, and tomato sauce are additional nods to "the Italian culture that's so much a part of New York," he said. The result is a light meatball that's touched with spice, and paired with both the crisp (pickled carrot, cucumbers) and the creamy (spicy mayo, garlic butter, tomato sauce).

✳ ✳ ✳

In a large bowl, combine the veal, hoisin sauce, basil, and rice. Season with salt and pepper to taste. Sauté one meatball over medium heat to check the seasoning; adjust if necessary. Roll the veal mixture into balls around 1-inch in diameter and refrigerate for a few minutes until firm.

Add the tomatoes to a large pot and crush lightly. Stir in the fish sauce.

When the meatballs are firm, place the sauté pan over medium heat. Lightly brown the meatballs in the pan. Drain on paper towels and add to the pot with the tomatoes. Simmer the meatballs until cooked through, about 15 minutes. If using immediately, keep them warm.

Preheat a toaster oven. Spread each baguette half with garlic butter, and then toast. Spread each toasted side with the spicy mayo. Lay the cucumber slices evenly on the bottom halves of toast, and top with an even layer of the pickled carrots. On the opposite side of each toast half, lay the cilantro sprigs. Fill each sandwich with four meatballs, including a few tomatoes in each. Close each sandwich, cut in half, and serve.

GARLIC BUTTER

MAKES 1 CUP

½ **pound (2 sticks) unsalted butter, at room temperature**
1 **tablespoon minced garlic**
Pinch of salt

Combine the butter, garlic, and salt and mix well. Refrigerate until needed.

PICKLED CARROTS

MAKES ABOUT 2 CUPS

3 **large carrots, julienned on a mandoline**
¾ **cup sugar**
1 **cup apple cider vinegar**
1 **tablespoon salt**

Combine the carrots, sugar, vinegar, and salt and mix well. Marinate for at least 2 hours.

SPICY MAYO

MAKES ABOUT 1 CUP

½ **cup mayonnaise**
¼ **cup ketchup**
1 **tablespoon plus 1 teaspoon Sriracha sauce**

Combine the mayonnaise, ketchup, and Sriracha in a bowl and mix well.

BAOGUETTE BÁNH MÌ WITH DAIKON PICKLE

MICHAEL "BAO" HUYNH ✳ BAOGUETTE ✳ WWW.BAOGUETTE.COM

❶ Ⓗ

SERVES 4

4 petit baguette rolls or 4
    (8-inch) sections cut from
    regular baguette
Mayonnaise
Maggi Seasoning Sauce or soy
    sauce
16 slices boldly flavored meat,
    Pâté (recipe follows), or
    cold cuts, sliced and at
    room temperature (aim for
    2 kinds, 8 slices each)
1 thin cucumber (pickling or
    English variety), cut into 12
    to 16 strips
8 to 12 cilantro sprigs,
    roughly chopped
1 jalapeño pepper, cut into 12
    or 16 thin slices
Daikon and Carrot Pickle
    (recipe follows)

THE story reads like an especially over-the-top work of fiction: Teenage Vietnamese refugee arrives in New Jersey with practically nothing and ultimately achieves massive success through self-branded Manhattan sandwich empire. Yet that's pretty much the sum of Chef Michael "Bao" Huynh's trajectory.

In a city where Vietnamese bánh mì is all the rage, there's much to be said for timing, of course. But given how often the Baoguette sandwiches—crispy on the outside and brimming with heat, crunch, and savory fillings—have won out in national taste tests and competitions against a variety of other types of sandwiches, you've got to believe Huynh has built something special.

Talent is certainly part of it: Huynh was a well-known chef prior to the whole bánh mì thing. But the full-circle-ness of this particular concept—finding success in the street foods of your past—is certainly telling. Especially since Huynh isn't the only key player in Baoguette. His wife, Thao Nguyen, had worked for years at her family's restaurant in Da Nang, Vietnam. She developed the menu and collaborated with him on the recipes.

Fittingly, for this book, Huynh chose the traditional bánh mì, an easy-to-make and delicious point of entry to both his personal style (layered and robust) and Vietnamese cuisine (strong, clear tastes). "My wife and I grew up eating these in Vietnam," he said. "When I moved to the U.S., I would make them whenever I felt homesick. Thao likes hers really spicy, so when we decided to open Baoguette, we made sure to offer a range of spiciness." Similarly, here, Huynh's recipe comes with choices and options—you can prepare a basic version in minutes, or roll up your sleeves and go all out, making your own pickle and/or traditional pâté.

Slice the bread lengthwise and then use your fingers or a bread knife to hollow out the insides, making a trough in both halves. Discard the extra bread or save it for another use, such as breadcrumbs. Generously spread both bread halves with mayonnaise. Drizzle in some Maggi Seasoning Sauce or soy sauce. Start from the bottom portion of bread to layer in the meat, cucumber, cilantro, pepper, and Daikon and Carrot Pickle. Close the sandwich, cut it in half crosswise for easy eating, and enjoy.

DAIKON AND CARROT PICKLE (DO CHUA)

MAKES ABOUT 3 CUPS

- 1 large carrot, peeled and cut into thick matchsticks
- 1 pound daikons, each no larger than 2 inches in diameter, peeled and cut into thick matchsticks
- ½ cup plus 2 teaspoons sugar, divided
- 1 teaspoon salt
- 1¼ cups distilled white vinegar
- 1 cup lukewarm water

Place the carrot and daikons in a bowl and sprinkle with the salt and 2 teaspoons of the sugar. Knead the vegetables for about 3 minutes, expelling the water from them. They will soften, and liquid will pool at the bottom of the bowl. Stop kneading when you can bend a piece of daikon so that the ends touch but the daikon does not break. Drain in a colander and rinse under cold running water and then press gently to expel extra water. Return the vegetables to the bowl.

To make the brine, in a bowl, combine the remaining ½ cup sugar, salt, vinegar, and water and stir until the sugar is dissolved. Pour over the vegetables (the brine should cover the vegetables). Let the vegetables marinate in the brine for at least 1 hour before eating. They will keep in the refrigerator for up to four weeks.

NOTE: "Make this Daikon and Carrot Pickle once and then tweak the recipe to your liking," said Huynh. "Variations include adding tangy-sweet-pungent pickled shallots (cu kieu) to the mixture, as well as making it heavier on the carrot side than the daikon side. I prefer to keep a higher ratio (say 2-to-1) of daikon to carrot as I like the mild bite of daikon radish. I like a tangy-sweet flavor, whereas you can alter the ratio of sugar to vinegar to make the brine sweeter, and hence affect the pickle's flavor."

PÂTÉ

- **1 pound pork liver (trim any excess tissue and wash well and dab dry)**
- **½ pound pork fat (or pork belly)**
- **½ pound ground pork (for a smoother, more liver-flavored pâté, use less ground pork)**
- **2 garlic cloves**
- **2 shallots**
- **½ teaspoon five-spice powder**
- **½ teaspoon soy sauce**
- **2 tablespoons fish sauce**
- **2 tablespoons sugar**
- **1½ teaspoon salt**
- **1 tablespoon freshly cracked peppercorns**
- **1 tablespoon Chinese cooking wine (if unavailable, try dry sherry)**
- **1 whole egg and 1 egg yolk**
- **30 slices of bacon (about 2 store-bought packages)**

Preheat the oven to 350°F. Cut the liver and pork fat into small pieces, add to a food processor, and give it a few pulses. Add the ground pork, garlic, shallots, five-spice powder, soy sauce, fish sauce, sugar, salt, and pepper. Process until smooth.

In a mixing bowl, incorporate the meat and liver mixture with the wine and eggs. Line bottom of a baking dish or loaf pan with overlapping pieces of bacon and then fill with the meat mixture. Cover the top with pieces of bacon. Place the mixture into the oven in a larger baking pan and add enough water to cover two-thirds of the pan. Bake for 1 to 1½ hours. The pâté will contract and the juices will be on the bottom. Allow to cool; it will soak up the juices and fat as it does so. Remove the pâté from the pan and remove the excess bacon.

NOTE: Just about any kind of meat—from chicken and turkey to any and all kinds of pork—works here. For a vegetarian version, try frying tofu or your choice of mushrooms (look for meaty-tasting one, like portobello) in a little cooking oil and a few shakes of the Maggi or soy sauce, until brown. Cooked lentils, or even leftover soup, with the excess water drained out is another option.

Japanese Chicken Curry Roll

ANITA LO * ANNISA * WWW.ANNISARESTAURANT.COM

1 **P**

THE cooking of Anita Lo reflects an apt kaleidoscope of cultures. Raised in Michigan by a Chinese mother who'd grown up in Malaysia, Chef Lo studied cooking in France, then returned to New York and worked at several restaurants, including Chanterelle, headed by her mentor, David Waltuck. She skyrocketed to fame by earning two stars from *The New York Times* and winning an *Iron Chef* competition against Mario Batali. Eventually, she toured Mediterranean Europe and Southeast Asia, tasting the food that was to inspire this small, well-revered West Village restaurant. She'll typically pair steak tartare with Korean chili, barbecued squid with Thai basil, and tiny soup dumplings with foie gras.

Like Chef Lo's background, this sandwich defies categorization. "This is a Japanese curry, made with roux. It came to the Japanese via the British, and was (oddly) considered Western. So it's a multicultural curry, right up my alley. At Annisa, we serve it often for 'staff meal' over rice, [sometimes] with a fried egg," she said.

SERVES 4

7 tablespoons unsalted butter,
   divided
1 onion, minced
1 garlic clove, finely chopped
¼ teaspoon grated ginger
3 tablespoons all-purpose
   flour
1 pound boneless and skinless
   chicken thighs, cut into
   ½-inch dice
2 to 3 tablespoons Madras
   curry powder
Pinch garam masala
Salt and pepper
2 cups chicken stock
4 frozen rotis, defrosted
   (available in Southeast
   Asian and South
   Asian grocery stores) .
1 tablespoon beni shoga
   (unsweetened pickled
   ginger)
2 tablespoons thinly
   sliced scallions (about 2
   scallions)
¼ cup cucumber, thinly sliced
   (about ⅓ cucumber)

NOTE: You can substitute the chicken with different ingredients, such as shrimp, beef, ground pork, or portobello mushrooms. Adjust cooking times accordingly.

Place a pot over medium heat. Add 3 tablespoons of the butter, and swirl as it melts to coat the bottom of the pot. Add the onion and sweat, stirring until the onion is translucent, but not brown (about 5 minutes). Add the garlic and ginger, and stir again. Add the flour, and stir to break up lumps. Cook for 3 minutes. Add the chicken thighs and season with curry powder, garam masala, and salt and pepper to taste. Add the chicken stock and stir vigorously, incorporating any browned bits on the bottom of the pot. Bring to a boil, and then reduce heat and simmer, stirring occasionally until the chicken is cooked through and sauce is very thick, about 30 minutes. Season with salt and pepper to taste.

Place a sauté pan over high heat, and add 1 tablespoon of the remaining butter. Swirl as it melts to coat the pan. Turn heat to medium high, and add a roti. Cook until golden brown, then flip and cook the other side. Repeat with the remaining roti. Place each pan-fried roti on a plate, and divide the curry evenly among them. Sprinkle scallions and cucumber over the curry. Roll up each roti and serve. If packing to take with you, roll each roti in a combination of parchment paper (on the inside) and tin foil (on the outside).

TONKATSU SANDO

ABE HIROKI ∗ EN JAPANESE BRASSERIE ∗ WWW.ENJB.COM

1 **P**

SERVES 2

1 pound high-quality pork loin, cut into 2 or 3 ½-inch cutlets

Salt and pepper

½ cup flour

2 eggs, beaten

½ cup panko breadcrumbs

2 cups vegetable oil

½ cup Tonkatsu Sauce (recipe follows; also available in Asian grocery stores)

4 teaspoons red miso paste

2 teaspoons mayonnaise (preferably Japanese Kewpie)

½ cabbage head, shredded

8 slices white bread

WE'VE seen a few *izakaya* (Japanese pubs serving small dishes) in New York, but none quite like this one. EN Japanese Brasserie is grand in scale, with soaring ceilings, a large showcase kitchen, an elegant *shochu* bar, and spacious, sink-into seating. Chef Abe Hiroki's artisanal touches (handmade tofu, house-made soy sauce, house-fermented miso) and luxe ingredients (braised Berkshire pork belly, miso black cod) elevate the restaurant into something not only completely unlike a pub, but *haute* and yet comfortable (a word on the house tofu: It's the kind even tofu detractors can fall in love with.)

Still, this lunch item—a fried pork cutlet with a lovely, traditional sauce—is tried-and-true pub fare. What's more, it translates well into home kitchens: it's crisp, juicy, lovely to look at, and difficult to mess up. "Tonkatsu Sando reminds me of the fried chicken sandwiches I ate growing up in Atlanta," said owner Jesse Alexander. "It's the only sandwich we have in Japan," added Chef Hiroki, who points out that "sando" means sandwich in Japanese. This sandwich is delicious cold, easy to pack (wrap the pork separately), and pairs well with potato salad and draft beer.

* * *

Score each pork cutlet 3 or 4 times to prevent it from curling. Season the pork with salt and pepper. Place the flour, eggs, and panko crumbs into three separate bowls. Dust each cutlet with the flour, and then dip into the eggs. Coat, thoroughly, with the panko crumbs. Heat the oil in a skillet over high heat, until shimmering. Add one cutlet, and fry for 2 to 3 minutes on each side. Using tongs, remove each cutlet and place on a paper towel. Repeat with the remaining cutlets. Combine the Tonkatsu Sauce, red miso, and mayonnaise. Dip each cutlet in the sauce. Top it with even portions of the cabbage, and serve warm or cold between 2 slices of white bread.

TONKATSU SAUCE

¼ cup Worcestershire sauce
2 tablespoons ketchup
1 tablespoon soy sauce
Fresh-cracked black pepper

Combine the Worcestershire sauce, ketchup, soy sauce, and pepper to taste. Chill.

NOTE: For a healthy leftover, try drizzling the Tonkatsu Sauce over ripe tomatoes and avocados. Another take: fry panko-crusted tomatoes as you would the pork, crumble ripe avocado over them, and drizzle both with Tonkatsu Sauce.

ADOBO PULLED PORK BUN

KING PHOJANOKONG JR.

KUMA INN, UMI NOM * WWW.KUMAINN.COM * WWW.UMINOM.COM

2 **P**

SERVES 6

3 pounds pork shoulder
   (preferably bone-in), cut
   into 4-inch cubes
8 garlic cloves, crushed
1 teaspoon black peppercorns
5 bay leaves
1 cup rice wine vinegar
¾ cup soy sauce
¾ cup water
½ cup coconut milk
6 frozen mantao, or steam
   buns (available at Asian
   grocery stores)
Pickled Jicama and Carrots
   (recipe follows)
Hoisin sauce

NOTE: The longer the Adobo sauce
keeps, the better it gets (within limits, of
course). So feel free to make this ahead
of time.

THAI-FILIPINO Chef King Phojanokong Jr. honed his skills under the tutelage of Daniel Boulud and David Bouley. His breakout move? Opening a Lower East Side Asian "tapas" spot called Kuma Inn. One could easily spend the evening ordering repeats of one or two of the intriguing crowd favorites, such as the Chinese sausage seasoned with Thai chili, the sticky rice with pork and shrimp, or this sandwich, an adobo-style pulled pork stuffed into a steamed bun.

"Adobo is the Filipino national dish. It's so rich. My mom cooked it once a week [using] both pork belly and chicken," said Chef Phojanokong, who now has a second restaurant in Brooklyn. Our version is adapted from Kuma Inn's and uses pickles that "cut through the richness of the pork," said the chef.

* * *

In a large stockpot, combine the pork, garlic, peppercorns, bay leaves, vinegar, soy sauce, and water. Let stand for 1 hour, or cover and refrigerate overnight.

If refrigerated, bring the pork to room temperature before bringing to a boil over high heat. Reduce the heat, and simmer 2 hours, or until fork-tender. Add the coconut milk. Pull the pork into tender strips. Drizzle each frozen bun with a teaspoon of water, wrap in a paper towel, and microwave on high for 45 seconds, until soft. Cut open, lengthwise. Fill with ⅙ of the pulled pork, and 1 to 2 tablespoons of the cooking liquid. Add the Pickled Jicama and Carrots and hoisin sauce to taste.

PICKLED JICAMA AND CARROTS

2 carrots, julienned
½ jicama, julienned
¾ cup sugar
1 cup apple cider vinegar
1 tablespoon salt

Combine the carrots, jicama, sugar, vinegar, and salt and mix well. Marinate for at least 2 hours.

Chapter 8

THE LATIN SANDWICH

TWENTY-SEVEN PERCENT OF NEW YORKERS ARE OF HISPANIC OR LATINO origin, according to the U.S. Census Bureau. Into the backbone of New York street food is woven a distinctive heat and richness. And from the savory aromas of tortas and cemitas to the hundred and one "best" cubano places to delicate Spanish bocatas, sandwiches are a critical part of the formula.

Fusing Latin flavors into a sandwich is, some would argue, about as inspired as it gets. The rich flavors manage to feel extra indulgent when nested into sandwiches, moist bread soaking up sauce and delectable ingredients piled high on one another hitting you all at once with heat and spice and savoriness. Often, it's all cooled off with white cheese (a perfect complement to the ever-present avocado), crema (a lighter variant of sour cream), or both.

For the initiated, "tortas" refers to the broadest of categories—thick bread brimming with meat or fish, avocados, tomatoes, onions, and lettuce. Some combination of beans, peppers, cheese, and crema often round things off. The permutations and variants, not to mention sauces, are endless.

"Cemitas" are distinguished by lighter, fluffier bread, and a somewhat shorter combination of the same ingredients (each one therefore packs a bigger punch). The "Cuban"—ham, roast pork, Swiss cheese, pickles, and mustard—has a totally different flavor profile. But in the salty meat and the melted white cheese taste, you can still see how both may have evolved from similar roots.

Over the past few years, Latin sandwiches have been making their way into a whole host of new contexts. Part of this has to do with the cuisine itself. So familiar and popular are the flavors that the demand is growing. Spanish small plates took off and never stopped; they fit beautifully into New York's around-the-clock dining scene. And as Latin cooks and chefs continue to reinterpret and build on traditional cuisine, the presumptions appear endless—and diners couldn't come out more ahead.

✳ ✳ ✳

Pambazo

NACXITL GAXIOLA ✳ LA SUPÉRIOR ✳ WWW.LASUPERIORNYC.COM

2 **P**

SERVES 4

4 soft rolls (preferably Mexican teleras, or other 6-x-4-inch rolls), halved lengthwise (available in Mexican grocery stores)

2 small white potatoes, peeled and cut into ¼-inch dice

5 tablespoons lard or vegetable oil, divided

10 to 12-inch section chorizo Toluqueño, casing removed (available in Mexican grocery stores)

Salt

Pambazo Salsa (recipe follows)

4 cups shredded lettuce

¼ cup Mexican cream (available in Mexican grocery stores)

1 small white onion, thinly sliced

¼ cup Cotija cheese, grated (available in Mexican grocery stores)

4 pickled jalapeños en escabeche, sliced (sold in jars)

L A Supérior gave Mexican food lovers great reason to rejoice. When this restaurant opened in Williamsburg, Brooklyn, in 2008, its whimsical décor, reasonable prices, and hip location were pleasant, but mere bonuses to the fanatically authentic tacos (something New Yorkers longed for) and other street food. For anyone who knows Chef Nacxitl Gaxiola, the exacting dishes are no surprise: He hails from Mexico City, collects Mexican cookbooks, and has an abiding passion for—as well as an encyclopedic knowledge of—chiles and chile-based sauces.

The Pambazo is a wonderful example. "This sandwich is as prevalent on the streets of Mexico City as hot dogs in New York," said Chef Gaxiola. Despite the long list of often-specialty ingredients, the sandwich isn't difficult to make. The chiles (two types) are lightly toasted, then soaked, crushed, fried, and fried again (while on the roll). Chorizo and potatoes are cooked separately. The resulting sandwich is rich, varied, and gorgeously balanced.

✳ ✳ ✳

Tear out a portion of the fluffy white insides of the teleras. If the rolls are fresh, leave them out overnight to harden. Place the potatoes in a pot and cover with water. Cook for about 20 minutes, until tender.

While the potatoes are cooking, make the Pambazo Salsa. Add 3 tablespoons of the lard or oil to a large skillet. Turn the heat to high. Add the chorizo, and crumble while frying, until well-browned and nearly crispy, about 6 minutes. Drain the potatoes. Turn off the heat under the chorizo. Add the potatoes, and toss to combine. Season with salt to taste.

Dip the inside of each roll half in the salsa. Spread the salsa to all corners. Heat a clean griddle or pan. Heat ½ tablespoon of the lard or oil. Toast a roll (2 halves) on all sides until light brown. Repeat with the remaining rolls. Set aside.

In the same griddle or pan, reheat the chorizo mixture. Add even portions of the mixture to each roll (2 halves). Add even portions of the lettuce, cream, onion, cheese, and pickled jalapeños. Serve hot.

PAMBAZO SALSA

1 medium plum tomato

2 cups water

3 tablespoons brown or raw sugar

1 teaspoon salt

5 dried mulato chiles, stemmed, deseeded, and deveined (available in Mexican grocery stores)

4 dried guajillo chiles, stemmed, deseeded, and deveined (available in Mexican grocery stores)

¼ small white onion (preferably including ⅛ broiled onion)

5 garlic cloves (preferably including 1 roasted garlic clove)

¾ teaspoon dried oregano

½ teaspoon dried marjoram

¼ teaspoon cumin

½ teaspoon allspice

¼ teaspoon fresh-cracked black pepper

2 teaspoons ground cloves

⅛ teaspoon dry avocado leaf, crushed (available in Mexican grocery stores)

¾ cup white vinegar

Salt

¼ cup lard or vegetable oil

Preheat the oven to 275°F. Roast the tomato, about 30 minutes (if you have a salamander or torch, see note). Bring the water to a boil. On a separate burner, heat a skillet. Add the chiles, and toast lightly, about 2 to 3 minutes. Dissolve the sugar and salt in the boiling water. Pour the boiling water over the toasted chiles. Soak the chiles until completely soft, about 20 minutes. Drain the chiles, reserving the liquid. Place them in a blender. Add the roasted tomato, onion, garlic, oregano, marjoram, cumin, allspice, black pepper, clove, avocado leaf, and vinegar. Blend until smooth. If the sauce is too thick for your liking, add some of the reserved chile liquid. Season with salt to taste. Place a skillet over high heat. Heat the lard or oil until smoking. Add the chile mixture, standing back to avoid splatters. Fry for 10 to 15 minutes, stirring constantly. Check the seasoning, and salt again to taste, if necessary. Let cool.

NOTE: Frying Pambazo Salsa is a reduction process that concentrates and intensifies the flavors. Be careful: If you're doing it correctly, the sauce will splatter, so stand back.

CRISPY BEER-FRIED TILAPIA SANDWICH

JULIAN MEDINA ✻ TOLOACHE, YERBA BUENA

WWW.TOLOACHENYC.COM ✻ WWW.YBNYC.COM

1 **P**

NOTE: Why fry in beer? "Really, the reason to include beer as an ingredient for fried food is as a quick leavener," said beer brewer Rich Higgins. "Since beer is essentially liquid bread, beer's a fried food batter waiting to happen—add a little flour and egg for structure, and you're ready to go. Beer's carbonation will help to build an airy fried crust that's not too dense or soggy."

SOMETIMES in New York you walk into a certain kind of restaurant on a certain kind of night and feel like you just stepped into your friend's welcoming, slightly fabulous apartment—and there's an epic dinner in store. It's the ultimate what's-behind-the-unassuming-door sensation, and it's just the kind of energy that Mexican-born Chef Julian Medina seems to be able to create time and time again. His cuisine is rich and homey, the sorts of things you'd hope to get from a grandmother who trained at, say, some kind of Mexican Cordon Bleu. (Medina himself honed his skills with his father and grandfather, and later, with Richard Sandoval in New York.)

The sandwich Medina has chosen here is something he says is representative of his roots and the Mexican fare he turns out at Toloache, his Midtown flagship. (Medina also owns and runs Yerba Buena and Yerba Buena Perry in the East and West Villages; both have a more pan-Latin influence). "Fish sandwiches are something I ate every summer as a kid growing up at the beach in Acapulco," he said. "To this day, I almost always order a fish sandwich if I see it on a menu. When I opened Toloache, I just knew I had to have a great one. Truthfully I love any kind of fish sandwich, but this one is truly special. The fish is made with a tempura batter, Baja-style, and is served on Mexican bolillo bread. I dress it with a tamarind vinaigrette immediately after it comes out of the fryer, so it soaks in both tangy and sweet flavors. Then I make a chipotle cabbage slaw that's spicy and citrusy. Without much effort, you really have a lot going on—sweet, tangy, citrusy, and spicy."

For the batter: Mix the water, beer, and salt together in a bowl and then slowly whisk in the flour until smooth. Fold in the egg white, and set aside in the refrigerator.

For the sandwiches: Cut the rolls in half lengthwise and lightly toast for 1 minute. Heat the oil to about to 300°F in a frying pan or cast-iron skillet over medium-high heat. Spread the flour onto a plate. Season each tilapia fillet with salt, coat with flour on both sides, dip into the batter, and fry—turning repeatedly—until crisp and golden brown. Pat the fish dry with a paper towel and sprinkle with more salt. (If you have to do this in batches, make sure the olive oil has returned to 300°F before resuming.) For every sandwich, place a tilapia fillet on the bottom half of a roll. Cover with a generous amount of coleslaw, and close the sandwich with the other bread half. Serve immediately.

SERVES 4

BATTER

- **1 cup cold water**
- **½ cup beer, preferably Negra Modelo (a full-flavored dark brew)**
- **1 teaspoon kosher salt**
- **1 cup all-purpose flour**
- **1 egg white, beaten into soft peaks**

SANDWICHES

- **4 Mexican bolillos (or Italian rolls)**
- **3 cups olive oil for frying**
- **4 (6-ounce) tilapia fillets**
- **Salt**
- **1 cup all-purpose flour**
- **Jicama and Cabbage Coleslaw (recipe follows)**

JICAMA AND CABBAGE COLESLAW

MAKES ABOUT 2¾ CUPS

- **1 cup jicama, peeled and thinly sliced**
- **1 cup Napa cabbage, thinly sliced**
- **½ cup red cabbage, thinly sliced**
- **¼ cup freshly squeezed lime juice**
- **2 tablespoons mayonnaise**
- **1 teaspoon honey**
- **1 teaspoon adobo (the sauce chipotles are canned in)**
- **Salt**

In a bowl, mix together the jicama and cabbages. Season the salad with the lime juice, mayonnaise, honey, adobo and salt to taste. Serve at room temperature.

CHICKEN TINGAS
(MEXICAN-STYLE PULLED CHICKEN)

DAVID SCHUTTENBERG ∗ CABRITO ∗ WWW.CABRITONYC.COM

2 **H** MAKE WITH WHITE MEAT ONLY AND HALVE OR ELIMINATE THE CHEESE.

QUICKIE TINGAS PRIMER

Adobo: Spanish for sauce or seasoning marinade. In Mexican and Southwestern cuisine, the adobo is generally stewed in with tomatoes, as it is here.

Tingas: A shredded and stewed Mexican meat dish.

Papalo: An intense Mexican herb (it's been called "cilantro on steroids"), available in most Mexican groceries.

Queso Oaxaca: A white, semi-hard cheese like mozzarella.

SINCE it opened in 2008, Cabrito—"goat" in Spanish—has been turning out toothsome, critically praised, and vivid Mexican fare in a cozy West Village space that as chef/owner David Schuttenberg is quick to point out, is a "little bit rock 'n' roll." Before becoming a chef, Schuttenberg worked on Wall Street, and at Cabrito you can practically taste his pleasure over having traded a cubicle for his own restaurant. (Chef Zakary Pelaccio, for whom Schuttenberg cooked at Fatty Crab, and businessman Rick Camac are also partners.)

Schuttenberg's chicken tingas are a great example of both the open-mindedness and the dedication he's sinking into the venture: "A previous sous chef of mine brought his family recipe for tingas to me, and we adapted it until we were happy with the results," he said. "It's since become one of our most popular items. The big constant between his family recipe and the one we do here is Mexican Coca-Cola. Sweetened with real sugar, not high fructose corn syrup, it has a more pleasant flavor when reduced in the sauce. To that base, you then get smoke and heat from chipotle chiles, and acidity from vinegar and tomatoes. It's a powerful flavor combination."

TINGAS

¾ cup extra virgin olive oil, divided

1 small onion, julienned (about ½ cup)

5 or 6 garlic cloves, sliced (about ¼ cup)

8 plum tomatoes, seeds removed, julienned

8 ounces Mexican Coca-Cola (or any similar cola made with cane sugar)

1 cup Chipotle Vinegar Adobo (recipe follows)

1 bay leaf

4 skinless boneless chicken breasts

SANDWICHES

4 sesame seed rolls

8 ounces queso Oaxaca (if unavailable, substitute mozzarella)

1 (14-ounce) can refried beans

2 sprigs papalo (if unavailable, substitute cilantro)

Chicken Tingas

½ head iceberg lettuce, shredded

1 whole avocado, sliced thinly

For the tingas: Preheat the oven to 250°F.

Heat ½ cup of the olive oil in a medium saucepan over a low flame. Add the onion and garlic and sweat them until tender and translucent, but not brown, about 8 minutes. Add the tomatoes, and cook them until they begin releasing their juices, about 5 minutes. At that point, pour in the Mexican Coke and Chipotle Vinegar Adobo. Add the bay leaf. Simmer the mixture over low heat for 30 minutes to marry the flavors and to reduce the liquid.

Heat a Dutch oven or other heavy cooking pot over medium-high heat. Add the remaining ¼ cup olive oil. When hot, sear the chicken until golden brown. Turn over and sear quickly on the other side. Pour the sauce over the chicken, cover the pot, and place in the oven. Cook until the meat is completely tender, about 45 minutes. For breasts only, aim for 45 minutes. If you're using legs as well, leave those in for 2 hours, removing the breasts when ready. When the chicken has cooled, shred the meat and toss it with some of the remaining sauce. The mixture should be thick and moist, but not saucy.

For the sandwiches: Halve the rolls crosswise, add an ounce of cheese to the top side of each, and toast them until the cheese has melted. Smear a bit of the refried beans on the bottom of each bun, place 3 or 4 leaves of papalo on the beans and then evenly pile the tingas mixture onto each bottom bun. Finish each with the shredded lettuce, a quarter of the avocado slices, and the top half of the bun.

CHIPOTLE VINEGAR ADOBO

15 dried chipotle chiles
½ medium white onion
½ cup cider vinegar
2 tablespoons lime juice
2 tablespoons orange juice
1 tablespoon honey
Salt

Bring a small pot of water to a boil. Remove the stems and seeds from the chiles. Place a dry cast-iron skillet over medium heat. When hot, toast the chiles until deep red-brown, taking care not to burn, about 20 seconds. Place the chiles in a glass bowl and pour enough boiling water over them so they're just barely covered. Cover the bowl with plastic wrap and let the chiles rest for 15 minutes. Place the cut side of the onion half in the same cast-iron skillet over medium heat and toast until it's blackened, about 8 minutes.

Strain the chiles, saving the water. Combine the chiles, onion, vinegar, lime juice, and orange juice in a blender and purée on high until a smooth paste forms, adding a little of the chile water, if needed, to achieve a nice smooth texture. Season with honey and salt to taste, and set aside.

CHILORIO TORTAS
(MEXICAN-STYLE PULLED PORK SANDWICH)

RICHARD SANDOVAL ∗ MAYA, PAMPANO, ZENGO ∗ WWW.RICHARDSANDOVAL.COM

2 **P**

SERVES 4

- 10 pasilla chiles, seeded (mild-to-medium chile, can substitute with poblano if unavailable)
- 4 guajillo chiles, seeded (medium chile, can substitute with ancho if unavailable)
- 1 quart water
- 12 garlic cloves
- 2 teaspoons dried oregano
- 2 teaspoons black peppercorns
- ½ teaspoon cumin
- 1¼ cup white wine vinegar
- ¼ cup plus 2 tablespoons canola oil, divided
- 1 pound shredded pork shoulder (available from your local butcher or deli)
- 4 teaspoons salt, divided
- 1 cup cooked black beans
- 4 bolillo or hero rolls, havled lengthwise
- ½ small white onion, sliced (optional)
- 4 tablespoons crema fresca or sour cream

MEXICAN Chef Richard Sandoval had already won the prestigious Toque d'Oro—his country's highest culinary honor—for his fresh, refined approach to Latin cuisine by the time he moved to New York in the early 1990s. Back then, high-end Mexican food was such a rarity that French fare wound up seeming a surer way to start a career.

Come 1997—and two popular French eateries later—things felt different. Now, he was well positioned to launch his own venture, one closer to his roots and culinary interests. Maya, a spot devoted to the earthy, bold flavors of Mexico, drew New Yorkers from all boroughs to the Upper East Side.

Ultimately, the restaurant's success allowed Sandoval to expand across the United States and eventually as far afield as Dubai. In Manhattan, meanwhile, Sandoval kept introducing new kinds of Mexican flavors. Pampano, a Midtown venture with opera singer Placido Domingo as a partner, launched in 2003, introducing diners to the clean ceviches and other preparations that constitute Mexican coastal fare. Zengo, his newest eatery (opened with executive chef Akhtar Nahwab underscores just how far the cuisine has come—diners are now embracing Latin-Asian fusion.)

Sandoval took this opportunity to put his spin on the traditional torta, a personal favorite. "People don't think of Mexico as having actual bread sandwiches, but tortas are a favorite street food. They're very much part of our culture," he said. "Savory fillings are piled onto crusty, oval shaped bolillo bread or soft, round telera rolls. For this one, I've added warm black beans and cool crema fresca for contrasting flavor and texture."

Soften the chiles in boiling water. Remove them, saving a small amount of the water. Combine the chiles, garlic, oregano, pepper, cumin, and vinegar in a food processor. With the machine running add just enough of the reserved water to make a paste.

In a saucepan, heat a ¼ cup of the canola oil over medium heat. When the oil is hot, add the shredded pork and fry for about 3 minutes, or until light brown. Add the blended mixture, and stir until it all thickens (the sauce should still be moist, but not liquid). Add 2 teaspoons of the salt.

In a different pan, heat the remaining 2 tablespoon of canola oil. Add the black beans, smashing them up as they fry until they form a paste. Season with the remaining 2 teaspoons of salt. Toast the bread. Spread 2 tablespoons of the refried beans on each roll bottom, and divide the pork mixture among the sandwiches. Add the onion slices and crema fresca or sour cream to taste.

NOTE: Pork is an excellent source of vitamin B6 (good for energy, brain and skin health, and even mood), as well as selenium, protein, and thiamin.

Tuna Bocata

SEAMUS MULLEN ∗ WWW.SEAMUSMULLEN.COM

1 P H

SERVES 4

1 (5-ounce) can tuna (preferably a Spanish brand such as Bonito del Norte or Ortiz Spanish)

1 tablespoon chopped chives

1 tablespoon diced shallots

1 tablespoon capers or chopped caperberries

½ cup pickled peppers (to get really authentic, look for guindilla—semi-sweet and hot)

1 tablespoon lemon juice

1 tablespoon extra virgin olive oil

Lemon zest

¼ cup chopped black olives

2 tablespoons mayonnaise

Salt and pepper

8 slices sourdough Pullman bread

2 free-range eggs, cooked for 6 minutes in simmering water

NOTE: Tuna is exceptionally high in lean protein and a good source of omega-3 fatty acid. It also contains impressive amounts of vitamin D (believed to reduce inflammation and contribute to weight loss), which is difficult to come by in most foods.

SEAMUS Mullen's cooking has been praised by critics over and over again for their mouthwatering take on small plates, among them tapas and—you knew this was coming—bocatas, traditional Spanish snack sandwiches known for its intense, delicious flavor. In spite of their diminutive size, bocatas are crammed with pungent local flavors and textures—think fresh olives, high quality oils, creamy mayonnaises and aïolis, strongly spiced meats, and a touch of lemon.

Mullen grew up on an organic farm in Vermont, where he gained a deep knowledge of and appreciation for how food is sourced. A high school exchange in Spain not only cemented his passion for food but also rooted it in that country's strong, salty, memorable tastes. In addition to top positions in New York and San Francisco, he's trained and cooked in and around Barcelona. "Simple, elegant, and absolutely delicious, bocatas really embody so much of the best of Spanish cuisine," he said. "For me, the tuna is a particular favorite. The added flavors are clean and complex— olive, onion, capers, lemon, and oil, for example—and each contributes another interesting, harmonious layer. The end result is truly satisfying."

* * *

Combine the tuna, chives, shallots, capers, lemon juice, olive oil, lemon zest to taste, olives, mayonnaise, and salt and pepper to taste in a bowl. Distribute the mixture evenly on the slices of bread, and top with the hard-cooked egg and the peppers. Cover with the remaining bread and cut each sandwich into quarters.

Cuban Sandwich

ALFREDO TECO ∗ CAFÉ HABANA ∗ WWW.CAFEHABANA.COM

2 **P** **M** 1 DAY

WHEN he opened Café Habana in 1998 in a corner space near Soho, all founder Sean Meenan wanted to do was bring his love of Cuba (where he'd spent several months) and Mexico to his favorite city. The restaurant quickly became one of New York's favorite Cubano spots.

"This sandwich isn't entirely authentic," he admitted, explaining that "chipotle mayo adds a Mexican flair, and is a nod to Mexican street food," which Meenan said is the best in the world.

∗ ∗ ∗

Set the pork on a work surface. Using a sharp paring knife, make 1-inch-long slashes in the skin, about 2 inches apart. Rub the garlic into the slashes and along the underside of the pork. In a large glass or ceramic bowl, combine the vinegar with the lime, grapefruit and orange juices, oregano, pepper, adobo seasoning, and Sazón. Stir in the bell pepper and onion, and then add the pork, skin side up. Refrigerate overnight (or up to three days), turning the meat once or twice. Bring to room temperature before cooking.

Preheat the oven to 400°F. Transfer the pork and its marinade to a roasting pan. Cover with foil and roast for about 3 hours, or until the meat is very tender. Let cool in the liquid. Transfer the pork to a cutting board and discard the skin and fat. Strain the pan juices into a glass measure and skim off the fat. Slice or shred the meat before serving.

SERVES 6

- 1 (8-pound) pork shoulder, boned
- 1½ tablespoons minced garlic
- 1 cup plus 2 tablespoons white vinegar
- ¾ cup fresh lime juice
- ¼ cup fresh grapefruit juice
- ¼ cup fresh orange juice
- 2 tablespoons dried oregano, crumbled
- 1 tablespoon freshly ground black pepper
- 1 teaspoon Goya adobo seasoning
- 1 teaspoon Goya Sazón with Coriander and Annato
- 1 large green bell pepper, coarsely chopped
- 1 medium onion, coarsely chopped
- 1 cup mayonnaise
- 8 canned chipotle chiles in adobo
- 6 long sandwich rolls, halved lengthwise (preferably white and fluffy)
- 6 thin slices Black Forest or other organic sliced ham
- 12 thin slices Swiss cheese
- 2 kosher dill pickles, thinly sliced lengthwise
- Salt

In a food processor, combine the mayonnaise and chipotles and process until smooth. Spread the cut sides of the rolls with the chipotle mayonnaise. Assemble the sandwiches with even portions of the ham, cheese, pickles and Mexican Roast Pork. Top the meat with a spoonful of the pork pan juices and season with salt. Close the sandwiches and tuck in any overhanging filling.

Set a large griddle over moderately low heat. Arrange the sandwiches on the griddle and cover with a large baking sheet weighted down with several heavy skillets. Cook the sandwiches, turning once, until they are crisp outside, about 6 minutes. Transfer the sandwiches to a cookie sheet and bake until the cheese is melted, about 8 minutes. Cut the sandwiches in half and serve immediately; pass the remaining pan juices separately.

NOTE: *Medianoche*, which means "midnight" in Spanish, is a close cousin of Cuban sandwiches. The difference is that Cuban sandwiches are made with white sandwich rolls, and *medianoche* are made with egg bread, similar to challah. That *medianoche* are preferred during or after a night out in Havana proves that the Cuban appetite for rich bread comes out after dark.

Chapter 9

The Seafood Sandwich

* * *

FOR 183 YEARS—FROM ITS OPENING IN 1822 UNTIL IT WAS RELOCATED TO THE Bronx in 2005—the Fulton Fish Market was widely considered to be the most important wholesale fish market in the United States. In some cases, fish from New England would be shipped through Fulton, just to be trucked back up to be sold in the states from which they came.

All this is to say that New Yorkers have long been a little spoiled when it comes to seafood—a good thing since they also seem to be incredibly receptive to the stuff. To thank in part, of course, is the city's eclectic population. From Scandinavian open-faced shrimp sandwiches to the fried fish and tartar sauce of Brittany's coast (cook it in beer and you're channeling the coast of Mexico), there's a taste and technique for just about every palate and occasion.

Situated as it is geographically, New York also benefits from a range of distinctly American influences. New Englanders are never short on options for an absolutely authentic Maine lobster roll, while Marylanders can haggle over which beach-town-trained chef gets the crab cake right. Southerners, for their part, can rest assured there's somebody who migrated up a few states and knows how to fry up a mean catfish po' boy. The competition among chefs to best each other at these very specific, very beloved specialties has yielded some pretty splashy press—and satisfied diners.

As the demand for healthful, sustainable fish has grown, New York chefs have risen to the challenge, creating easy, approachable preparations—be they grilled trout or shrimp salad—that fit into busy lives. Put simply, and as you'll see in the coming pages, the New York fish sandwich is taking off.

* * *

Pan Bagnat
(Niçoise Salad Sandwich)

ALAIN ALLEGRETTI * ALLEGRETTI * WWW.ALLEGRETTINYC.COM

1 **H**

SERVES 4

FILLING

4 large breakfast radishes,
    sliced fine

½ cucumber, peeled, seeded,
    sliced fine

1 large or 2 small red bell
    peppers, roasted and sliced
    fine

1 stick celery, sliced fine

2 cans tuna fish packed in
    olive oil, flaked with a fork

8 marinated anchovies, cut
    into ½-inch pieces

16 Niçoise (or kalamata)
    olives, pitted and sliced

½ cup basil, sliced fine

24 fava beans, blanched and
    peeled (optional)

Salt and fresh-cracked black
    pepper

LEAVE it to a chef from Nice to imbue his Flatiron restaurant with old-fashioned sensibilities like vintage crystal and cordial, Old World service. Allegretti's eponymous restaurant provides a lovely, low-key source for Côte d'Azur dishes and across-the-border pastas.

At lunch, his Pan Bagnat—sort of a Niçoise salad in a roll, flies out of the kitchen. You can taste the nostalgia here, and it's Allegretti's own. "My friends and I would go to the beach in Nice, and take these sandwiches wrapped in paper. At lunchtime, we'd unwrap them, brush off the sand, and devour them. They tasted just like the ocean," said Allegretti.

* * *

For the filling: In a mixing bowl, combine the radishes, cucumber, bell peppers, celery, tuna, anchovies, olives, basil, and fava beans. Mix well. Season with the salt and pepper to taste. Keep in mind that the anchovies and tuna fish are already salty.

For the sandwich: Combine the vinegar with the olive oil. Add salt and pepper to taste and whisk to emulsify. Brush the mixture thoroughly on the inside of each roll. Line each roll bottom with 1 to 2 leaves of the lettuce, 1 slice of the tomato, and even portions of the egg. Spoon even amounts of filling on each roll bottom. Top the sandwiches, press gently to secure, and serve.

SANDWICHES

2 tablespoons red wine vinegar

4 tablespoons extra virgin olive oil

Salt and fresh-cracked black pepper

4 soft rolls, whole wheat or white, at least 4 inches long, split lengthwise

1 small head butter lettuce, washed and dried

1 large heirloom tomato, thinly sliced

2 hard-boiled eggs, thinly sliced

Pan Bagnat Filling

GRILLED PORTUGUESE SARDINE SANDWICH

BRIAN BISTRONG * BRAEBURN * WWW.BRAEBURNRESTAURANT.COM

1 **P** **H**

SERVES 2

2 (6-inch) baguettes, halved
    lengthwise

Salt and pepper

6 sardines, filleted, marinated
    for an hour in olive oil and
    lemon zest

4 to 6 cipollini onions,
    marinated in olive oil and
    balsamic vinegar, sliced
    (available at specialty
    grocery stores and delis)

6 thin slices Parmesan cheese

1 tablespoon lemon juice

2 tablespoons olive oil

½ cup baby arugula

NOTE: You can find sardines marinated in oil and lemon at specialty grocery stores and delis. Or, you can use a tin of sardines in oil and add fresh-grated lemon zest to it. If you can't find pre-marinated cippolini onions, then marinate onions with the zest of half a lemon, 2 tablespoons of extra virgin olive oil, and 1 tablespoon balsamic vinegar. The mixture will keep for months.

THIS West Village restaurant merges some of the most formidable forces in the New York restaurant world. Both John-Paul O'Neil and Brian Bistrong started young, pursuing hospitality degrees and growing up in New York's best restaurant empires. Chef-owner Bistrong cooked at Bouley Bakery, and later at the retail chain Citarella. General Manager-owner O'Neil honed his front-of-house talents at Danny Meyer's Eleven Madison Park. After stints at the Four Seasons (O'Neil) and Ritz-Carlton (Bistrong), both returned to New York, and sealed their partnership.

We asked Chef Bistrong to give us a sandwich that would utilize his barbeque expertise. "When I worked for Citarella, one of my favorite dishes was a grilled sardine with marinated onions and Parmesan crumble," he said. In sandwich form, the dish is easy to make, good for you, and highly packable (Chef Bistrong tucks them into special-order picnic baskets). If you can find them, use Portugese sardines.

* * *

Preheat an outdoor or stovetop grill. Season the bread with salt and pepper to taste. Grill lightly until marks show. Set aside. (If you don't have a grill, then broil the sardines for a few minutes on each side, and toast the garlic- and tomato-rubbed bread.)

Grill the sardines, skin side down, for 00 minutes. Flip over and grill the other side for a few seconds. (If using tinned sardines, drain, wrap in foil, and heat over the grill.)

Place 3 sardines on each baguette bottom. Add even portions of the onions and Parmesan cheese. Combine the lemon juice and the olive oil. Pour the lemon mixture over the arugula. Add to the sandwich. Cover each with the baguette top to make the sandwich.

FRESH SEAFOOD DUO

JOSH CAPON ∗ LURE FISHBAR ∗ WWW.LUREFISHBAR.COM

TO change with the times is a skill—you have to be open-minded, willing to listen and take feedback, and most certainly risk some unfamiliar waters. The reward, of course, is that if you do it well, you stay relevant and your influence just gets bigger. Case-in-point: Lure Fishbar, a sleek, nautically themed haven of fresh catches of all shapes and sizes that opened in 2004 in a subterranean spot on Mercer and Prince.

What's interesting here is that when it opened the restaurant wasn't as new as one might think—earlier, it had been an equally popular place called Canteen, which had the same owners (John McDonald and Josh Pickard) and even the same chef, Josh Capon. Capon's ability to completely redefine his cuisine—he went from truffled macaroni and cheese to a menu of artfully prepared seafood dishes—impressed critics and diners alike. Today Lure is considered a downtown mainstay, and Capon's cooking positively soars. Among the sandwich recipes he suggested for this project, each seemed better than the last (which we didn't want to give up either)—we couldn't narrow things down past two. Below, the winners, with Capon's comments.

GRILLED BROOK TROUT ON FOCACCIA
WITH SPINACH, ROASTED PEPPERS, AND TOASTED PINE NUTS

SERVES 4

1 **P** **H**

BALSMIC VINAIGRETTE

¼ cup Dijon mustard
1 cup balsamic vinegar
¼ cup red wine vinegar
4 cups olive oil
Salt and pepper

SANDWICHES

4 brook trout fillets
Salt and pepper
Olive oil
4 cups baby spinach
1 roasted yellow pepper*,
    julienned
1 roasted red pepper*,
    julienned
¾ cup toasted pine nuts†,
    divided
1 cup Balsamic Vinaigrette
    (recipe follows)
4 pieces rosemary focaccia (4
    × 8 inches)

This came from a lunch dish that we serve at Lure. We had always made it as a salad, but one day we had some focaccia around and a customer asked for a fish sandwich. We put the two together, and it's turned into one of those "of course" moments. There was no going back. Now, we offer the dish both ways.

* * *

For the balsamic vinaigrette: Combine the mustard and vinegars in a blender. Blend on high and slowly drizzle in the olive oil until emulsified. Season with salt and pepper to taste. This mixture can be stored in the refrigerator for up to two weeks.

For the sandwiches: Season the trout fillets with salt and pepper to taste, and rub with a little olive oil. Either grill on a hot grill or grill pan over medium-high heat or bake in an oven at 400°F. The fillets will cook quickly, about 5 minutes or 2½ minutes each side if cooking on a grill.

In a large mixing bowl, toss together the spinach, roasted peppers, and ½ cup of the pine nuts and season with salt and pepper to taste. Dress with enough balsamic vinaigrette to evenly coat the greens.

Slice the focaccia in half and warm the slices on the grill or in the oven. Place a cup or so of the salad mixture on the each of the bottom pieces of focaccia and spread evenly. Top each bottom with a piece of trout and a few roasted peppers and the remaining pine nuts. Drizzle with some of the balsamic vinaigrette and cover with the other piece of focaccia. Serve while warm.

*NOTE: To roast peppers in the oven, set the temperature to 425°F and place the peppers on a foil-covered baking sheet. Leave them in for 30 to 40 minutes, turning about three times so the color stays even.

†NOTE: To toast the pine nuts, heat them a skillet with just a splash of olive oil on medium-low heat. Move the pan frequently to keep the nuts from burning.

WARM SHRIMP AND SCALLOP CIABATTA POCKET
WITH TOMATO CONFIT, GRILLED RED ONIONS, AND ARUGULA   **SERVES 4**

2 ⓗ

TOMATO CONFIT

2 (28-ounce) cans plum
     tomatoes
4 garlic cloves
1 cup extra virgin olive oil
6 sprigs fresh thyme
½ bunch fresh basil
1 teaspoon dried oregano
Salt and pepper

SANDWICHES

16 U-16 shrimp, peeled,
     deveined, and sliced in half
1 pound Nantucket Bay
     scallops
Salt and pepper
Extra virgin olive oil
Juice of 1 lemon, divided
½ cup white wine
1 cup fresh basil leaves, torn
¼ cup fresh oregano leaves
4 ciabatta rolls
4 cups arugula
2 large red onions, sliced and
     grilled or sautéed

This is my interpretation of a dish my wife and I had in Portofino, a small town in Italy on the water. It was such a perfect light lunch, one that I will never forget. They served some toasted slices of ciabatta on the side, and I remember assembling each piece with some of the tomato confit and arugula and a squeeze of lemon. With a glass of pinot grigio, sitting outside on a warm summer day, I remember thinking that it doesn't get much better.

* * *

For the Tomato Confit: Preheat oven to 350°F.

Drain the water from the tomatoes. Place them in a large baking dish and add the garlic, oil to taste, thyme, basil, and oregano and season with salt and pepper. Cover the mixture with tin foil and bake for 45 minutes. Let cool, and roughly chop it. You can store this in the fridge for up to five days.

For the sandwiches: Season the shrimp and scallops with salt and pepper to taste. Heat the olive oil in a skillet over medium heat. Sauté the shrimp and scallops for 2 minutes or until half cooked. Squeeze half the lemon and pour the white wine on the scallops and shrimp. Add 3 cups of the Tomato Confit, the basil leaves, and the oregano leaves. Warm the ciabatta rolls in the oven. Toss the arugula with the other half of the lemon juice, salt and pepper to taste, the grilled red onions, and about 1 teaspoon of olive oil. Slice the ciabatta pockets about two-thirds of the way down to open them. Don't slice them all the way; you want to form a pocket. Stuff the pocket with the shrimp and scallop mix, dividing it up equally and with a good amount of tomato. Top with the arugula mixture, garnish with a wedge of lemon, and serve.

LOBSTER ROLL

REBECCA CHARLES ✳ PEARL OYSTER BAR ✳ WWW.PEARLOYSTERBAR.COM

2 **P**

A native New Yorker, Chef Rebecca Charles grew up summering in Maine—as her family had been doing for generations, thanks to her grandmother Rebecca "Pearle" Goldsmith, who had been an opera singer at the Met. From that perspective, it was fitting that Chef Charles be the woman generally credited for bringing the lobster roll craze to New York.

Since its opening in 1997, Pearl Oyster Bar (named after the grandmother, not the jewel) was a runaway hit. Perfectly suited to Cornelia Street, a tiny pocket of the West Village that actually does have a bit of New England to it, the restaurant drew crowds and out-the-door lines almost immediately. Everyone from Mario Batali to Tony Soprano (on an episode) weighed in, as did the critics—again and again—on Pearl's perfect Lobster Roll.

Over the years, Charles has been praised for everything from the meat-to-mayonnaise ratio to the way she gets her buns to crisp, butter-cooked perfection. Here, she spills the details, along with some additional tips. "At Pearl Oyster Bar, we serve the lobster roll in a way that Mainers would consider pretty upscale," she explained. "We fill the bun with the lobster salad, sprinkl ...tn chopped chives and put it next to a big pile of shoestring fries, with a garnish of baby greens. If you want to go totally authentic, the traditional garnish is a couple of slices of bread and butter pickles and a bag of potato chips."

NOTE: Culls are lobsters that have just one, or no, claws and are therefore cheaper than others. Stay away from pre-cooked lobster meat, which is generally overcooked, probably not fresh, and definitely overpriced.

SERVES 4

4 to 4¼ pounds lobster meat
  (one lobster per person)
1 celery rib, chopped very
  finely
Squeeze of lemon
½ cup mayonnaise (Pearl
  Oyster uses Hellman's/Best
  Foods)
Salt and pepper
2 teaspoons unsalted butter
4 top-loading hot dog buns,
  preferably Pepperidge
  Farm

NOTE: "Long ago, I realized that hot dog buns were like washing machines: you have top loaders and side loaders," said Charles. "Top loaders are very popular in New England, where they put all kinds of food in hot dog buns. The quintessential Maine Lobster Roll is made with a top loading bun, so the sandwich sits up properly. New York City, on the other hand, is a side loading town. I had to call Pepperidge Farm corporate headquarters just to get the top loaders for the restaurant. No New England lobster shack would have spent the money on an expensive bun like that but I like the brioche-quality and now, of course, everyone uses them."

To cook and prepare your own lobster (optional): Throw the lobsters into a large pot of rapidly boiling water and boil for 7 to 10 minutes for each 1 to 1½ pounds; they will float when they're done. When done, put the lobsters in a large amount of ice water for 10 minutes to stop the cooking and cool thoroughly. Remove them and drain.

Lightly crush the tail with the heel of your hand to crack the shell. Bend the sides of the shell back and remove the tail in one piece. Separate the claw from the knuckle. Next, hold the claw in one hand and whack the top with the back of a chef's knife, giving the blade a little twist at the end. If you do this right, it will separate the shell into two pieces. Wiggle the thumb part back and forth and pull it off. If you're lucky and careful, the thumb meat will remain attached. Pull the claw meat out. With the small end of a fork or spoon, pry the meat out of the upper portion of the knuckle. Put the spoon end in again and break off that piece of empty shell. Pry the meat out of the remaining piece of shell. Cut the tail meat in half lengthwise and then into ¾-inch chunks. Pull the claw meat apart with your fingers because there is cartilage in the claws that needs to be removed.

For the salad: Rough chop the lobster meat into ½- to ¾-inch pieces and add to a bowl with the celery, lemon juice, mayonnaise, salt, and pepper. Mix the ingredients until thoroughly combined. Cover and store the lobster salad in the refrigerator until you need it, but no longer than overnight.

For the sandwiches: Melt the butter on low-medium heat in a small saucepan. Place the hot dog buns on their sides in the butter. Flip the buns over a couple of times so that both sides soak up an equal amount of butter and brown evenly. Remove the buns and stuff them with the lobster salad.

CRISPY SKATE SANDWICH

POLO DOBKIN * DRESSLER, DUMONT, DUMONT BURGER

WWW.DRESSLERNYC.COM * WWW.DUMONTRESTAURANT.COM

1 **H**

SERVES 4

1 cup all-purpose flour

Salt, black pepper, and
   cayenne pepper

½ cup milk

1½ cups oil, such as vegetable
   or grapeseed

1 pound skate, cut into 4 or
   more fillets

4 soft bread rolls (such as
   brioche, potato, or country
   white), toasted and halved

½ cup Tarragon Tartar Sauce
   (recipe follows)

4 leaves Bibb lettuce

1 small tomato, sliced

1 small red onion, sliced

DUMONT, America's would-be fourth television network, never came to fruition. But the name became a household name in Williamsburg, Brooklyn, when owner Colin Devlin snatched the sign from the network's defunct former offices to open DuMont, a neighborhood burger joint with a large outdoor garden. The success of DuMont spawned a mini-empire that now includes DuMont Burger and Dressler, an upscale bistro mere blocks away.

At DuMont Burger, Chef Polo Dobkin wanted to introduce a fish sandwich to balance out the burger-happy menu. "Tempura batter proved messy, so we created this skate sandwich instead," he said. The homemade tartar sauce is intensely lemony. "I like my tartar sauce bright, with decent acidity. Lemon juice helps balance out the fat from the skate," he explained.

* * *

Place the flour in a wide platter. Season with the salt, pepper, and cayenne to taste and stir to combine. Pour the milk into a similar platter. Line a third platter with paper towels. Position all three platters next to the stove. Heat the oil in a high-sided sauté pan or skillet. When the oil is shimmering, drop a pinch of flour into it. If it sizzles, it's ready.

Dip a skate piece into the milk, and then the flour. Slide it quickly into the skillet. Fry the skate until crispy, 1 to 1½ minutes. Using tongs, flip the skate onto the other side, and cook for another 1 to 1½ minutes. Transfer the skate onto the towel-lined platter. Season the skate with salt and pepper to taste. Repeat the process until all the skate has been fried. Spread about 2 tablespoons of Tartar Sauce on each roll half. Add 1 leaf of the lettuce and 1 slice each of the tomato and onion. Divide the skate evenly among the roll bottoms. Cover with the roll tops and serve.

214

TARRAGON TARTAR SAUCE

1 cup mayonnaise

Heaping ¼ cup chopped
   cornichons

Heaping ¼ cup chopped (or 9
   slices) bread and butter
   (or other sweet) pickles

Large handful fresh dill,
   chopped

4 stalks fresh tarragon,
   chopped

¼ cup fresh lemon juice
   (about 2 lemons)

Salt and fresh-cracked black
   pepper

Combine the mayonnaise, cornichons, pickles, dill, tarragon, lemon juice, and salt and pepper to taste. Using a rubber spatula, mix all of the ingredients together.

Seared Tuna Sandwich with Apple, Jalapeño, and Mint

ALEXANDRA GUARNASCHELLI ✳ BUTTER ✳ WWW.BUTTERRESTAURANT.COM

1 **P** **H** OPT FOR A LOW-FAT OR FAT-FREE YOGURT INSTEAD OF MAYONNAISE.

SERVES 4

2 small, firm and crisp apples, such as Pink Lady, washed, dried, cored, and thinly sliced

1 jalapeño pepper, washed and thinly sliced

½ lemon, peeled and thinly sliced, all pits removed from the slices

2 tablespoons packed chopped fresh mint leaves

Salt and black pepper

2 tablespoons cooking oil, such as canola, extra virgin olive, or grapeseed

12 ounces raw tuna, bloodline and skin removed

Ground white pepper

8 slices whole-wheat sandwich bread

Mayonnaise or a low-fat or fat-free Greek yogurt

WHEN Butter opened nearly ten years ago—near the downtown Public Theater—it quickly became a place to be seen. Early on, the buzz was all about the glamorous indoor forest of faux birch trees and the celebrity sightings, but these days, it's just as likely to be about Alexandra Guarnaschelli, the restaurant's accomplished executive chef. (You might also recognize her from not one but two Food Network shows, *The Cooking Loft* and *Alex's Day Off*.)

Having launched her career working under chefs such as Guy Savoy and Daniel Boulud, Guarnaschelli quickly made a name for herself through her passion for fresh seafood and organic ingredients. Her creations have a clean and refined appeal that's perfectly reflected in the easy, surprisingly inventive recipe she's chosen here. "I love this sandwich because fresh tuna is, to me, so elegant," she said. "Cooked medium rare, it really is a protein that makes a sandwich more special. The heat from the jalapeño slices and the crispness and sweetness of the apple contrast each other. The mint adds freshness. The sum total is something that's substantial, yet light and refreshing."

✳ ✳ ✳

In a large bowl, combine the apple, jalapeño, and lemon with the mint leaves. Mix to blend, and season with salt and black pepper to taste. Set aside.

In a large skillet, heat the oil. When it begins to smoke lightly, season the tuna with salt and white pepper. Place the tuna in the center of the skillet and sear it for about 2 minutes on each side. Remove the tuna from the pan and place it on a flat surface. Use a sharp knife to cut the meat into thin slices. Set aside.

Toast the bread in a toaster or conventional oven (arrange on a baking sheet—you can drizzle with a little oil if you like—and let cook on "broil" until the bread is light brown). When done, arrange 4 slices of bread on a flat surface. Spread a touch of the mayonnaise or yogurt on each. Top with the slices of tuna, apple mixture, and salt and black pepper to taste. Cover with the other bread halves, cut in half, and serve immediately.

NOTE: You'll often see lemon juice on fasts and cleanses because it's believed to help balance the body's pH. Interestingly, during digestion, lemon turns from acid to alkaline bicarbonate, which actually neutralizes the body's own acidity and helps us release toxins. As for the apples, not only are they high in digestion- and metabolism-promoting fiber, they're also replete with pectin and other enzymes that gently aid in breaking down and ridding the body of potentially irritating food particles.

CATFISH PO' BOY WITH PICKLED SLAW

PRESTON MADSON ✳ FREEMANS, PEELS ✳ WWW.FREEMANSRESTAURANT.COM

1 **H** PAN-FRY THE FISH IN JUST A FEW TABLESPOONS OF OLIVE OIL.

SERVES 4

2 cups cornmeal

1 cup flour

2 teaspoons smoked paprika

⅛ teaspoon ground black pepper

½ teaspoon mustard powder

4 teaspoons celery salt

4 catfish fillets, cut into 1-inch strips

⅓ cup (or more) cooking oil, such as olive or canola (for a lighter version, use just 1 to 2 tablespoons)

4 hoagie rolls

Pickled Slaw (recipe follows)

BACK in 2004, at the end of an unnoticed alley on New York's Lower East Side, a clubby, heavy on the taxidermy restaurant appeared. Like its owners, Taavo Somer and William Tigrett, Freemans staffers somehow managed to make the "Victorian" and "Mountain Man" hybrid seem like a feasible—and, in fact, strangely enviable—style choice. Cocktails were old school, the spinach artichoke dip was a hit, and patrons flocked. Things haven't slowed down.

Himself scruffy and slightly roguish, with a penchant for sustainable seafood and wild game, Chef Preston Madson fits right into the Freemans aesthetic. Here, Madson's opted for a nostalgic favorite, with savory, crisp, and even meaty tastes he deftly balances with the textures and sourness of pickled vegetables.

"Due to my Southern upbringing, I grew up eating quite a bit of fried catfish," Madson explained. "Even living here in New York City, I actually make this sort of thing. It reminds me of home, my family and my roots. This particular version is a tribute to my mother, who is the best southern cook that I know."

* * *

Mix together the cornmeal, flour, paprika, pepper, mustard powder, and celery salt. Dredge the catfish strips in the mixture.

For deep-fried fish: Pour cooking oil in a heavy pan so it's about ¼-inch deep. Gently lay the breaded catfish in the oil and fry until golden brown. For a lightly fried variant: Heat 1 to 2 tablespoons oil in pan and sear fish on both sides until golden brown. Place the fried fish on a paper towel to remove excess oil. Fill each hoagie roll with the fish and pickled slaw and serve immediately.

PICKLED SLAW

4 cups thinly sliced cabbage

1 cup grated carrot

2 small red onions, thinly
   sliced

4 tablespoons thinly sliced
   jalapeño pepper

2 cups water

1 cup white wine vinegar

2 tablespoons salt

4 tablespoons sugar

Combine the cabbage, carrot, onion, and jalapeño in a bowl. In a small saucepan, combine the water, white vinegar, salt, and sugar and bring to a boil. Pour the liquid over the slaw mixture and allow to cool.

Maryland Crab Cake Sandwich With Chili Aïoli

MIKE PRICE * MARKET TABLE * WWW.MARKETTABLENYC.COM

1 **P**

SERVES 6

CRAB CAKES

½ medium onion, finely
   minced

1 stalk celery, finely minced

2 tablespoons butter, divided
   (plus more, if needed)

2 eggs

2 tablespoons mayonnaise

2 tablespoons Dijon mustard

1 teaspoon lemon juice

1 teaspoon Old Bay

1 tablespoon chopped
   parsley

Salt

2 pounds fresh Maryland
   jumbo lump blue crab

½ cup plain breadcrumbs

SANDWICHES

6 brioche or hamburger
   buns, toasted

Chili Aïoli (recipe follows)

6 crab cakes

4 lettuce leaves, such as
   Boston

1 large steak tomato, sliced

MARKET Table is the kind of neighborhood restaurant you'd pretty much travel to any neighborhood to get to. Peer through the big windows, and the space is always packed with diners. The glow of the room, especially in spring when it's filled with cherry blossoms, could definitely induce a major press-your-nose-to-the-glass moment.

Chef-owner Mike Price is the guy to thank for all that. Having grown up working on his parents' farm and eventually cooking in a local crab house in Chesapeake Bay, he's retained a connection both to the ingredients themselves and to the whole experience of eating. Here, he shares—what else?—a recipe for Maryland crab cakes that reflects a healthy bit of both. "Crab cakes are absolutely one of my favorite things to make. I use very little filler in my recipe, which means it's not too carb heavy on bread," he said. "The Chili Aïoli features one of my favorite ingredients, sambal olek, which adds a really nice spicy depth. I also just have to say, Maryland blue crab makes it that much better. Try to use it whenever possible."

* * *

For the crab cakes: Sauté the onion and celery in 1 tablespoon of the butter over medium-low heat until they're translucent and tender. Remove from heat and chill in the refrigerator.

Beat together the eggs, mayonnaise, Dijon mustard, lemon juice, Old Bay, parsley, and cooled onions and celery. Adjust seasoning with salt and/or Old Bay. Place the crab meat in a bowl and gently toss in the egg mixture, being careful not to break up the lumps of crabmeat. Add the breadcrumbs and very gently toss again. Allow the mixture to rest in the refrigerator for about 15 minutes. If cakes are too moist to hold together, add another bit of breadcrumbs. Sauté the cakes over medium heat in 1 tablespoon of the butter until golden brown.

For the sandwiches: For each sandwich, smear the bun—top and bottom—with chili aïoli. Top with crab cakes, lettuce, and tomato. Serve cocktail sauce and/or cider vinegar if desired.

NOTE: In 2008, Mike Price married his wife, Alice, at Market Table. A version of these crab cakes was cooked up by Price's Market Table co-owner and friend, Joey Campanaro, of the neighboring Little Owl (both had worked at Tribeca's The Harrison years ago).

NOTE: The concept of crab cakes, it turns out, came to the Atlantic coast along with its first English settlers. The word itself has been traced back 1930, when *The New York World's Fair Cookbook* ran a "Baltimore Crab Cake" recipe.

CHILI AÏOLI

MAKES ABOUT ½ CUP

½ cup mayonnaise
1 teaspoon sambal olek (Sri Lankan chili sauce, available at grocery stores or online)
1 teaspoon lemon juice
1 teaspoon chopped parsley
Salt to taste

Mix the mayonnaise, sambal olek, lemon juice, parsley, and salt together in a bowl.

(FRENCH) FRIED FISH SANDWICH

CYRIL RENAUD ✳ BAR BRETON ✳ WWW.CHEFPIANO.COM

1 **P**

SERVES 4

4 eggs

½ cup all-purpose flour

2 cups breadcrumbs

4 (¼-pound) fluke or mahi
mahi fillets

Salt and pepper

Vegetable oil

1 baguette, sliced into
quarters

Breton Tartar Sauce (recipe
follows)

4 ounces frisée

4 radishes, julienned

1¼ teaspoons olive oil

2 teaspoons red wine
vinegar

WHAT do you do when you've cooked at countless great restaurants in Paris and New York, run your own highly successful place for years, and, well, pretty much "made it"? In Chef Cyril Renaud's case, you shift gears, close the fancy place (Michelin-starred Fleur de Sel), and open a cozy neighborhood spot in New York's Flatiron district where you can cook the stuff you grew up with. Specifically, dishes from Brittany, a coastal region in western France, known for crêpes and seafood. This fried fish recipe is especially close to Renaud's heart.

The care with which he's interpreted the sandwich comes through strongly in the flavor, which is deliciously light. What follows is Cyril's own description (it's pretty winning): "I *love* this sandwich. I remember my mother making it for me when I was a child. My friends would all clamor for pieces, so I even started having my mother make extras for them. I became very popular because of her. Over the years, I've refined some things, and created an original tartar sauce with mint leaves and pepperoncini, but I've been careful to preserve all those rich, approachable, original flavors."

✳ ✳ ✳

Beat the eggs in a bowl. Pour the flour into a second bowl and the breadcrumbs in a third bowl. Season each fish fillet with salt and pepper to taste. Heat 2 inches of oil in a saucepan over medium-high heat. Press each fillet in the flour, coating both sides, and then in the egg. Coat each fillet with the breadcrumbs, covering both sides. Fry the fish in the hot oil to a golden brown on both sides. Remove the fish from the heat.

Cut each baguette quarter in half, lengthwise. With a spoon, spread the tartar sauce on both sides of the baguette and add the fish. In a bowl, combine the frisée and the radishes; season with the olive oil, vinegar, and salt and pepper to taste. Serve alongside or—for a little extra contrast—inside the sandwich.

BRETON TARTAR SAUCE

4 tablespoons mayonnaise

2 mint leaves, chopped

½ teaspoon capers

1 cornichon, chopped

1 small green pepperoncini,
   chopped

Salt

Pepper

Mix the mayonnaise, mint, capers, cornichon, pepperoncini, salt, and pepper together in a bowl.

Scandinavian Cold-Water Shrimp Sandwich

MORTEN SOHLBERG * SMORGAS CHEF * WWW.SMORGASCHEF.COM

IF anything, New York is a city of little discoveries—be it suddenly seeing a rooftop garden (maybe on a street you've passed a hundred times) on your way to work, or realizing your local deli actually serves something delicious. In 2003, Norwegian Chef Morten Sohlberg and his wife, entrepreneur Min Ye, had the idea of opening a chain of Scandinavian restaurants around the city (keep in mind, this was well before IKEA took root in Brooklyn). Though little known, the cuisine—with its emphasis on freshness and spot-on flavoring—stood to have a broad reach, they believed. Sohlberg and Ye opened the first Smorgas Chef (meaning "Sandwich Chef" in, believe it or not, Swedish, Norwegian, *and* Danish) on Stone Street in the Financial District, where it was an instant hit with investment bankers looking for a fast and delicious lunch.

Today, the couple runs four busy outposts (among them, one in Midtown's Scandinavia House, and another that serves primarily crêpes), and their success has led to teaching positions for both in restaurant and small business management. Here, Sohlberg offers up a Nordic classic—and hugely popular menu item. "Cold-water shrimp have a distinctly sweet and fresh flavor. Eating them on sandwiches is as commonplace throughout Scandinavia as hot dogs are in the U.S. In fact, there are even shrimp sandwich stands," he said. "When I created this recipe for the restaurants, I thought about sitting at the pier in Oslo as child, waiting and waiting for the fishing boats to arrive. We would peel and eat the shrimp right out of the bucket. Add fresh dill, salty caviar, bread, and a little lemon, and you've got an irresistible explosion of tastes."

SERVES 4

1 pound cold-water shrimp, cooked and peeled

¾ cup Dill Sauce (recipe follows)

4 slices white country bread, toasted with butter

1 cup shredded romaine lettuce leaves

1 lemon, sliced

Fresh dill, for garnish

Red and/or black lump caviar, for garnish (optional)

NOTE: "Cold-water shrimp are uniquely flavorful just as a type of shrimp, but it's the way they are harvested that really sets them apart," said Sohlberg. "They're cooked in huge barrels right on the fishing vessel, immediately after they're taken from the ocean. And they're cooked in the same salt and mineral-rich seawater that the shrimp live in. That's what makes them so exquisite. However, if you can't find real cold-water shrimp, here's a trick: Cook any raw shrimp preferably with head and peel on in your own seawater: Just add 1.2 ounces of sea salt to each quart of fresh water. Submerge the raw shrimp in the boiling 'seawater' and remove from heat, steep for 5 minutes and cool."

Put the cooked shrimp in small bowl and toss with Dill Sauce until thoroughly coated. Line the toast up on a serving plate, and top the toast with the shredded lettuce to form a "nest" for the dill-shrimp mixture. Place the shrimp on top of lettuce, and garnish with dill, lemon slices, and—if you like—caviar and serve.

DILL SAUCE

½ cup mayonnaise
¼ cup sour cream
Juice of ½ lemon
3 tablespoons fresh dill, finely
   chopped
1 teaspoon red lump caviar
Salt and pepper

Place the mayonnaise, sour cream, lemon, and dill in medium-size bowl and mix with a whisk until thoroughly combined. Season with salt and pepper to taste. If well covered, this keeps in the refrigerator for up to two weeks.

Chapter 10

THE SWEET SANDWICH

---
* * *

ASIDE FROM A HANDFUL OF STANDBYS (ICE CREAM SANDWICHES, PB&J), WE weren't at all sure that sweet sandwiches would be easy to find in New York. But upon closer inspection, we spotted them. They were in the macarons in Angela Pinkerton's petit four service at Eleven Madison Park, and the brown sugar "whoopie" cookies at the celebrated (and amazingly still-quaint) Magnolia Bakery. Then, chefs began turning in their recipes. Some, such as Australian kitchen whiz Shaun Hergatt, gave us recipes that waxed nostalgic about their childhood. Other chefs created dessert sandwiches specifically for this book, such as Janssen Chen's Sweet Miso Focaccia, or the Banana Pudding with Chocolate Ganache by the duo behind Sugar Sweet Sunshine, a wildly popular Lower East Side bakery.

In keeping with the city's culinary trends, the sandwiches in this chapter are cutting edge—and often involve chocolate. Even the simplest of our sweet sandwiches use tricks taught in culinary school to enhance flavors and achieve balance. For example, any chef worth her salt knows that salt—even just a touch—improves sugar. Salt emphasizes the fruit in Bklyn Larder's Almond Butter and Strawberry Jam Sandwich, the chocolate in The Tangled Vine's Pan con Chocolate, and the caramel in Eleven Madison Park's pink peppercorn macaron. Upping the ante, smoked salt underlines the nuttiness of Jimmy's No. 43's Elvis Tea Sandwich, and lends a pleasing dimension to Anarchy In A Jar's Key Lime Marmalade. Speaking of marmalade, the bitterness of the zest of those limes tones down the sweetness in a Key Lime Ice Cream Sandwich. These next recipes will sweeten your lunch box.

---
* * *

1,000-YEAR-OLD ICE CREAM SANDWICH

DAVID ANDREWS, PASTRY CHEF ∗ ANGELO SOSA, TOP CHEF FINALIST

❶

SERVES 10

**Cocoa Nib Cookie (recipe
follows)**

**1,000 Year Old Caramel
(recipe follows)**

**2 pints vanilla bean Haagen
Dazs ice cream**

XIE xie means "thank you" in Mandarin Chinese, and expresses the gratitude of this former Buddakan chef and *Top Chef* finalist for his passion: cooking innovative Asian dishes. In Xie Xie, Chef Sosa's recent sandwich shop near Times Square, he offered sweet glazed pork tucked into a trio of steamed buns, char-grilled Vietnamese beef, tilapia deliciously (and surprisingly) infused with dill.

This sweet sandwich was a dessert at Xie Xie, and a riff on the so-called 1,000-year-old egg, a Chinese delicacy in which a hard-boiled egg is cured in clay, ash, and salt for weeks or months, until the yolk turns blackish green. The ice cream and cookie form a backdrop to a black caramel center. "I asked my pastry chef, David Andrews, to create this sandwich as a nod to tradition, while stepping into the future," said Chef Sosa.

∗ ∗ ∗

Place one cookie on a plate. Top with some caramel. Add 1 scoop of ice cream and the second cookie. Repeat with all 20 cookies.

1,000 YEAR OLD CARAMEL

3½ cups cream
10 tablespoons unsalted butter
1½ teaspoon salt
2½ cups sugar
1 teaspoon vanilla extract
1 teaspoon gel-based, jet
   black food coloring
   (optional)

Bring the cream, butter, and salt to a boil over medium heat. Place the sugar in a small saucepan over medium-high heat. Caramelize the sugar until amber, about 5 minutes. Add the caramel to the cream mixture. Finish the caramel with the vanilla and the food coloring, if using. Cool and chill until ready to use.

COCOA NIB COOKIE

⅓ cup cocoa nibs (available at specialty grocer or online)

¾ cup sugar

½ cup brown sugar

12 tablespoons unsalted butter

1 egg

6 ounces dark chocolate, melted

2 cups all-purpose flour

1 teaspoon baking soda

1 teaspoon salt

Preheat the oven to 325° F. Line a half-sheet pan with wax paper. Place the cocoa nibs in a coffee grinder, and grind. Combine the sugars, butter, and cocoa nibs. Mix well. When fluffy, add the egg; then the melted chocolate. Sift in the flour, baking soda, and salt. Roll out the cookie dough into a thin sheet on a cutting board lightly dusted with flour. Using a 3-inch round cookie cutter, cut out 20 cookies. Place the cookies onto the sheet pan. Bake for 5 minutes. Turn each cookie, and bake another 5 minutes.

SWEET MISO FOCACCIA

JANSEN CHAN ✳ OCEANA ✳ WWW.OCEANARESTAURANT.COM

2 **P** **H** HALVE THE CREAM CHEESE AND OPT FOR LOW-FAT OR FAT-FREE.

NOTE: Miso is high in "umami," that same savory taste you get in meat and cheese (also, interestingly, mushrooms and tomatoes). Since the flavor is so tied to savory and hearty meals, when it's present in lean foods, researchers are starting to believe it may have the ability to trick the body into thinking it's had something richer and more calorie-dense than what it actually got. A number of recent studies have found that when this taste alone (no extra fat or calories) is added to food, people report feeling sated sooner.

FOR nearly twenty years, Oceana has maintained a sterling reputation as a top seafood destination—a place you go when you want the fish to all but melt with flavor. So it was notable that when the restaurant moved from its refined Upper East townhouse to a breezier, more contemporary space near Times Square, the new reviews devoted precious ink to praising pastry chef Jansen Chen's ambitious dessert program.

Before attending Le Cordon Bleu and working under Alain Ducasse, Chan was an architect (he actually had a strong hand in designing Oceana's kitchen). It's a vocation he says he loves for the same reasons he does baking—the puzzle of building something from the ground up, adding layer on layer to make it look solid and effortless. Indeed, Chan's desserts have time and again been praised for their structural beauty and for the clean innovative tastes.

Chan grew up cooking a dessert a day with his Chinese father, and lately those Asian influences have turned into a source of inspiration. "Using miso paste in a traditional foccacia was an organic marriage of two loves. The salty, heartier flavors of miso contrasts well with the sweet, dried fruits and help make the foccacia chewier and tender," he said. "Sandwiched with simple, rich cream cheese and crisp, sweet apples, this is a great any-time snack or a perfect breakfast/brunch item."

✳ ✳ ✳

Soak the raisins and dried cranberries for 30 minutes in warm water. Strain and reserve.

In a mixer with a dough hook, mix together at low speed the flours, sugar, and yeast. Add the salt, miso, molasses, and water. Keep the mixer on low until the dough comes together. Then, increase the speed to medium and mix for 10 to 15 minutes, until the dough is elastic and smooth and forms around the hook. At this point, add candied oranges, raisins, and cranberries. Place the dough in a greased bowl and wrap well in plastic wrap. Store in a warm spot for an hour (not too close to the oven or it will rise lopsided), or until the dough has doubled in size.

Meanwhile, line the bottom a 13 × 9-inch baking dish with parchment paper and grease all the sides as well as the paper. Punch down the dough and gently stretch it to fill the pan. With your fingers, poke dimples in the dough. Place a greased plastic wrap on top of the dough and return the pan to the warm spot for another hour.

Preheat the oven to 425°F. When the dough has doubled in size, remove the plastic wrap and bake the entire focaccia for 30 minutes, or until golden brown. Allow the focaccia to cool on a wire rack. Remove the edges from the cooled focaccia and cut it into 12 equal portions (three by four). Cut each focaccia in half horizontally and spread the cream cheese on the bottom layer. Place apples slices on top of the cream cheese. Return top layer and slice sandwiches on a diagonal.

SERVES 12

1 cup raisins
1 cup dried cranberries
2¾ cups all-purpose flour
1 cup bread flour
1 tablespoon sugar
1 tablespoon dried yeast
2 teaspoons salt
¾ cup white miso
2 tablespoons molasses
3 cups water, at room temperature
1 cup chopped candied orange
24 ounces cream cheese
4 apples (sweet and crisp, such as Pink Lady), sliced into ⅛-inch pieces

Lamington Sandwich

SHAUN HERGATT * SHO SHAUN HERGATT * WWW.SHOSHAUNHERGATT.COM

1 **P**

SHO Shaun Hergatt is named after its chef, an unassuming Aussie who honed his signature French cooking in five-star hotels such as the Ritz-Carlton and the Setai Miami. The restaurant's vast size (12,500 square feet), imaginative displays (Japanese scrolls, a light-filled wine "gallery"), and luxurious surfaces (mother-of-pearl bar, silk walls) culminate in a single focal point: a glass-enclosed showcase kitchen behind which Hergatt and his staff prepare refined dishes such as peekytoe crab with galangal gelée and sweet uni, saffron-crowned Maine lobster, and tender veal with morels and potato almondine croquette. The chef's subtle palate, delicate techniques, and pan-Asian sensibilities have earned him two *New York Times* stars and rave reviews all around.

And yet there's nothing the chef craves like Lamingtons, the epitome of Australian comfort food. These "Australian s'mores"—a sponge cake filled with jam and dipped in chocolate and coconut—were Hergatt's after-school treats.

"Mom used to make Lamingtons when we finished school. 'Here's your Lamington and your glass of juice,' she'd say. Now, I make them for visiting Australians [who dine at SHO]. One time, I surprised some friends, and they began crying at the table; they hadn't had a Lamington in so long," he said.

SPONGE CAKE

4 eggs

¾ cup sugar

1¾ cups all-purpose flour

3 teaspoons baking powder

**5 tablespoons unsalted butter,
melted**

½ cup corn syrup

⅓ cup milk

CHOCOLATE GANACHE

**17½ ounces baking chocolate,
semi-sweet or dark**

1 pint (2 cups) heavy cream

SANDWICHES

**1 (12-ounce) package
shredded coconut**

**1 (10- to 13-ounce) jar of
raspberry jam (you may
use strawberry jam)**

For the sponge cake: Preheat the oven to 325°F. Using an electric mixer, beat the eggs and sugar for about 5 minutes, or until light and foamy. Sift together the flour and baking powder. In a separate bowl, combine the butter and corn syrup. Fold the flour mixture into the egg mixture using a rubber spatula. Add the milk. Add the butter mixture. Line a baking sheet with parchment paper. Spread the batter in the pan. Bake for 8 minutes, or until a toothpick inserted in the middle of the cake comes out clean.

For the chocolate ganache: Break the chocolate into 1-inch chunks. Prepare a double boiler. If you don't have one, fill a pot with water, and fit a metal bowl above the water line. Place the chocolate chunks and the cream in the metal bowl. Heat the water to boil. Turn the heat down, and stir the chocolate occasionally, until it is fully melted and incorporated into the cream.

For the sandwiches: Place the shredded coconut in a bowl. Cut the cake in half to form two 13 x 9-inch rectangles. Spread the jam evenly over one half. Place the other half on top. Slice the layered cake into even squares, about 2½ inches wide. Dip each square into the chocolate ganache. Immediately drop each square into the bowl of shredded coconut. Working quickly, coat the entire square with the coconut. Place the squares on a large platter or sealable container. Cover and chill. When the chocolate hardens (about 1 hour), the sandwiches are ready to serve.

ELVIS Tea Sandwich

JIMMY CARBONE * JIMMYS NO. 43 * WWW.JIMMYSNO43.COM

①

BEER aficionado Jimmy Carbone opened this subterranean East Village gastropub as a quiet place where he could pop a brew and cook for his friends—many of whom are cooks from the likes of Jean-Georges and WD-50. Soon, those cooks were taking turns manning the tiny kitchen, and using Chef Carbone's minimalist equipment—a couple of hot plates, a small oven, no stove, and little working room—to one-up one another in turning out delicious grub such as lamb riblets and roasted shisito peppers. The restaurant received Slow Food's "snail of approval" and made a name for remarkable, beer-friendly creations.

This sandwich, also favored by Elvis, represents one of Chef Carbone's favorites. Fair warning: There's no tidy way to eat it. Even if you fill it thinly (and really—why would you?), and toast until crusty, the almond butter and honey will melt into a fine, runny goo. It makes a good breakfast or snack, but Carbone has something else in mind. "Eat it hot with a cold glass of beer," he said.

* * *

Peel the bananas. Mash them in a bowl. Spread 4 slices of the bread with the mashed banana. Spread 4 slices of the bread with the almond butter. Drizzle as much honey as you prefer. Sprinkle with smoked sea salt to taste. Join the banana slices with the honey-almond butter slices. Heat a skillet. Add the butter. When it melts, add a sandwich and fry until golden, about 2 to 3 minutes. Flip the sandwich and repeat. Cut each sandwich into triangles, and serve.

SERVES 4

- 2 bananas
- 8 thin slices white bread (preferably Pepperidge Farm)
- 6 to 8 ounces almond butter (about 1 cup)
- Local honey
- Smoked sea salt
- 4 tablespoons unsalted butter

NOTE: Legend has it that the sandwich that Elvis Presley actually favored contained not just warm bananas, peanut butter, and honey, but also pickles, bacon, and mayonnaise. We thought we'd stick to something more universally delicious, but feel free to build on our version.

KEY LIME ICE CREAM SANDWICH, WITH MARMALADE

LAENA MIRA MCCARTHY * ANARCHY IN A JAR * WWW.ANARCHYINAJAR.COM

1 **P**

SERVES 4

KEY LIME ICE CREAM

1 pint premium vanilla ice
cream, softened
1 tablespoon key lime zest
2 tablespoons key lime juice

KEY LIME MARMALADE

8 key limes
1 cup sugar
⅛ teaspoon smoked salt
(look for naturally smoked)

BROOKLYN'S booming cottage food industry is well exemplified by this talented jam producer. During the day, Chef Laena Mira McCarthy is a Pratt Institute professor; during her off hours she fashions jams out of local fruits and aromatics. The bright, simple flavors stand out in her fresh, pectin-free jams, such as the key lime marmalade with smoked salt.

By itself, the marmalade pairs well with nut butter (McCarthy recommends cashew) on whole grain bread. But tucked in a brownie crust and smeared with key lime-"tinted" vanilla ice cream, the marmalade imparts surprising dimension.

"This recipe seemed like a classic combination: key lime pie and ice cream. [But] the tart flavor of marmalade balances the sweetness of the ice cream and brownie," said Chef McCarthy. She recommends brownies by Baked (in Red Hook, Brooklyn), or Ghirardelli's rich, simple brownie mix, available in most grocery stores (prepare the recipe according to the mix, then spread onto a buttered 15-×-10-inch jelly roll pan).

* * *

For the Key lime ice cream: Mix the ice cream, lime zest, and juice in a bowl. Cover and freeze.

For the Key lime marmalade: Scrub the limes. Cut them into thin slices and then quarter each slice. Combine 2 cups of water and the lines in a saucepan over medium-high heat. Bring the limes to a boil. Reduce the heat, and simmer for 10 minutes.

Add the sugar, and bring to a second boil. Remove from heat. Cool to room temperature, about 1 hour. Place the saucepan back on the heat. Bring to a third boil. Reduce heat, and simmer for approximately 15 minutes, or until the jam has reached 220°F or is set (spoon some onto a dish, set it in the fridge for a few minutes, and if it wrinkles when pushed, it's ready). Do not overcook, or the marmalade will solidify or caramelize. Add the smoked salt, and bring to a fourth boil. Turn off the heat. Stir to distribute the zest and let cool. The marmalade can be stored in the fridge for up to two weeks.

For the chocolate brownie crust: Preheat oven to 350°F. Butter a 15-x-10-inch jelly roll pan. Line with parchment paper, leaving a 2-inch overhang on the two shorter sides. In a medium bowl, whisk together the butter and sugar until combined. Whisk in the egg, vanilla, and salt until combined. Add the flour and the cocoa, and mix until smooth (don't overmix or the batter will be sticky). Using a spatula, spread the brownie batter in the baking pan. Bake until the edges of the crust begin to pull away from the sides of the pan, 10 to 12 minutes. Cool completely.

For the sandwiches: Using a long spatula, swirl 2 tablespoons of the marmalade into the ice cream. Lift the brownie crust onto a work surface (if using Chef McCarthy's recipe, use the built-in paper overhang). With a serrated knife, halve the crust crosswise. Place half of the crust, flat side down, on a large piece of plastic wrap. Spread the crust with 1 tablespoon of the marmalade and then ½ to 1 pint of ice cream. Top with the remaining half of the crust, flat side up. Press firmly. Return the ice-cream "sandwich" to baking pan, and wrap tightly in plastic. Freeze until firm, about 2 hours.

Unwrap the sandwich. Using a serrated knife, cut into 8 rectangles, wiping the blade clean between each cut. Serve immediately, or wrap individually in plastic, and freeze up to one week.

CHOCOLATE BROWNIE CRUST

8 tablespoon (1 stick) plus ½ tablespoon unsalted butter, melted
½ cup sugar
1 large egg
1 teaspoon pure vanilla extract
½ teaspoon salt
½ cup all-purpose flour
¼ cup unsweetened cocoa powder

NOTE: Key limes are smaller, rounder, and brighter than classic (Persian) limes. They are also tarter, with thinner rinds that yield big flavor and less bitter pith.

PINK PEPPERCORN AND CARAMEL GANACHE MACARON

ANGELA PINKERTON * ELEVEN MADISON PARK * WWW.ELEVENMADISONPARK.COM

2 **P** **M** 1 TO 2 DAYS

**MAKES 25
SANDWICHES**

1½ cups almond flour
1½ cups confectioners' sugar
½ tablespoon ground pink
   peppercorns
3 eggs, separated and divided
½ teaspoon egg white
   powder (available at
   baking supply stores)
¾ cup sugar
Pink food coloring
Caramel Ganache (recipe
   follows)

WHEN Eleven Madison Park opened in 1998, it was a gleaming jewel in the Danny Meyer empire—but not the biggest or brightest. For years, its stunning location—a landmark Art Deco building with a marble entry, soaring ceiling, and picture-perfect views of Madison Square Park; classic Danny Meyer hospitality—warm, inviting, the antithesis of stiff; and undeniably *haute* and yet current French menu somehow failed to elevate the restaurant above rave—but hardly stellar—reviews.

Things have recently changed. Meyer's group hired Swiss chef Daniel Humm, along with a remarkably young, biologist-turned-pastry chef named Angela Pinkerton. A few short years later, the team earned an extraordinary four stars from *The New York Times*, a James Beard nomination for best chef, and other uncommon kudos. EMP took its rightful place in New York's dining hall of fame.

Despite its plush vibe and high-minded cuisine, the restaurant exudes a youthful playfulness that is showcased well in this delicious macaron. Here at EMP, we like to have fun, said Pinkerton. "We do a selection of macarons for our 'petit four' service. [As a play on the ubiquitous salted caramel macaron,] we paired pepper (which goes with salt), and chocolate (which goes with caramel). The end result is . . . sweet and savory . . . with a caramel-like texture. It's like eating a candy bar," she adds.

* * *

Preheat oven to 265° F. Position a rack in the center. Cover a baking sheet with a slipat or parchment paper.

Blend the almond flour with the confectioners' sugar and pink peppercorns in a food processor for 30 seconds. Drizzle in half the egg whites. Blend to make a smooth wet paste. Transfer to a large mixing bowl. Cover with a wet towel.

Whisk together the remaining egg whites and egg white powder in a 5-quart (or larger) stand mixer. Place the granulated sugar in a small pot (preferably copper). Use your hand to mix ¼ cup water into the sugar, making a slurry. Make sure there are no sugar crystals stuck to the side of the pot. Cover the pot and place over medium heat.

When the sugar is at 239°F (115°C), whip the egg white mixture to soft peaks. At 244.4°F (118°C), slowly stream the hot sugar syrup down the side of mixer bowl while continuing to whip. Whip to stiff peaks. Color to the desired shade.

Remove the wet towel from the almond paste. Fold meringue into the almond paste with a rubber spatula, until smooth and well combined. Continue folding until the mixture loosens. The crests and lines from folding should slowly disappear. Be careful not to over fold the batter or the cookies will be too flat.

Immediately transfer the batter to a piping bag fitted with a number 803 or 804 round tip. Pipe silver-dollar size rounds onto the prepared baking sheet. Dry at room temperature until a thin crust is formed, but the cookie is still soft in the center, 30 minutes to 1 hour depending on the humidity in the air. Bake for 12 to 15 minutes, rotating the pan 180 degrees halfway through. Cool completely.

Pipe a dot of caramel ganache onto the flat bottom of a cookie. Place another cookie, flat side down, on top of the ganache to form a sandwich. Place the macaron on a tray. Wrap it gently with plastic wrap. Repeat with the remaining cookies. Refrigerate overnight. When ready to serve unwrap and allow cookies to come to room temperature.

NOTE: Although French, the word *macaron* is derived from *maccherone*, which is Italian for crushed almonds. The smooth cookie—simultaneously chewy and airy—is made from peaked egg whites, almond flour, and sugar, and often filled with cream, butter, or in this case, chocolate-caramel ganache. *Macarons* are related to, but distinctly different from, American macaroons, a sweeter, nuttier cake that often contains shredded coconut.

NOTE: Although they are the size and shape of peppercorns, so-called pink peppercorns are actually dried berries from a South American rose tree. They are peppery, sweet, and pungent.

CARAMEL GANACHE

- ½ cup plus 2 tablespoons sugar
- 1 tablespoon corn syrup
- ¼ cup plus 1 tablespoon heavy cream, warmed
- 1½ teaspoons salt
- 3 tablespoons unsalted butter, softened
- 3.5 ounces milk chocolate (preferably Valrhona's Jivara Chocolate 40%), melted
- 1.2 ounces bittersweet chocolate (preferably Valrhona's Araguani Chocolate 72%), melted

Place the sugar and corn syrup in a small pot over a medium flame. Cook the sugar mixture until it reaches a dark caramel color and begins to smoke, about 10 minutes. Stir in the warm cream. If the mixture bubbles and spurts, lower the heat. Add the salt, and stir. Add the softened butter, and stir. Pour the mixture over the melted chocolate. Stir to incorporate. Cool completely (preferably overnight, in the refrigerator). Bring the ganache to room temperature before using.

ALMOND BUTTER and STRAWBERRY Jam Sandwich

ANDREW FEINBERG ✳ BKLYN LARDER ✳ WWW.BKLYNLARDER.COM

1 **P** **H**

IT was the same story with first-time visitors as with regulars. Nearly everyone who came to Franny's, Andrew Feinberg's popular restaurant in Brooklyn's Park Slope, clamored to know where the restaurant sourced its hand-crafted cheeses, fine honeys, olive oils, artisanal ice creams, and cured meats—that is, when they were not crafted in-house. This gave Feinberg and his wife, Francine, the inspiration to open up a retail shop, and Bklyn Larder was born.

The store sparkles. Up front, panini and sandwich makers stand at the ready. Mid-counter, staff is prepared to answer questions about olive oils, cheeses, and vinegars, or bottle the house-specialty brands.

Bklyn Larder's Almond Butter Sandwich makes use of the store's fine provisions to "bring you straight back to your childhood," said Feinberg. The recipe uses freshly ground almond butter (more nutritious than most commercial peanut butters), enhancing the clean nuttiness of almonds with sea salt and a touch of sweet butter.

✳ ✳ ✳

Spread the butter on 4 slices of the bread. Sprinkle each buttered slice with a pinch of sea salt. Spread the almond butter on the other 4 slices of bread. Spoon the jam on the buttered slices. Close the sandwiches. Cut into quarters, and serve.

SERVES 4

⅓ to ½ stick unsalted butter, at room temperature

8 slices hearty multigrain bread

½ teaspoon sea salt (such as Maldon or fleur de sel)

¾ cup almond butter (preferably freshly ground)

8 tablespoons Moulin Mahjoub, or other high-quality strawberry jam

S'MORE

SUNCHAR RAYMOND * PASTRY CHEF, UNION SQUARE EVENTS * WWW.USHGNYC.COM

2 **P**

YIELDS 20 TO 30 COOKIES

GRAHAM CRACKER SQUARES

1¼ cups cake flour

1½ cups graham cracker crumbs

1 teaspoon baking soda

1 teaspoon cinnamon

1 teaspoon salt

2 sticks (½ pound) unsalted butter, softened

1 cup dark brown sugar

2 tablespoons honey

2 tablespoons whole milk

THIS sweet, classic treat was specifically created for Sandwiched, Union Square Event's pop-up café at the Whitney Museum of American Art.

"Because people are so passionate about this little sandwich, we wanted to make sure and get it just right. After months of research (and taste testing), we felt we'd nailed it with the flavor of the chocolate and the texture of the homemade graham cracker," said Sunchar Raymond, pastry chef of Union Square Events.

Slice the graham crackers, marshmallow, and chocolate ganache as fat or as thin as you like, and set out for your guests to compile, buffet style. Eat them cold, or warmed in the microwave for about 10 seconds so that the ganache pools over the marshmallow sides.

* * *

For the graham cracker squares: Preheat the oven to 350°F. Line two baking sheets with parchment paper or silicone baking mats.

Whisk together the cake flour, graham cracker crumbs, baking soda, cinnamon, and salt in a large bowl.

In a separate bowl, beat the butter, dark brown sugar, honey, and milk until light and fluffy, scraping the sides of the bowl as necessary. With the mixer on low speed, add the dry ingredients to the creamed butter mixture, mixing until barely combined. Mix slowly until the dough is uniform.

Turn the dough onto a lightly floured surface. If the dough is sticky, place a sheet of parchment paper on top of it. Using a rolling pin, roll the dough into a square ¼-inch thick. Using a sharp knife, slice the dough into 2½-inch squares.

Using the tip of a fork, lightly score each square down the center, so that it resembles a graham cracker. Lay the square on the baking

CHOCOLATE SQUARES

1½ cups bittersweet chocolate morsels

½ cup milk chocolate morsels

1½ cups heavy cream

2 tablespoons light corn syrup

2 tablespoons unsalted butter, softened

MARSHMALLOW SQUARES

1¼ cups confectioners' sugar, divided

½ cup cold water

3½ envelopes (2 tablespoons plus 2½ teaspoons) unflavored gelatin

2 cups granulated sugar

½ cup light corn syrup

½ cup hot water

¼ teaspoon salt

2 teaspoons vanilla

sheets, 1 inch apart. Bake until the square tops are lightly golden, about 15 minutes. Let the square rest on the baking sheet for 10 minutes. Transfer to a wire rack. Cool completely.

For the chocolate squares: Place the chocolate morsels in a large, heat-proof bowl. Line a large baking sheet with parchment paper.

In a heavy-bottomed pot, bring the cream and the corn syrup to a boil over medium-high heat. Pour the cream mixture over the chocolate. Remove from heat. Allow the mixture to cool for 30 seconds.

Gently whisk the chocolate and the cream together until fully incorporated. Whisk in the softened butter.

Pour the chocolate mixture onto the sheet tray. Using a spatula, spread it to ¼-inch thickness. Place the tray, uncovered, in the freezer until set, 30 to 45 minutes. Once set, cut it into 2-inch squares. Keep chilled until ready to assemble.

For the marshmallow squares: Grease a large metal baking sheet. Line it with parchment paper. Dust with ½ cup of the confectioners' sugar. Add the cold water to the bowl of a standing mixer. Sprinkle the gelatin over it. Let stand until soft, about 5 minutes. Add the granulated sugar, corn syrup, hot water, and salt to a medium, heavy-bottomed saucepan. Turn heat to low. Stir gently until the sugar is dissolved.

Increase the heat to medium. Bring the mixture to a boil, without stirring. Add a candy thermometer and allow the mixture to boil, still without stirring, until it reaches 240°F, about 10 minutes. Immediately remove the pot from the heat. Pour the sugar mixture over the gelatin mixture, stirring until the gelatin is dissolved.

Using a stand mixer fitted with a whisk attachment, beat the gelatin mixture on high speed until it is white, thick, and tripled in volume, about 8 minutes. Pour the mixture onto the prepared baking sheet. Sift ¼ cup of the confectioners' sugar over the top. Chill the marshmallow, uncovered, until firm, about 2 hours.

Dust a large cutting board with ¼ cup of the confectioners' sugar. Run a thin knife around the edges of the baking sheet to loosen and then quickly turn the marshmallow out onto the prepared board. Gently remove the parchment paper. If the marshmallow is sticky, dust with ¼ cup of the confectioners' sugar.

Using a large, greased knife, cut the marshmallow into 2-inch squares. Store them, wrapped tightly in plastic wrap, on a parchment-line sheet tray until ready to assemble.

For the sandwiches: If making ahead, store each component unassembled. Just before serving, take 1 graham cracker square. Add 1 chocolate layer square. Add 1 marshmallow square. Top with another graham cracker square. Continue assembling s'mores until the ingredients run out.

BROWN SUGAR WHOOPEE COOKIE WITH MAPLE CREAM CHEESE ICING

SINA CLARK, HEAD BAKER ✳ MAGNOLIA BAKERY ✳ WWW.MAGNOLIABAKERY.COM

② **P**

MAKES 1½ DOZEN SANDWICH COOKIES

BROWN SUGAR COOKIES

1 (8-ounce) package cream cheese, at room temperature

8 tablespoons (1 stick) unsalted butter, at room temperature

⅜ cup maple syrup

1 teaspoon vanilla extract

3 cups confectioners' sugar

MAPLE CREAM CHEESE ICING

1 (8-ounce) package cream cheese, at room temperature

8 tablespoons (1 stick) unsalted butter, at room temperature

⅜ cup maple syrup

1 teaspoon vanilla extract

3 cups confectioners' sugar

LIKE the happy coincidence of a Reese's Peanut Butter Cup, this sweet sandwich is a tasty accidental pairing by the celebrated Magnolia Bakery. The maple cream cheese icing was originally created to go with the bakery's pumpkin cupcake. But folded into the bakery's classic brown sugar cookie, bakers found it irresistible: a delicate, chewy cookie with creamy cupcake icing.

"The flavors of brown sugar and maple complement each other so well; it's like an autumn afternoon in your mouth. It makes me think of hot apple cider, leaves blowing around, and colorful wool sweaters," said Bobby Lloyd. Great on their own, it's hard not to nibble on cookies or icing before joining the two.

✳ ✳ ✳

For the brown sugar cookies: Preheat the oven to 325°F. In a mixer or food processor, beat the butter and sugars until light and fluffy. Add the eggs one at a time, until completely incorporated. Add the vanilla extract and mix well. In a mixing bowl, sift together the flour, baking soda, and salt. On the lowest speed of the mixer or processor, add the sifted ingredients in three parts. Be careful not to overmix. Pause between additions to scrape the sides and bottom of the bowl, using a rubber spatula. Line an ungreased cookie sheet with parchment paper or foil. Using an ice cream scoop, scoop golf ball–sized balls of cookie dough and place on the sheet 1½ inches apart. Bake until the edges are golden brown, 10 to 14 minutes. Cool the cookies on the cookie sheet for 2 minutes. Transfer to a wire rack.

For the maple cream cheese icing: Cut the cream cheese into 1-inch cubes. In a mixer or food processor, combine the cream cheese and butter, beating on medium speed until smooth. In a liquid measuring cup with a pour spout, combine the maple syrup and vanilla extract. Turn the mixer speed to low, and add the syrup mixture to the cream cheese mixture in a thin stream. Sift the confectioners' sugar into a large bowl. Add half the sugar to the cream cheese mixture and mix on the lowest speed until smooth. Stop the mixer. Scrape the sides and bottom of the bowl. Add the remaining sugar (1 ½ to 2 cups), and mix until smooth.

For the sandwiches: Spread a ½ to ¾-inch layer of icing on one cookie, then top with another. Continue until all the cookies are used.

Banana Pudding Sandwich
with Chocolate Ganache

DEBBIE WEINER AND PEGGY WILLIAMS ✳ SUGAR SWEET SUNSHINE ✳ WWW.SUGARSWEETSUNSHINE.COM

1 **P**

ONLY a place this sweet and folksy could open in the dead of winter, and still call itself 'sunshine.' Friends Peggy Williams and Debbie Weiner opened the doors of Sugar Sweet Sunshine in 2003, bringing moist cupcakes and buttery cookies to the Lower East Side. The ring of the bell on the door is accompanied by the smell of butter, and the sight of smiling bakers spooning muffins into tins.

This sandwich is built from one of the bakery's bestsellers: banana pudding with Nilla wafers. The pudding is spooned into brioche, over a layer of chocolate ganache. "We serve the pudding fresh, but after a day, the wafers get super soft. We also recommend adding a slice of sandwich meat for an interesting contrast," said Chef Weiner, suggesting turkey or prosciutto.

✳ ✳ ✳

For the banana pudding: Using a hand mixer, blend the water, condensed milk, and pudding powder until combined. Place in the refrigerator and chill for at least 4 hours, until set.

Using a hand mixer, whip the cream until firm, but not clumpy. With a rubber spatula, gently fold the pudding mixture into the cream, until thoroughly integrated. In a large mixing bowl, layer the cookies, whipped cream, and bananas, and repeat until complete.

For the chocolate ganache: Place the chocolate chips in a large bowl. On the stove, heat heavy cream until just about to boil. Pour hot cream over chips. Allow to stand 5 minutes and stir until smooth. Alternately, place the chips and cream in a large microwave safe bowl and microwave 1 minute. Stir and heat for an additional minute, in 30 second increments, if necessary, until smooth.

For the sandwiches: Place about 2 tablespoons of the banana pudding on each roll bottom. Drizzle with 1 tablespoon of the ganache. Repeat if desired.

MAKES 8 TO 10 SANDWICHES

BANANA PUDDING

¾ cup cold water

½ cup plus 3 tablespoons sweetened condensed milk

⅓ cup instant vanilla pudding powder

1½ cups heavy cream

1 box Nilla wafers

2 to 3 bananas, sliced

CHOCOLATE GANACHE

6 ounces semisweet chocolate chips

½ cup heavy cream

SANDWICHES

8 to 10 soft rolls (such as brioche), split lengthwise and toasted

NOTE: Remaining pudding and ganache may be stored in refrigerator up to four days.

Pan con Chocolate

DAVID SIEGAL ✳ THE TANGLED VINE ✳ WWW.TANGLEDVINEBAR.COM

SERVES 4

3 ounces dark chocolate (at least 61% cocoa)
4 pieces baguette, sliced 4½ inches thick on the bias
Drizzle extra virgin olive oil (about 4 teaspoons)
Sprinkle of sea salt

NOTE: Believe it or not, the dark chocolate and olive oil make this an antioxidant-packed dessert that's low in saturated fat.

FOR restaurants, New York's Upper West Side can be a tough place to break in. It's a low-key, long-term residential neighborhood, and people don't like to cheat on their regular spots. Like any small town, it can take time to win trust. The Tangled Vine, however, has been an exception. A relatively new restaurant (opened in early 2010), it seems to have slipped right into the rhythm of the area.

This may have something to do with the nature of the venture—classy, comfortable, dedicated to serving food that's good for you, and driven by some well-established names behind the bar. Evan Spingarn, author of *The Ultimate Wine Lover's Guide*, has built a list of more than 160 bottles, all with an eye toward the organic, biodynamic, and sustainable. That theme is echoed in the kitchen, where Chef David Siegal—who first got noticed cooking for Jean Georges, David Bouley, and Charlie Palmer, among others—has crafted a clean, organic menu that's incredibly rich on flavor, thanks in part to his passion for Spanish Catalan cooking.

Siegal's Pan con Chocolate was one of the first things he served guests when Tangled Vine opened, and it's been a draw ever since. Thick slices of toasted bread are generously covered in melted chocolate, the flavor deepened by olive oil and enhanced with coarse salt. Siegal says he learned about the dessert—featuring an impressive four key ingredients of the region's cuisine—while staying just north of Barcelona. "Each of these components offers something unique: The chocolate adds richness and sweetness, the olive oil adds fat and a floral aroma, the bread offers texture and the sea salt brings everything together," he said. "It's like listening to Led Zeppelin—there's only four guys playing, but it sounds like they have a massive orchestra behind them."

Melt the chocolate in a double boiler, and toast the bread. Brush each slice of bread generously with the melted chocolate. Drizzle the olive oil over the top of every sandwich, and finish with a sprinkle of sea salt on each.

NOTE: For this dish, look for Spanish olive oils that use Arbequina olives, suggests Chef Siegal. They're known for their fresh, fruity taste, which will offset the heaviness of the bread and chocolate.

NOTE: A version of this dish dates back to World War II. Chocolate was rationed, and—both to make it last and to improve their other meager supplies—Spaniards would spread it on toast, eating it for breakfast with a little salt and oil.

BEST-EVER CHOCOLATE CHIP COOKIE ICE-CREAM SANDWICH

JENNIFER YEE ✳ AUREOLE ✳ WWW.CHARLIEPALMER.COM

NOTE: Researchers writing in the *Journal of the American Medical Association* found that not only did eating 30 calories' worth of dark chocolate containing 30 milligrams of polyphenol antioxidants (most commercial brands have several hundred milligrams) each day have significant positive effects on blood pressure, but—believe it or not—those improvements were deemed in the study to be comparable to what some patients saw on beta blockers.

JENNIFER Yee's desserts are certainly beautifully built (she has a degree in architecture) and well described (she's a pretty gifted wordsmith). Yet the truly amazing part about this star pastry chef is how feet-on-the-ground delicious even her most fancy creation is. It's not something you might say about everyone with her level of artistry, but Yee is exactly the kind of person you'd want to make your birthday cake.

In that sense, it's no surprise that this Cordon Bleu graduate has landed at Charlie Palmer's Aureole. The restaurant's approachable take on high-end food—along with Yee's own long-standing working partnership with Executive Chef Christopher Lee (the two cooked together previously, and they're getting raves for the way their dishes play off each other)—seems a perfect fit.

Here, Yee pulled out all the taste stops: "Everybody loves a cookie, and there's no better cookie than a great chocolate chip," she said. "Here, I've paired my favorite cookie with a creamy but not too rich milk ice cream to create a fun crowd pleaser. These cookies have the right balance of brown sugar sweetness and dark chocolate bitterness. The coffee extract in the dough, plus the Maldon salt sprinkled on top, make them absolutely addictive."

✳ ✳ ✳

For the milk ice cream: Prepare an ice bath by adding ice water to a large bowl. Put another bowl in the ice water, making sure it stays dry. In a pot on the burner, boil the milk with the corn syrup and fondant, whisking constantly. In a separate bowl, whisk together the milk powder and ice cream stabilizer. Sprinkle this dry mixture into the boiling milk mixture. Whisk to incorporate the dry ingredients. Boil for another minute before straining into the top bowl in the ice water. Allow to cool completely, stirring occasionally. Freeze in an ice cream machine according to the manufacturer's instructions. Store the ice cream in the freezer to get semi-firm.

For the cookies: Preheat the oven to 325°F.

Beat the butter with the sugars using an electric mixer. Add the eggs, one at a time, scraping the batter down with a spatula after each addition. Add the vanilla and coffee extracts.

In a separate bowl, combine the flour, baking powder, baking soda, fine sea salt, and chocolate chunks, making sure to stir everything together well. Now, stir the dry ingredients into the wet ones, using an electric mixer on low speed. You'll probably need to do it in three additions. Remember to scrape the bowl well between each addition. Continue to mix the batter until all of the flour is absorbed into the dough. Then, split the dough into 3 evenly sized pieces and roll them into 2-inch diameter logs. Wrap each log individually in plastic wrap, and freeze until firm.

Once firm, take out the logs one at a time cut into ½-inch slices. Place the slices on a parchment-lined sheet tray 2 inches apart. Sprinkle each disc with a pinch of Maldon sea salt, and bake until the edges have dried, but the centers are still soft, 10 to 12 minutes. Remove from the oven and allow to cool completely on the tray. Once cooled, the cookies should still be soft and chewy.

Sandwich assembly: When the cookies are baked and cooled, turn half of them upside down on a tray. These will be the bottoms of the sandwiches. Using a 2-ounce-size ice cream scoop (or approximate), place a scoop of the milk ice cream on each of the bottom cookies. Top with another cookie and press down slightly to ensure it adheres to the ice cream.

SERVES 12, ABOUT 2 SANDWICHES EACH

MILK ICE CREAM

- **4 cups whole milk**
- **¼ cup corn syrup**
- **6 ounces fondant (also called white icing)**
- **1 tablespoon dry milk powder**
- **1 teaspoon ice cream stabilizer**

COOKIES

- **½ pound (2 sticks) butter**
- **1 cup brown sugar**
- **¾ cup sugar**
- **2 eggs**
- **½ teaspoon vanilla extract**
- **½ teaspoon coffee extract**
- **3½ cups all-purpose flour**
- **1 teaspoon baking powder**
- **1 teaspoon baking soda**
- **1 teaspoon fine sea salt**
- **3 cups chocolate chunks or chips (preferably around 70% cocoa)**
- **2 teaspoons Maldon sea salt for sprinkling**

Chapter 11

WHAT TO DRINK WITH YOUR 'WICH

* * *

A GREAT SANDWICH IS A HIGHLY LIKABLE EXPERIENCE. WHETHER SOFT AND squishy, crusty and golden, or nutty and nourishing, it's typically made to be held. Fillings are often playful, balanced, surprising—and expertly designed to jive.

Take the time and care to match that sandwich with a worthy beverage, and the experience has the potential to be more than just likable. New possibilities (and flavors) open up. Another dimension blooms. The minuet becomes a symphony.

All this for a sandwich, you say? So let's just get that out of the way. The sandwiches in this book are cherry-picked and market-tested, and we think they're all pretty special. Be it a juicy souvlaki, a crispy skate fillet that's cornered the interplay between crispy and moist, or a springy beauty overflowing with arugula, some are a snap to make, and others take a bit of (enjoyable and enriching!) effort. Once it's in your hands, you can't wait to finish chewing so you can sink your teeth into the next amazing bite.

Now, pair it with something great to drink—and suddenly, blurry bites emerge into focus. Palates overwhelmed with richness are wiped clean for the next bite. Flavors build on flavors, and each compounds the other. Luckily, the principles of pairings are not difficult—once you have grasped the few simple rules, feel free to experiment and explore.

* * *

DO OPPOSITES ATTRACT, OR IS IT THE OPPOSITE?

To get started, forget the beverage. Take a good look at the sandwich in question. Is it big and bold, or light and slight? Is it complicated, with a lot of ingredients, or simple, with just a few? Does it want to party, or chill? Answers to these questions lead to the first, most important decision: to complement or to contrast?

Sometimes, you want the sandwich to match the drink. A single, big-flavored meat, like lamb shank, would pair beautifully with a single, big-flavored drink, like a full-bodied, ripe Bordeaux. That's big to big, and it's simple, bold, and perfect. Another example:

> **Delmonico's Classic NY Cheesesteak** (page 122) consists of filet mignon beef tips, veal jus and rich, gooey cheese. "This calls for a big juicy red wine, or a stout that's lighter than Guinness, such as Black Butte Porter, by Deschutes Brewery," said Cameron Bogue, bar manager of Chef Daniel Boulud's Café Boulud.

In a similar vein, a light sandwich often calls for a light drink that avoids overwhelming.

> When asked what he'd pair with **Magnolia Bakery's Brown Sugar Whoopee Cookie with Maple Cream Cheese Icing** (page 248), Chef Tyler Kord said, quite simply, New York tap water. "The minerals make a nice chaser, and there's fluoride for your teeth," he added, only half joking.

When the sandwich is complicated, you need to shift gears. For, say, a rich sandwich with a lot of interesting flavors, introducing a similarly complex drink adds confusion, not clarity. It's time to introduce contrast.

> Take **Fort Defiance's Muffuletta** (page 32), a jaw-challenging monster stuffed with Italian deli meats and antipasto-rich olive salad. The meat's fatty and rich, and the salad's acidic, and salty. This sandwich already has complexity to spare.

> Rather than muddle the flavors with something similarly big, John Slover, wine consultant at Bar Henry, suggests a cleansing drink, like a pilsner. "You want to get out of its way," said Slover. With every sip of the pilsner, your palate gets a clean start.

The contrast rule works especially well when pairing sandwiches with wine. If there are condiments involved, look for wines that are light in body, low in alcohol, with zero tannins, he says. Acidity cuts through fat and mayonnaise, he says, which suggests lively whites such as Austrian Grüner Veltliners (made for relish, pickles, and sauerkraut, he says). If you'd rather go with a red, gamay, found in Beaujolais-Villages, is a good pick, as are reds from the Loire Valley in general, and cabernet francs or light American pinot noirs.

If the sandwich is spicy, look for off-dry (or slightly sweet) German whites, another great contrast. A good contrast could also involve texture:

Jimmy's No. 43's Elvis Tea Sandwich (page 237) is a lovely combination of bananas, honey, and peanut butter sealed in toasted white bread. "Peanut and nut butters are really fun with beer, mostly because of texture. Think about carbonation and the power of a creamy, super-carbonated Belgian blonde to lift the oily stickiness of peanut butter from your mouth, drawing you to the next bite," said Justin Philips, founder of Beer Table, a customized tasting room, where beer is promoted as food.

Sometimes, the choice between complementing and contrasting isn't always obvious—it's one or the other, and you've got to just commit.

Travertine's Grilled Hanger Steak and Mint Pesto Sandwich (page 94) contains stinky gorgonzola. "It's great to pair a powerful blue cheese with a super-stinky spontaneously fermented beer. But it's also really satisfying to pair it with a gooey, sweet barley wine—for contrast," said Philips.

TECHNICOLOR SANDWICHES

Now here's where things get more complicated. Drink experts—particularly mixologists—like to take the complement/contrast game a step further, with some free association. Think of it as the art behind the science of pairing. Sample this:

"Untoasted white bread reminds me of a tea sandwich," said Don Lee, of Chef David Chang's Momofuku mini-empire. For him, the association conjures cucumber slices, laid on crustless bread. So Lee recommends pairing **EN Japanese Brasserie's Pork Tonkatsu Sando** (page 182), made with untoasted white bread, with a simple cocktail of muddled cucumber topped with gin ("like a sour, mintless Tom Collins," he said).

Sound good? Let's try another. Bogue of Café Boulud likes to use the classic wine pairing rules above as a launch point for his free associations—with spirits. To wit:

Daniel's Croque Monsieur (page 103) combines high-end ham with melted Gruyère, fine Béchamel, and Pullman bread. "With this rich sandwich, I'd pair a full-bodied, big oaked chardonnay: It's got some acidity, some oak, and a lot of body," he said.

Fair enough. So we need a spirit that is also acidic, with slight oak, and a lot of body. Bogue suggests lightly oaked rum. He then builds on the rum to create a daiquiri de poire (pear daiquiri). Shake together 2 ounces Flor de Cana (Nicaraguan rum), ¾ ounce lime juice, ¾ ounce simple syrup (optional replacement: Ronin pistachio syrup),

½ ounce Clear Creek Poire Williams (pear brandy). The acid cuts through the richness of the sandwich, and the sweetness of the drink brings out the sweetness of the ham. Voila!

Part of what's fun about this is that off-the-cuff pairings don't always have to contain alcohol. Here are a few examples:

As explained in **Annisa's Japanese Chicken Curry Roll** (page 179) recipe, the sandwich is a fusion that hails from both Japan and Great Britain, via the colonies. The natural association is with lassi, a thick yogurt drink popular in India. "Fermented yogurt drinks are common in Japan," said Lee, adding that curry rolls remind him of a kid's meal: soft, comforting, and kind of fun. So for this sandwich, he recommends Yakult, a Japanese yogurt drink.

Chef Tyler Kord, the wizard behind No. 7 Sub, pairs his own **General Tso's Fried Tofu Sandwich** (page 160) with chocolate milk. "It's like a chocolate-covered pretzel, with a little horseradish and tarragon. Or maybe it's more like [author] Robert Jordan drinking absinthe [because of tarragon's strong licorice notes], but with chocolate and tofu, if they had had tofu in Hemingway's *For Whom the Bell Tolls* . . . but on a sub," he added. We didn't really follow that last one, but hey, it's *his* fantasy sandwich pairing.

Sometimes, a pairing is just a personal recipe for nostalgia:

Chef Kord likes Dr. Brown's Cel Ray soda with **Tribeca Grill's Lamb Pastrami** (page 116)— mainly because pastrami and Cel Ray remind him of going to the New York Deli in Richmond, Virginia, every Saturday with his late Grandpa Joe. But it's a good pairing.

Getting back to alcohol, here's one we love:

Bogue would pair **Corton's Welsh Rarebit with Marrow Crust** (page 113) with a zinfandel/merlot blend, or a Bordeaux to match its richness. The spirit translation is a rye old-fashioned on ice (rye isn't as sweet as bourbon, and ice will get it to open up, Bogue reasons). Because the sandwich is too rich to easily digest, he then adds Cynar, a lightly bitter digestif made with artichokes, which are in turn a traditional European accompaniment to meat and marrow. The recipe? Two ounces of rye (Bogue favors US1 by Michter's), ½ ounce Cynar, and a dash of celery bitters (or Angostura bitters). Stir, strain, and serve over fresh ice.

Whoa! We realize that if you're new to this, it probably sounds like you've got to sprout a sixth sense overnight to intuit the right drink. But listen, you've been drinking liquids and eating foods all of your life. You know what you like, and you know what tastes good together. Add a bit of research, maybe look at a cocktail blog or two, and the rest is all delicious fun and discovery.

Beer, Wine, or What?

You'll note that a lot of our pairing examples involve beer. Pairing bread with beer is a no-brainer: "Malty flavors will work naturally with bread, almost regardless of style," said Philips, adding that the comparison, flavor-wise, is pure "apples to apples."

It's trickier—albeit equally rewarding—to pair a sandwich with wine, cocktails, or other drinks. Again, this is both art and science: Just trust your instincts and don't be afraid to experiment.

MORE SANDWICH PAIRINGS BY CAMERON BOGUE

Picholine's Tartiflette (page 58): Bogue recommends a big, hoppy, acidic full-bodied IPA, such as Dogfish Head 60-Minute or 90-Minute, to combat the crispy potatoes, bacon, and powerful melted Reblochon.

Kefi's Chicken Souvlaki (page 84): Bogue concluded that this herbaceous, garlicky, and lively sandwich suggested a sauvignon blanc. Taking that a step further, the Classic Aviation: 2 ounces gin, ¾ ounce maraschino liqueur, ½ ounce lemon juice.

Nikk Cascone's Simple Salmon Sandwich (page 28): Bogue liked Victory Prima Pils from Pennsylvania to go with the citrus-bright aioli.

Eleven Madison Park's Pink Peppercorn Macaron (page 240): Bogue liked Lindemans Kriek beer, a Belgian beer that's sweet and slightly tart, with cherry notes (aged in the cask).

MORE SANDWICH PAIRINGS BY DON LEE

Baoguette's Báhn Mì with Daikon Pickle (page 176): Lee recommended a classic Vietnamese drink, such as fresh-pressed sugarcane juice. "Sugarcane will destroy your juicer, so you can't juice it at home," he said. But he recommends going to your nearest Asian grocery store to buy sugarcane juice. If you like, you can spike it, too—Lee recommends gin. In the alternative, beer works; "microbreweries are popular in Vietnam," Lee added.

Kuma Inn's Adobo Pulled Pork Bun (page 184): Adobo is cooked in vinegar, said Lee. He instantly thought of a tall and fizzy drink, something less acidic, such as spiked iced tea. "The bitterness will wash away the heaviness of the sandwich, without the acidity," he added.

Num Pang's Hoisin Veal Meatball (page 174): This sandwich is heavy with a lot of fat, so go with something carbonated, said Lee. He recommends matching the basil in the sandwich with muddled Thai basil paired with fresh limes, adding 2 ounces of rum and then topping the whole thing off with Goya-brand Tamarind Soda (lighter than other brands, he said).

MORE SANDWICH PAIRINGS BY JOHN SLOVER

508's Smoked Turkey and Brie (page 34): "Cheese is traditionally tough to pair. I would say a demi-sec Champagne with high dosage [added sugar, which indicates high residual sugar]," said Slover. He recommended a 1996 Salon Blanc de Blanc: "It's a very restrained, tightly wound Champagne that evolves slowly in the glass, with beautiful lime, chalky minerals, and clean, fine bubbles," he said. Of course, it's also over $200, so you could go with a prosecco.

Savoy's BBQ Duck Confit (page 127): For the gamy notes in the duck, Slover recommends a southern Rhone wine. If money's not an object, go with Domaine de la Solitude 2005, Châteauneuf-du-Pape (it's got nice roasted aromas, says Slover). Or, Domaine Saint Damien Gigondas 2006 would be more price-friendly.

Nikki Cascone's Simple Salmon Sandwich (page 28): Unlike Bogue, who suggested a beer pairing for this sandwich, Slover went with wine. Any coastal white will do, he says, naming Portuguese wines such as Albariño and vinho verde, French Chablis, or Cassis Blanc, an Italian blended Vermentino. These wines are high in structure and acidity, due to the richness of the limestone soil, he says.

Commerce's Israeli Workingman's Lunch (page 152): A light and summery hefeweizen will pair well with the bright citrus notes and lemon in this dish, says Slover.

BEER + SANDWICH Q&A BY JUSTIN PHILIPS

What kind of beers go with deli-style sandwich meats?

Typically, I would pair medium-bodied mild styles like ambers and dry stouts with pork and/or beef, particularly braised meats such as brisket, or anything with a more mellow, but deep and potentially earthy undertone. As for wheat beers and more soft, refreshing beers, I'd try spicy flavors like spiced, cured meats, i.e. sopressata, or maybe even some fishy things like oil-cured sardines.

What beer best tones down Sriracha or an even spicier sauce, such as guajillo chili paste?

I'd suggest thinking about sugars and carbonation. I love spicy foods, and generally think that having a beer with a slightly higher density helps maintain the flavor of the spice without allowing [the spice] to hurt you.

Would you generally keep a beer within the same continent as a sandwich? Laotian beer with Cambodian sandwiches? etc.

Absolutely not. I am much more interested in finding flavor relationships rather than making assumptions that region has anything to do with flavor as it relates to food cultures and style (author's note: there is probably room for disagreement in the drinks community on this one).

What is one great all-around beer that goes with nearly everything?

Bayerischer Banhof Leipziger Gose.

What are one or two crazy specialty beers that you love, and are real finds that you think our sandwich-loving readers should know about?

Brasserie des Franches-Montagnes Abbaye de St. Bon-Chien and J. W. Lees Harvest Ale.

What's a beer that goes great with desserts, particularly chocolate?

Goose Island Bourbon County Stout.

ACKNOWLEDGMENTS

First off, a huge thank you to the ninety-four chefs and restaurateurs—not to mention their tireless assistants, publicists, spouses, and partners—all of whom truly shaped this book. Your ideas, personalities, and enthusiasm turned this from a fun idea into something real, exciting, and tangible.

Next up, we'd like to thank the our extraordinary team of astute and adventurous home cooks who donated their time, kitchens, opinions, and palates to making sure our recipes were user-friendly, mouthwatering, and totally memorable.

NIKHIL CHANDHOK	STEVEN LONG (SUPERTESTER EXTRAORDINAIRE)
SUE CONSTANTINE	VICTORIA LOUSTALOT
TERESA FAUDON	NALIN PATEL
AARON FOX	ANTHONY PIETRO
ED FRIEDRICH	JACKIE POTTS
MATTHEW FROMKIN	LISA SKYE
JENNIFER GILHULY	MAGDALENA SPIRYDOWICZ
MARISSA GOLDBERG	ANDREW SPRAGGS
HAYLI HALPER	CATHERINE STEWART
TANYA JOHNSON	CALVIN SWAIM
DANIELLE KING	KIRI TANNENBAUM
ZACK AND ALICE KNOTTS	EMMA THOMAS
NUSHIN KORMI	MICHAEL TULIPAN
FRANK LEONE	SHEILA WARREN

A special thank you to our editor, Geoffrey Stone, and our agent, Joelle Delbourgo. Lastly, much love and gratitude to our friends and family—your support and encouragement kept our sandwich spirits soaring. Sara and Jean especially acknowledge their parents, without whose love and dedication this book would not be possible.

INDEX